METAPHYSICS EXPLAINED SERIES: BOOK 1

UNDERSTANDING

METAPHYSICS

USING PSYCHOLOGY TO BETTER UNDERSTAND
METAPHYSICAL EXPERIENCES

DR JIMMY HENDERSON

MYEBOOK
WE EMPOWER AUTHORS

DEDICATION

The book is dedicated to all the spiritual teachers (some unseen) who have assisted me in this work.

Also dedicated to you, the reader, those brave souls who are prepared to walk this path of inner exploration and unfoldment.

TABLE OF CONTENTS

ACKNOWLEDGEMENTS

I wish to thank my editor and publisher, David Henderson of www.myebook.online for his assistance in the completion, publication and marketing of this book. This has been a long and difficult process and I am grateful for all the help received from friends and helpers along the way. For those of you also wishing to publish I would suggest visiting his website.

PREFACE

'The one who follows the crowd will usually get no further
than the crowd. The one who walks alone is likely to find
himself in places no one has ever been.'

Albert Einstein

WHO IS JIMMY HENDERSON?

As a young boy from a broken home, I had very humble beginnings.
Money was tight, and being quite a few years older than my younger
siblings, I felt lonely and abandoned by my absent father. I was quite
sickly, spending most of my adolescent years introverted and withdrawn.
In hindsight, the 'gifts' I got from this period of my life were the ability
to be alone with myself, to think deeply and sensitively, while from my
struggling mother I gained inner strength and faith.

In the early seventies, if your family was not wealthy, you had
to be content to miss university and either take up a trade or enter the
government service. I enjoyed science as a school subject and after school
took the opportunity to enter the police force as a trainee radio technical
specialist, which offered a better salary. The drawback was that I had to
do the police training and later also border duties which involved being
exposed to violence and danger. However, I believe that this training and

the conflict experiences were formative and indeed necessary, as my self-esteem and confidence grew as a result and I was able to advance in the police ranks over 30 years to reach the rank of Senior Superintendent and became the Commander of the Durban Technical Unit and later Regional Head of Human Resources Management.

LOOKING BACK

It is now strange to look back and see how these different experiences shaped my interest in metaphysics, as it was during the first of these border excursions in 1974 that I first came into contact with the books of Lobsang Rampa, an Eastern sage who many of you might know as one of the first mystics to put his metaphysical experiences into popular paperback form. His books certainly piqued my interest, but it was only during my last border trip in 1978 that I came across members of the Rosicrucian Order, a society dedicated to metaphysical study and practice which interested me even further. Upon my return I joined the local lodge, signed up for the studies and over 35 years later, am still a member. I attribute my present metaphysical interest and work to my studies with this Order as well as the many metaphysical and esoteric books I have read and the spiritual teachers who have helped me during this time.

THE STORY CONTINUES

By this time I had also developed an interest in psychology and began with undergraduate studies in 1982. A little later I joined Lifeline, a non-profit organisation involved in lay crisis counselling, and spent over 30 years with them as a counsellor and trainer.

In the mid-eighties, I began preparing the draft for a metaphysical book which I tried to publish. Many of you will laugh, or perhaps cry if you knew of the challenges that faced aspirant writers at that time.

Fortunately, I had the moral support of a dear friend from the Order who was a published author and she kept me motivated.

The traditional publication route in this country was almost impossible. Imagine completing a 300- page manuscript on a typewriter (no computers in those days), making copies and packing them for postage to overseas publishers, as I could find no local publishers in my genre in those days before online search engines. Apart from the expense, the turnaround time for packing, posting and receiving a written reply was three to four months, and each time the manuscript was rejected for obscure reasons. In some cases, it was simply returned unopened. After a period of two years during which I sent the manuscript to a number of different overseas publishing houses, I gave up, feeling disillusioned, and put away the whole idea of becoming a writer.

The big change came in the mid-nineties, when, as a result of political changes in the country, I found myself removed from my top work position and my career effectively came to a halt. I admit I took it very badly, as up to that time I had been very driven and ambitious. Things came to a head around the year 2000 when the sky literally turned grey and I entered the dark night of the soul, a period of depression brought on by long-standing feelings of helplessness and hopelessness which took me many years to overcome (or at least, to manage). During this time I applied for, and was given, early medical retirement, having already served 30 years.

This time of loneliness and feelings of abandonment took me back to my childhood days when I had experienced similar feelings, but fortunately this time I was an adult and had better skills to deal with it. Looking back, this dark period was also a 'gift' in that it allowed me to release my driving ambition and the insidious promptings of my ego which brought on the pain and anguish. In other words, this experience had allowed me to rediscover myself and start afresh. As a result, I threw myself into intense metaphysical study to find meaning in my life, self-published my first manuscript and took the time to complete my psychological studies. After 35 years of study. I graduated in 2016 at the age of 64 with a doctorate in psychology.

During 2005 I was fortunate to have found a publisher in Cape Town who helped me publish my second and third metaphysical books and more recently another publisher who has assisted me with a number of short guides on counselling.

I suppose that at this time many of you will ask why, as a fully-fledged cognitive scientist with a background in science, technology and psychology, I would still be interested in metaphysics. At first glance, they seem to be so far apart. However, what I have learnt from my studies and my past experiences is that, if we take the time to look deeper, many metaphysical or so-called 'spiritual' phenomena can be explained with science and psychology. And this is what I try to show in this book. This approach of explaining metaphysics and *'spirituality'* in terms of psychology and the activity of our minds is called *psycho-spirituality*.

PSYCHO-SPIRITUALITY

Linking spiritual or metaphysical experiences to the operations of our minds does not mean that I consider them any less real or without value, in fact, just the opposite. Making use of real-life examples backed up by accepted scientific and psychological research, these experiences should be more credible to those of you still *'sitting on the fence'* so to speak, when it comes to metaphysics. Metaphysics simply means 'that which goes beyond physics'. This implies that, although we metaphysicians might begin our search for truth with science and psychology, we delve deeper to uncover higher, potentially hidden principles.

The problem is that a *fear of the unknown* holds us back from so many new and exciting experiences found just outside our comfort zone. This fear is the result of our early conditioning by our parents, teachers and friends. Having doubts about something stops us from exploring new ideas and prevents us from ever reaching a deeper understanding of ourselves and of our reality. Surprisingly, this fear is kept going by our egos. It is almost as if they do not want us to find a deeper truth and wish to keep us bound to a sort of lower *ego-consciousness*, in which we focus only on ourselves and our own selfish needs. This action of the ego also keeps us tied to a certain view of reality. Everything that does not fit this view is seen as a threat. In fact, our egos actively fight to protect their sovereignty, prompting us to become angry and lash out at anything or anyone seen as a possible threat.

Most people believe their version of the truth to be the only correct one. To see this in action, we only have to look at the powerful emotions and violence due to clashes of political, ideological, religious or cultural beliefs in the world today. In most cases, this fear of the new, unknown and extraordinary is due to a simple lack of insight and understanding. The result? We are afraid to look beyond our past experiences or present beliefs for the answers to important questions.

I am not saying that you have to accept everything that is written in this book. Maintain an open mind and perhaps you will find something useful and valuable to add to your own view of life.

A MULTI-DIMENSIONAL APPROACH

As far as my *psycho-spiritual approach* in this book is concerned, in my earlier publication *Multi-Dimensional Thinking* I introduced the idea that we will only find deeper levels of truth if we are prepared to move outside of the 'box' of day-to-day thinking. I introduced a *multi-dimensional approach* to problem-solving in which I used logic and reasoning to draw facts and research from a colourful mix of science, psychology, philosophy, theology, symbolism and metaphysics until I arrived at the essence of the problem. In other words, in this book, I will once again be *crossing the lines or boundaries* of different fields of knowledge and drawing from, and comparing ideas from each of these fields.

I found that when I used this approach I was able to superimpose ideas from these different areas, broadening my perspectives and view, and answers spontaneously began to present themselves. In psychology, this is called an '*immediate insight*' into problem-solving. My earlier book *Multi-Dimensional Thinking* will give you a greater understanding of this approach.

ENDNOTES

I know that it may be difficult to get hold of the information I have listed as sources, so I have used *online references* as much as possible and put in endnotes in the case of difficult concepts and ideas. The numbered endnotes are explained and linked to their online sources at the end of each chapter. I hope this makes the book easier to read.

REAL-LIFE EXAMPLES

I have also included quite a few real-life examples in the text to show you how the skills should be applied and to point out the kind of inner experiences that can result from the exercise. I hope you find them interesting and informative. Names have been changed to ensure confidentiality.

A GRADED APPROACH

I introduce a graded approach to learning in this book by grouping the chapters into three different themes increasing in difficulty, starting with those chapters which fall under the introductory theme; 'The start of metaphysical understanding', then moving onto those chapters associated with the intermediate theme, 'The application of metaphysical principles' and finally, dealing with the most complex ideas and practices in the final chapters under the heading of 'Advanced metaphysical work'.

YOUR OWN PERSONAL JOURNEY

I really want you to see this book as a guide along your own personal journey into the knowledge of metaphysics and a process of self-development which will take you through to self-actualisation. If you can identify with and enjoy the processes as much as I do then I will have succeeded in my goal with this book. Remember that higher guidance will be with you every step of the way. Keep an open mind, take courage and make a commitment to move forward with me into the light of a new reality and understanding of yourself and the universe.

A SUMMARY OF THE CHAPTERS

'As long as your mind is free, you are free.'

J. Henderson

WHAT TO EXPECT FROM THIS BOOK

CHAPTER 1: INTRODUCTION

My first goal is to try to convince you that metaphysics itself is not as obscure, shadowy and frightening as it is made out to be and that we do, in fact, use so-called metaphysical practices every day without knowing it, as they are part of our normal personal growth and development.

You may find naturalist, evolutionary undertones in this book, but please don't be put off by the idea of *'evolution'*, as this does not mean that I believe that we descended from monkeys. One simply has to look deeper to see this. For instance, although we may have a common ancestor in some sort of genetic 'soup', our bodies have developed separately from other species for millions of years and we are the only species complex enough to support full self-awareness. I do touch on this issue in this book, but I give it a religious twist by linking it to the idea of the 'embodiment of the soul'.

CHAPTER 2: THE POWERS OF THE MIND

I begin by showing you how many metaphysical processes are simply latent abilities of our minds, especially the subconscious parts. I believe that 'mind' and consciousness are laced together to form the *golden thread* that links all knowledge, and go as far as saying that they are the keys to understanding the secrets of the universe. The reason I say this is because our minds are far more active than we ever realised in creating our *sense of reality*. In fact, I show how they can change or even 'add to' what we see and hear, influencing what we believe to be true. They are very *selective* in what they allow in, with the result that we tend to overlook important experiences and lessons which could otherwise change our beliefs about ourselves and reality.

CHAPTER 3: SELF-DEVELOPMENT

I assert that metaphysical development is really a natural part of our personal growth and show how it fits into an upward personal growth curve. I discuss the various stages of the growth curve, starting at the point when we first become aware of our need to grow, to the time that we begin to take action to simplify our lives, increase our mindfulness, quieten our minds and reach emotional wellness, to the final stage in which I show how metaphysical practices such as meditation and visualisation form the apex of the growth curve and how *spiritual wholeness* can be compared to self-actualisation.

CHAPTER 4: NEW SKILLS IN UNFOLDMENT

I introduce more advanced concepts and also deeper metaphysical processes for those of you ready to begin your personal growth. In this chapter I describe and explain in great detail the type of skills you will need and how you can develop them. These include *meditation* and *spontaneous visual imagery*[2], or simply 'spontaneous imagery'. This is an extremely powerful skill which will change your whole view of reality. I have personally used these exercises and know them to be effective, as will be seen in the real-life examples I present.

CHAPTER 5: A UNIVERSAL COLLECTIVE MIND

I combine scientific, psychological and metaphysical research to introduce you to the idea of the universe itself being linked to the actions of a *Universal Collective Mind*[3] and our existence to that of a Universal Soul, both aspects of a single creative source.

To continue, I show how the idea of a single 'mind-reality' underlying all of creation is supported by *quantum scientists*[4], who believe that their research shows that the Universe itself may, in some way, be conscious. In a conscious universe, everything, every part, would naturally be conscious in some way, with all living beings sharing in this one consciousness to varying degrees. Being plugged into a single *Collective Consciousness*[5] or in this case, a 'Universal Mind', can explain many of the so-called *spiritual* experiences and events in our lives which we, as yet, do not fully understand. For example, if we are all connected at a deep subconscious level it would be easy to communicate with one another as long as we are all on the same 'wavelength' (in the same state of mind).

THE QUANTUM MODEL

The *Quantum Model of the Universe* leads to new and exciting ideas, such as the view that we are all connected at a sub-atomic (energy) level and are different parts of a 'whole'. To support this idea further, I present ideas from systems theory in psychology as well as another scientific theory which suggests that the universe may be *holographic*[6]. This theory promotes the idea that what we see as reality is simply a hologram created by a Universal Mind. I know this is a radical departure from normal thinking, but it does explain several paradoxes in everyday life which I point out.

Next, I show that this idea of one Universal Mind is not new and has been around in different forms for many centuries, but is hidden in myths, analogies and metaphors. I open up and expose these metaphors and analogies to modern scientific research with the idea that you will at least consider the possibility of a single, conscious, collective source (or consciousness) in the universe. I believe the time has now arrived to re-examine this possibility in line with modern science and psychology.

ARCHETYPES

The idea of a single, Universal, Collective Mind also explains many age-old theological dilemmas. For example, how concepts of God are formed and how some people can have real, inner, personal experiences of 'deities' or celestial 'personalities' while others cannot, or simply do not believe in it. Using the framework of *universal archetypes*[7] as presented by Carl Jung, I offer an explanation for these experiences in terms of mental processes in this *collective* area of the subconscious mind and show the role of archetypes concerning all life and consciousness in the universe, including our own coming-into-being.

CHAPTER 6: THE SUBCONSCIOUS MIND

I introduce you to your own subconscious mind, its powers and its role in your metaphysical development and how important and necessary it is for your inner development to gain its cooperation. I also show you how to bring about and cement this relationship.

CHAPTER 7: ENGAGEMENT

I discuss a scientific approach to engaging the Universal Mind and communicating with archetypal personalities as well as other so-called 'spiritual' beings within its many dimensions. This is a very powerful section for which you need to have mastered meditation and spontaneous imagery for it to be effective.

CHAPTER 8: ENERGY

I discuss the metaphysical concept of energy, the different sources of energy in the universe, how to access and work with body-energy, and finally, how to use healing energies to assist others.

CHAPTER 9: NEW MENTAL SKILLS

I describe the latent powers of our minds and show how metaphysical practices can work to bring about a greater realisation of our authentic selves, our souls, and a mastery of will-power, intent and spontaneous imagery. This results in 'gifts' of lucid dreaming, telepathy, intuition, channelling and out-of-body experiences.

CHAPTER 10: INITIATIONS

Chapter 10 deals with rituals and initiations as well as the type of trials and tests and experiences you can expect during your metaphysical development.

CHAPTER 11: MENTAL CREATION

This is a very important chapter which unpacks the principles and methods of creating powerful thought-forms and how to project your consciousness into different dimensions of the Universal Mind. This section is not recommended for novices as it is quite demanding.

CHAPTER 12: NEW INSIGHTS

Finally, based on my experiences within a connected state while engaging with the Universal Mind as a 'collective', or *community of minds*, in this chapter I present some new ideas on what is consciousness, reality, the essence and power of love, the meaning of life and what happens after death. I also introduce you to the idea of world-service as a means of meeting your full potential.

WHAT I HOPE

I believe that the most important and exciting outcome of this book would be for you to accept that you are not bound by the limits of normal day-to-day experiences, but have an unlimited potential to grow, to develop and unfold *inwardly* to embrace all parts of your being. I invite, no, I challenge you, to open your minds and journey with me into the mysteries of your subconscious minds and ultimately connect and work with the one Universal Mind which is the source of all life and consciousness. I promise that you will all gain something from this experience.

ENDNOTE REFERENCES

1. Psycho-spirituality –finding relationships between spirituality and the workings of the mind https://www.yourdictionary.com/psychospiritual

2. Spontaneous visual imagery –what happens when visual images appear in our mind's eye unexpectedly without our own actions https://psychologydictionary.org/spontaneous-imagery/

3. Universal Collective Mind –the idea that there is only one mind in the Universe in which we all share. https://www.researchgate.net/publication/328538224_Universal_Consciousness_Collective_Evidence_on_the_Basis_of_Current_Physics_and_Philosophy_of_Mind_Part1

4. Quantum scientists –research which focuses on the relationships between sub-atomic particles, in this case, in support of a Conscious Universe. https://bigthink.com/philip-perry/the-universe-may-be-conscious-prominent-scientists-state

5. Holographic –research which suggests that the Universe behaves like a hologram https://phys.org/news/2017-01-reveals-substantial-evidence-holographic-universe.html

6. Collective Consciousness -The idea that we all share in one Consciousness https://www.thoughtco.com/collective-consciousness-definition-3026118 https://www.britannica.com/science/collective-unconscious

7. Universal archetypes –personality patterns said to exist within our subconscious minds http://www.soulcraft.co/essays/the_12_common_archetypes.html

THE START OF METAPHYSICAL UNDERSTANDING

CHAPTER ONE

INTRODUCTION TO METAPHYSICS

'The most beautiful and most profound experience is the sensation of the mystical.'

Albert Einstein

In this chapter, I introduce you to the concept of metaphysics, which I explain as 'the study and practice of principles going beyond normal, everyday scientific research and understanding'. In this case, my aim will be to try to show you that metaphysics is not what it is made out to be and can actually be seen as a legitimate part of normal human growth and development.

For instance, I show you how metaphysics can be reconciled with science, being based on sound psychological and scientific principles and go further by saying that we actually use metaphysical processes daily without our even knowing it. For example, when we use our imagination and see ourselves lying and enjoying ourselves on the beach we are actually accessing the same parts of our brains that we do during visualisation, and when we use positive thoughts and words to keep ourselves motivated during the day, we are simply duplicating common subliminal practices such as the use of affirmations and intentions.

For those who are concerned that metaphysics will clash with their religious values and beliefs, in this chapter I also show how metaphysics promotes an open spirituality, one which acknowledges the role of religion, but goes beyond dogma to stand firmly on fundamental spiritual principles which are at the heart of all religions.

Finally, I point out the close relationship between psychology and metaphysics as anchored in the all-important role of the activity of the mind in what we see and experience of the world and reality, especially the actions of our subconscious minds and the characteristics of consciousness itself. I show that consciousness is not just self-awareness but a fundamental principle of the Universe, an active, dynamic and transformative process.

Be prepared to open your minds and I will help you with your inner journey into the mysteries of your minds and the universe and show you the new worlds of perception and experience that come with a study of metaphysics.

WHAT IS METAPHYSICS?

Metaphysics does not stand alone. It links up with fields of study such as science, technology, psychology, philosophy and even theology, but the difference is that, in metaphysics there are no 'boxes' or limits to thinking. It goes beyond the 'rules' and boundaries set for these fields.

I know that many people are still suspicious or even critical of metaphysics, mysticism, or any teachings which do not fit into mainstream science or religion. People are uncomfortable with new concepts such as 'consciousness', 'interconnectedness', 'aura', psychic' and 'channelling'. Yet these are just new, broader concepts with the ability to draw science, psychology, philosophy and theology into a wider and more holistic framework of thinking which encourages free thought and avoids some of the pitfalls in these other fields of knowledge.

The problem is that we tend to fear anything that we do not understand. Much of the fear actually comes from the doubt, uncertainty and even confusion about what *metaphysics really is*. Metaphysics aims to highlight certain scientific and psychological principles which are not yet fully understood.

A MULTI-DIMENSIONAL APPROACH

If you ever wish to grow your thinking and understanding, you cannot expect it to always fit neatly into the boxes prescribed by traditional fields of knowledge. Be prepared to move 'out of the box' of everyday thinking and try out my *multi-dimensional approach*. With this method I superimpose facts from different fields of study as well as the lesser-known areas of symbolism and semantics, to explore the meaning of symbols and even the *metaphors* we use to arrive at creative solutions to word-problems, thinking dilemmas and paradoxes.

SUPERIMPOSED TRANSPARENCIES

In the days before digital projectors, we had to use a photocopier to make 'transparencies', a clear plastic sheet on which we would have typed information, a diagram or any picture we wished to share with the class or group. This sheet was placed on what was called an overhead projector, magnified by a strong lens and light, and projected onto the wall or a screen.

For the purposes of this analogy let us assume that, with regard to any issue, each field has only a single transparency on which there is an image representing their knowledge of this issue. Each transparency gives us as the viewer, only a single perspective from a specific point of view, but if we superimpose the transparencies one on top of another, we begin to see a far larger, more complex and more comprehensive image.

Each field of knowledge, whether it is science, psychology, philosophy or theology, has a set of rules, guidelines and boundaries which permits them only a single view or perspective. In thinking multi-dimensionally and metaphysically, I am opening every one of these 'boxes', looking inside and taking what I need to examine the issue from all possible angles. In this way, I get a complete view of reality, including possible hidden, universal principles.

CAN METAPHYSICS BE RECONCILED WITH SCIENCE?

'Everything is energy and that's all there is to it. Match the frequency of the reality you want and you cannot help but get that reality. It can be no other way. This is not philosophy. This is physics.'

Albert Einstein

Metaphysical ideas are often built on accepted and proven scientific and psychological theories. For example, the above quote by Albert Einstein highlights how he often seemed to combine science with spirituality. According to Einstein, science itself shows that our universe is actually one of pure energy. This means that, at a sub-atomic level, what we see as 'substance' is only different concentrations of energy-particles bound up in different ways. Psychologists share a similar idea, in that the current view is that the images we see of the world are actually put together in our minds. In other words, what we see and feel is the result of our *senses*, which, in terms of science, respond to different types and levels of energy.

This view is shared in metaphysics, but in this case, we take these conclusions one step further. Some quantum physicists have already suggested that this *sub-atomic energy* itself comes from a higher state, a conscious type of energy or 'consciousness' itself. In his article, *'The primacy of consciousness'*, Dr Peter Russel[1] theorises that material things have their beginning in a mind-essence, (called *'chitta'* in Sanskrit), which he says, is pure, concentrated consciousness.

Is this as far-fetched as it sounds? Let's look back to science where we find a recent discovery of a *universal field* which causes sub-atomic particles to come together and take on mass (the *Higgs-Boson* or 'God'-particle)[2]. Could this 'universal field' not be the conscious energy Dr Russel speaks about? This idea of a *pure state of consciousness with the power to create* is one of the building blocks of the idea of a Universal Mind giving rise to reality as we know it, and I am not the only one who believes this.

As an example, let's look at the following statement by Dr John Hagelin, a well-known particle physicist:

"And what we've discovered at the core basis of the universe, the foundation of the universe, is a single unified field of intelligence; a field that unites gravity with electromagnetism, light with radioactivity, with the nuclear force. So that all the forces of nature and all the so-called particles of nature – quarks, leptons, protons, neutrons – are now understood to be one. They're all just different ripples on a single ocean of existence that is the unified field... And that field is a non-material field. It is ultimately a field of consciousness and everything in the universe is nothing but that. Planets, trees, people, animals – we're all just waves of vibration of this underlying, unified, superstring field..."

Science is not so far removed from metaphysics when it comes to the nature of the universe. And there will be more examples of their agreement on some matters later on in the book.

I have thrown you in the deep end of metaphysics, but let's carry on!

WHAT DOES THE CHURCH SAY ABOUT METAPHYSICS?

'All religions, arts and sciences are branches of the same tree. All these aspirations are directed toward ennobling man's life, lifting it from the sphere of mere physical existence and leading the individual towards freedom.'

Albert Einstein

There is not such a big gap between metaphysics and church teachings as you might think. The main problem is that metaphysical concepts sound strange to many religious people.

If you look throughout history, you will see that meditation and contemplation have been practised by some priests and monks for many centuries. When it comes to dogma, theological beliefs about the *soul* and *divine spirit* form an important part of metaphysical philosophy.

It is true that metaphysics has the potential to give us a broader, more open-minded view of 'God' than many traditional scriptures. The reason for this is that most theologians believe that God can only be known through the Scriptures, whereas in metaphysics, it is believed that it is possible to have direct experiences of 'Source' through our minds during enhanced states of consciousness associated with meditation and contemplation. This, of course, opens metaphysics up to religious criticism.

I believe that the many concepts of God which exist in the world today are actually describing the same *spiritual* reality, but are merely presented differently because of different cultures, historical periods and the personal interpretations of religious leaders. For example, during ancient times when people were ruled by fearful, angry and vengeful monarchs, their view of God was one of a wrathful and even cruel ruler. However, in line with our present-day moral advancement, God is now accepted as benevolent and loving. If differing views of God are relative to circumstances and times, it would mean that recent metaphysical views of God should also be accepted.

METAPHYSICS AND RELIGION ARE REALLY NOT THAT EXCLUSIVE

I believe religious beliefs to be useful as long as they provide us with the opportunities, guidance and direction with which to arrive at a workable and fulfilling spiritual experience which we can call our own. Unfortunately, many people remain with a religious system that does not meet their spiritual needs simply out of fear. My problem is that many of these systems can be rigid, inflexible and closed to new ideas and so become fertile breeding grounds for the shadows of delusion or self-righteousness.

THE RELIGIOUS VIEW OF MAN COMPARED WITH METAPHYSICS

The following scenario highlights what I consider to be the most important difference between metaphysics and theology as taught in the churches. I was reading an article that compared the view of mankind presented by the churches with the view offered in metaphysics. According to the article, religion sees people as weak, fallen and sinful, whereas in metaphysics they are seen as magical, unlimited and powerful. For this reason, the article was quite critical of religion.

I am not naturally critical of any religion. I believe them all to be useful in giving guidance, but only insofar as they do not *enforce* specific dogma, punt their beliefs as the exclusive truth, or impose a self-righteous judgment on anybody else with a different belief.

I would say that, in the early phase of our moral and spiritual development, we all need what is called an '*external locus of control*', a strong framework which imposes spiritual ideas, values and behaviour on those of us who have not yet come to a good understanding of God, reality and ourselves. As we mature intellectually and morally, a new consciousness and understanding should arise in us, one bringing us to a new realisation of self, seen in psychology as the *higher or authentic self*[3]. Once we reach this new level of self-awareness we should be able to overcome, or at least manage, our evolutionary instincts, drives and needs, begin to think for ourselves, free ourselves from negative thoughts, and come to a new understanding of our purpose and place in the world. In this way, we begin to unfold more fully and acknowledge our *true higher selves* and its unlimited potential. This is simply the path of personal growth.

This new consciousness now gives us an *internal locus of control*, in which our conscience alone is enough to align us with the highest spiritual principles which govern our behaviour. In other words, this higher state of mind and consciousness empowers us to stand on our own two feet (spiritually) without the direction of any religious institution and bring out those characteristics called 'magical, unlimited and powerful' as explained by the author of the article.

Religion and metaphysics do not necessarily exclude each other. They both have merit. Religion plays an important role in the early stages of our moral and spiritual development, but becomes less of an issue after we achieve *higher-self-realisation*. At this time we take on the mantle of '*spirituality*', entering into a one-on-one relationship and personal communion with 'God', known in metaphysics by other names as well, such as 'Source', 'Being,' 'the Universe' or 'Spirit'.

DOES THIS MAKE PSYCHOLOGICAL SENSE?

'Relativity teaches us the connection between the different descriptions of one and the same reality.'

Albert Einstein

Metaphysics is not a scary or 'supernatural' process. In fact, I believe that it can be seen as part of a natural process of self-development, the top end of a gradual curve which includes the learning of new skills concerning feelings, thinking and perception. For instance, once we accept a higher, more moral and spiritual side to ourselves as seen in the idea of an *authentic self* in psychology, it can be argued that metaphysical unfoldment is the same as *self-actualisation*, and metaphysics is viewed as having the aim of reaching this self-actualisation.

I discuss the development learning curve in a later chapter.

When it comes to psychology, spirituality, as it is understood in metaphysics, actually links up with a psychological process called '*emergence*'. This concept explains what happens when several mind-processes combine to bring about a different state of mind and a completely new potential that was not there earlier. In other words, mental processes such as introspection, opening oneself to higher values and the learning of good behaviour through experience, could lead to a new state of openness, love, compassion and unconditional acceptance we could call 'spirituality'.

There are quite a few psychological theories on the activities of the mind that can be better explained using metaphysics which I will highlight later in other sections of this book. In the meantime, let us look at the contribution of metaphysics to the idea of 'consciousness' itself and also see how this description differs from other fields of knowledge. The development of consciousness is a key process in any programme of personal growth.

METAPHYSICS AND CONSCIOUSNESS

'Mind is consciousness which has put on limitations.
You are originally unlimited and perfect. Later you take
on limitations and become the mind.'

Ramana Maharishi – Indian Hindu sage

We normally explain 'being conscious' of something as being able to see, hear, smell or touch it, and self-awareness as being the *baseline state of mind* for all our experiences. In other words, our consciousness makes it possible for us to think, to reason, to know and understand ourselves, as well as what is happening in the world. However, in a metaphysical sense, consciousness is much more than this.

However, let's first see what else science and psychology have to say about consciousness.

CONSCIOUSNESS ACCORDING TO SCIENCE

Scientists see consciousness as simply arising from the activity of our brains and the same as self-awareness. Our level of consciousness can be measured scientifically using an EEG (Electro-encephalogram) and forms a continuum stretching from deep sleep to high mental activity. The higher our brain activity, the more awake or aware we are, (according to scientists anyway!).

A METAPHYSICAL VIEW OF CONSCIOUSNESS

This differs from metaphysicians who, although they accept the continuum of consciousness, point to other levels of *'altered'* or *'enhanced' consciousness* during which we can get amazing insights into everyday life, self and reality. Ironically, these enhanced states do not come from increased brain activity, in fact, just the opposite. In metaphysics we work with the lower end of the spectrum of brain activity and show how it has to be lowered for the more powerful states of consciousness to emerge. This is because our subconscious mind favours the lower frequencies, in other words, it 'wakes up', or becomes simply more active and dominant, when we sleep (or are close to sleep).

Let me explain this further: Brainwave patterns for normal, active minds run at about 12-30 cycles per second (cps) (This is also known as the Beta state). With metaphysical practices we can lower it to the Alpha state of 8-12 cycles (cps) or even further, down to the Theta state of 4-7 cps. This slows down our normal thinking until our brains are just idling or ticking over with no actual thought taking place, but we are still fully aware of what is happening on other levels. As I just said, the difference is that at low levels of brain activity *our subconscious minds are very active* and as a result, become the playground for metaphysical practices.

CONSCIOUSNESS AND THE 'NEW' SCIENCES (QUANTUM PHYSICS)

The differences in the views of consciousness between science and metaphysics are a bit blurred when we look at the relatively new science of *quantum physics*, a field in which physicists work with activities and processes at a sub-atomic level.

Metaphysics sees consciousness as something that exists *before* it becomes self-awareness and quantum physics also supports this idea that consciousness exists independently of our brains. I know that this is asking for a big shift in your present belief system, but if you can accept the idea that consciousness flows freely in the universe you will find answers to many of the paradoxes that science and psychology can't explain. These questions and metaphysical answers are highlighted and unpacked as the book progresses.

The present scientific view of consciousness is that it results purely from brain-activity. However, in metaphysics, as well as recent research into *quantum physics*, many forward-thinking scientists already believe in a flow of conscious energy through the cosmos, even comparing it to the flow of neural activity within the human brain. They find that the universe is so complex at a sub-atomic level that it could potentially be self-aware, forming a single cosmic or Collective Consciousness which expresses itself through many different life-forms.

Consider this famous quote by Nikola Tesla on the human brain *'The brain is only a receiver, in the Universe there is a core from which we obtain knowledge, strength and inspiration. I have not penetrated into the secrets of this core, but I know that it exists.'*

Other famous quantum physicists have also supported this idea of a universe composed of pure consciousness from which everything else is derived, an energy-based *'quantum reality'* or 'unified field', able to change its form and texture. Have a look at this quote from Albert Einstein:

'The field is the sole governing agency of the particle. We know, from the revelations of quantum physics, that this field, or all-pervasive space, is an information field within which everything in the universe exists. There is a non-local connectivity in the field – which must be a type of web, or super-fluid – enabling the instantaneous transfer of information from one body to another, one consciousness to another – and from the field itself, to all of life.'

This quantum view of the universe fits well with the metaphysical view of a conscious universe or a Universal Consciousness and Mind. This will be discussed a bit more in detail later on.

WHAT OTHER NEW SCIENTIFIC VIEWS OF CONSCIOUSNESS ARE THERE?

Some quantum scientists have suggested a link between consciousness and the complexity of the universe. This idea is important, as from an evolutionary science perspective, it is the complexity of the brain that allows for self-awareness. However, this has now been taken even further by some scientists, to the point of actually entering the realm of metaphysics. For example, research into *neuroscience combined with Information System Technology*[4] has led to the idea of IIT (Integrated Information Theory). The scientists putting forward this theory believe that when *free-flowing consciousness is concentrated*, self-awareness can arise in '*systems*' (biological as well as computer systems) which have the necessary complexity. As a result of this research, an Index of Consciousness (Phi) has been formed. This theory has implications for artificial intelligence (AI).

But it is the idea of a *free-flowing consciousness* that is so exciting and links up with metaphysics and supports the metaphysical argument that consciousness may be 'channelled' by the brain, but is not caused by it. In other words, these scientists also acknowledge a Universal Consciousness.

'Consciousness is a fundamental property of the universe. Wherever there is integrated information, there is experience.'

Christof Koch:
Chief Science Officer at the Allen Institute for Brain Science

I agree that all this is still only a theory, but if it can be proven, it will have far-reaching implications for our present understanding of consciousness itself. This whole idea of systems being linked to consciousness is important and it will be viewed later again in the *systems analogy.*

CONSCIOUSNESS AND SELF-AWARENESS

'Consciousness, like the universe, is ever- expanding, moving outwards to fill the framework of all possibilities.'

J. Henderson

PERSONAL GROWTH AND CONSCIOUSNESS

Personal growth can be seen as our consciousness struggling to unfold through our biological structures to allow us gradual mastery over our animal drives, instincts and destructive urges left over from earlier evolutionary stages. A good analogy would be that of a butterfly which has a larval stage as a caterpillar during which it struggles for survival, eventually forming a chrysalis and then emerging as an adult butterfly.

This bears a striking similarity to our human growth process. In the larval stage, (un-evolved mankind), we are just as primitive and destructive as the caterpillar, selfishly devouring everything in our path to satisfy our needs. Only later as we learn and mature and our chrysalis falls away (our bodily drives, instincts and destructive urges overcome), can our true selves (the butterfly) emerge.

To make this process a little more scientific, I offer you *four possible stages of consciousness* that occur as a result of evolution and continue later during our personal growth.

4 STAGES OF CONSCIOUSNESS

INSTINCTUAL CONSCIOUSNESS

The first stage of our evolution can be described as an *Instinctual Consciousness*. This is the mark of early man who had not yet achieved self-awareness and acted purely on instinct. The brain structures of embryonic homo-sapiens had not developed the complexity to support language or to *reflect on itself* and become self-aware. At this point there was no real thinking and consciousness was probably limited to moments of crude realisation based on associations. For instance, imagine a caveman being cornered by a sabre-tooth tiger and realising its association with death from his early learning experiences (having seen it kill others). This would give rise to an instinctual response of fear.

SCHEMATIC CONSCIOUSNESS

The next stage of the unfoldment of human consciousness would be linked to the development of those areas of our brains associated with self-realisation, language and thinking. This would bring with it 'self-awareness', but with an ego-driven mentality, a *Schematic Consciousness* in which people think only in terms of themselves and learnt programs (schemas and scripts) built up from rigid beliefs without any real independent or creative thought. For example, we often hear people using well-worn slogans and repetitive rhetoric when asked for their opinion without really thinking for themselves. Sadly, many people are still stuck at this level

I will go more deeply into this important issue of 'schemas and scripts' later.

COGNITIVE CONSCIOUSNESS

The third stage of human growth and development would bring with it a *Cognitive Consciousness*, when, as a result of education and mental maturity, a person begins to think less selfishly, more independently and is able to come up with creative, helpful ideas and discoveries. This level would be associated with those persons having a good understanding of themselves and their role and purpose in the world. A motivational speaker or manager who is able to encourage others with new ideas would be an example of someone working on this level of cognitive consciousness.

INTUITIVE CONSCIOUSNESS

Finally, we have the stage of *Intuitive Consciousness*, in which our pre-programmed thinking and reasoning gives way to an inner knowledge of *natural universal principles* which we use to explore and understand the mysteries of life and the universe. This can be likened to a study of philosophy and metaphysics. Apart from developing a deeper understanding, when this happens we reveal a more general attitude of *love and benevolence* towards all humanity and express a desire to help others and be more compassionate. An example of someone working on this level would be those with a deep insight into the human condition and who are engaged in *selfless service* to others.

Unfortunately, many of us are lagging behind and have not yet reached this intuitive stage.

HOPE FOR THE FUTURE

However, the signs for the future are good in that rapid moral advancement is now taking place and heralding a new global consciousness or awareness. People are becoming more involved and more aware of human and animal rights and are calling for ecological change. This change has been slow but noticeable. For example, commitment to the Covid-19 lockdowns has reduced air pollution in major cities around the world by 60% and allowed a large ozone hole at the Arctic Circle to heal itself.

Sometimes these changes are painful, but metaphorically, birthing pains are never pleasant but inevitable. And they bring with them a new form of life. There is a new interest in post-modern thinking in which people are becoming more perceptive and sceptical and less willing to blindly accept the power-play and ideologies of the world. People are beginning to feel more connected to others and the relationship between us and the cosmos is being seen as more important.

ENDNOTE REFERENCES

1. Dr Peter Russel – A researcher who maintains that consciousness exists before creation. https://www.peterrussell.com/SP/PrimConsc.php

2. Higgs-Boson or God particle – a sub-atomic particle said to be the cause of mass and is therefore involved in the formation of matter. https://www.scientificamerican.com/article/what-exactly-is-the-higgs/

3. Higher or authentic self – in psychology, regarded as the most real part of us, the true inner personality without the conditioning. It is said to house our highest moral and spiritual ideals. In metaphysics it's given a real and separate existence. https://www.psychologytoday.com/intl/blog/traversing-the-inner-terrain/201802/the-authentic-self

4. Neuroscience combined with Information Systems technology A number of scientists believe that , like an advanced AI computer, the complexity of the universe suggests that it could be conscious. https://www.psychologytoday. com/us/blog/mind-in-the-machine/201512/neurosciences-new-consciousness-theory-is-spiritual

CHAPTER TWO

THE POWERS OF THE MIND

'When you are inspired by some great purpose,
some extraordinary project, all your thoughts break their bonds:
Your mind transcends limitations, your consciousness expands in every
direction, and you find yourself in a new, great, and wonderful world.
Dormant forces, faculties and talents become alive, and you
discover yourself to be a greater person by far than
you ever dreamed yourself to be.'

Patanjali: Author of the Yoga Sutras

In this chapter I show how our minds are more active than we ever realised in creating our sense of reality, being able to filter, select, change, or even 'add to' what we see and hear in the world. This is important, as it influences what we believe to be true.

I also introduce you to two natural abilities of our minds, namely Synesthesia and Pareidolia, which provide the mental foundation for metaphysical experiences. In mapping out our minds in this way, its powers as well as its limits, we can avoid pitfalls in our thinking and set a baseline for what we know to be true in terms of our own personal experience. This will show us what is 'real' as opposed to what can be seen as an overactive imagination, an illusion or a 'quirk' of the mind.

I add a scientific flavour to our metaphysical view of the mind by introducing a computer metaphor to explain its operations in terms of information-processing. Using this computer metaphor, I discuss the subliminal 'programs' called schemas and scripts which are the reason that we have such rigid control by our minds over what we see and experience. I then show how we 'reprogram' them to allow us more flexibility and a wider and deeper view of self and reality.

Finally, I introduce you to the use of affirmations and how to set intentions, both psychological 'tools' to influence our minds at a *subconscious level*, as this is where most of the changes and development will happen if you choose to take the metaphysical path to self-actualisation.

OUR MINDS ARE THE KEY TO EVERYTHING

'Beware lest you lose the substance by grasping at the shadow.'

Aesop

THE DISTORTED LENS

The first question we have to ask ourselves is whether we are actually seeing things as they really are and hearing the words as they are really meant. We need to decide what is real and what is only our imagination or an illusion. In other words, how much of a role do our minds play in our perception of reality?

According to biology, our eyes are *receptors* which respond to different light-frequencies and the forms, colours and shapes that we see are formed from these frequencies and patterns of shadow and perspective. Our eyes translate an outside image into a set of neuron firing-patterns which become signals which are sent to imagery centres in our brains for translation and the images are then put together in our minds. It is the same with hearing. Our ears are also just sound receptors in which sounds are picked up, interpreted and translated into understandable words in our minds.

At first glance, it seems that we should be ending up with a reasonably accurate version of reality. But are we really? It's not as simple as that. In psychology, we learn just how active our minds really are in interpreting what we see and hear.

The truth is that our minds can alter, change, or even *augment* (add to) what we see and hear. We tend to see and hear *selectively* as a result of what is already in our minds, our past experiences and our personal *frames of reference*. A frame of reference is like a window or *filter* through which we see and judge the world. The problem is that it is made up of 'old stuff' which we have brought with us from our past, including assumptions, suppositions and negative feelings coming from our backgrounds and memories (some of which are not pleasant at all).

This 'filter' also houses our present cultural, religious and moral beliefs and convictions, personal agendas and dislikes and attitudes, which all have the effect of working together to act as a sort of narrow *lens* through which we view the world and try to make sense of what we see. All these bits and pieces covering our 'lens' mean that we see things in a *very selective and distorted way*, and the worst of all is that we use this 'data' to think and to arrive at conclusions and make decisions.

WE HEAR THROUGH 'CLOSED EARS'

When it comes to our hearing, we can actually choose to hear something that is being said or not, simply by shifting our focus and attention. For example, when we talk to someone we know at a party, we cut out all the other noisy conversations going on around us. In other cases, we can process a full conversation in our minds but choose to hear and remember only those words which are important to us. In this way, we lose the context of the conversation. This is why it is easy to misinterpret or misunderstand what someone else is saying. It happens all the time.

For example, the selective reporting sometimes seen in the media, where a person's words are misinterpreted or taken out of context by the interviewer, who is often listening with a certain agenda.

This brings us to an important point. What we see and hear in society and how we judge others depends to a large part on our own mindsets and ultimately, our personal issues and agendas. Usually, this just means that we are biased, but in worst-case scenarios, if our minds are filled with hate, fear and resentment, we will see only the negativity, chaos and suffering in the world, while people whose minds are filled with *loving thoughts* are more likely to see the world in a more positive light, even recognising the love and inherent goodness in people.

If our thinking can be influenced by personal feelings, our resulting thoughts become perceptions and are not accurate at all, at least certainly not a true reflection of things as they are. Skewed perceptions mean that our conclusions can be so out of touch that they are completely wrong, so it is not surprising that the world is in such a bad state.

SELECTIVE PERCEPTION AND METAPHYSICS

This lesson on our limited insight and perception is important for metaphysics, as having a narrow 'lens' or outlook on the world means that we each see what is out there in our own way, including our view of ourselves ('self'), reality and even our concepts of God. Selective thinking explains why we naturally have different views, opinions and beliefs about just about everything, as we always see things from our own personal perspective. It is important to remember this when working later with metaphysical processes.

THE COMPUTER METAPHOR

'Thinking and consciousness are not synonymous. Thinking is only a small aspect of consciousness. Thought cannot exist without consciousness, but consciousness does not need thought.'

Eckhardt Tolle: Spiritual teacher and
best-selling author

OPERATING THROUGH A KEYHOLE

You may have heard of doctors doing '*keyhole surgery*' when they only make small incisions and use a scope to work inside the patient. This would a good metaphor for the amount of *input* that our brains can actually process at any one time. I have used the word 'input' for a reason because I want to start using a *computer* as a metaphor for how our brains and minds actually work. This metaphor is often used in psychology.

CAN WE REALLY COMPARE OUR MINDS TO A COMPUTER?

If we had to try to compare our minds to a computer they would be like '*entry-level*' systems, very limited in processing. Consciously we can only work with a little information at any one time. It is as if the world out there is being fed to us through a 'two-wire system' and we end up only with bite (byte)-sized chunks of 'data' which we each believe to be the whole truth of the matter.

THE ANALOGY OF THE PUZZLE

There is a very good reason for this. If we give a large puzzle in a box to a group of small children, it is unlikely that they would ever be able to complete the puzzle, being so young and not able to think and reason well as yet. However, if we break up the puzzle into smaller pieces and give each child a piece to do on their own, be it a corner, part of a border, or a patch of colour, each child should be able to put together their small piece and then, if we put all them all together, the whole puzzle should take form.

This seems to be the case with us at the moment. Our processing abilities are simply not enough to give us a complete view of reality. But perhaps, like the children and the puzzle, we are actually supposed to share our thoughts and ideas and then the bigger picture will take shape. Hopefully I can help you put together some of your own pieces of the puzzle of life in this book.

SELECTIVE THINKING EXPLAINED BY THE COM-PUTER METAPHOR

If we again use the computer metaphor and go back to the previous section on selective thinking, we could say that our subconscious minds act as '*spam filters*' to block out most unnecessary stuff so that we don't overload our '*processor*' (brains). On top of this, the way we look at the world in terms of our past experiences, rigid beliefs and negative feelings, thoughts and perceptions, could also be seen as '*spam*', clogging up our processor. And we may even have a few 'viruses' in our computer (mind) due to our personal problems, stress and anxiety, which slow it down further.

I want to make a last comment using the computer metaphor before we move on. Research points out that most of us are lazy (in a mind-sense) and we do not like thinking deeply, as it is quite demanding to have to unpack and carefully evaluate everything that we see and hear. So we use '*macros*' or shortcuts in thinking such as *stereotyping*, *forming assumptions, guesswork and jumping to conclusions.* We have pre-set programs called *schemas* and *scripts* in our computers (minds) which are supposed to make our thinking quicker and easier, but they bring along their own set of problems. I will go into these schemas and scripts in detail later again, as they are very important to metaphysics.

COMMENT

The point that I am trying to make is that what we know of the universe and reality itself in terms of science at this time is not enough to regard it as the complete and final truth. The goalposts are moving back all the time in line with new scientific discoveries and technologies. Perhaps the time has come to give metaphysics a chance, as it works with universal principles and delves into those hidden areas of our subconscious minds often ignored by science and psychology.

HIDDEN POWERS OF OUR MINDS

'It is your mind that creates this world.'

Buddha

On the positive side, our minds also have other faculties that are very helpful in interpreting what is out there. In metaphysics, we focus on developing these faculties so that we can get a better view of reality and cope better with life. In this section, I discuss a few of them.

SYNESTHESIA

Being able to pick up impressions, sensations and feelings from inside and outside of ourselves and translate them into *colours or even images* is not supernatural or the stuff of fairy-tales. If you consult a psychological encyclopaedia you will come across a little-known term called *Synesthesia*[1], which describes when something picked up by one of our senses is translated into another sense-mode. For example, you must have read how some blind people claim to see music or feel textures as images or colours in their minds. In metaphysics, we believe that this power of our minds to change a sense-impression into a colour or an image is latent and only has to be developed.

Our minds already have the ability to convert *feelings into images* from memory. This is a simple process of association in which we link the feeling back to a memory of a past experience which gave us a similar feeling. An example would be images from old scary movies we saw years ago popping up in our minds when we feel afraid. This happens without us consciously doing it.

Exactly how and why this happens is not known, but it is probably a warning mechanism which evolved in pre-historic man with an image appearing in his mind as a result of cues warning him of any danger that was nearby. You must remember that language and thinking in words only came much later in our human development, and it is likely that early man's level of understanding was based more on *intuitive or instinctual impressions* and images arising from these impressions.

I am sure that many of you have experienced a sense of danger or discomfort in the past, walking through a rough area of town or even when driving through a nature reserve in which dangerous animals freely roam. Imagine how this feeling of discomfort gives rise to impressions of 'spikiness', or the colour red, or a vision of thorns flashing briefly in your mind. Metaphorically, thorns are prickly and dangerous and would symbolically mean danger. Similarly, think of a sensation of comfort or safety spontaneously producing a brief image of a 'safe' colour such as blue, or even objects such as 'bubbles' or 'cotton puffs', which we normally associate with comfort or harmlessness. You can now see how the sensation could be translated into a thought which gives rise to an image. In fact, this skill is currently widely used in neuro-linguistic programming.

WHAT GIVES RISE TO THE IMPRESSIONS, SENSATIONS AND FEELINGS?

The impressions, sensations and feelings we feel are normally linked to something outside of us. In everyday life, we speak of people giving off energy vibrations. For example, we say '*this or that person has a bad vibe*', or we say we can feel it when a person is looking at us. But is this true? And can we explain this scientifically or psychologically? Modern science tells us that our bodies have an *electrochemical nature* and can give off electro-magnetic waves. It seems that every living thing radiates emanations of some sort. For example, our hearts produce electrical impulses which we measure on an ECG (electro-cardiograph) and the EEG (Electro-encephalogram), measures the energy-impulses from our brains.

What is important is that we recognise the possibility that all living creatures, including us, give off characteristic patterns of energy which could be called *energy signatures*, typical of the life-form and even specific to individuals in much the same way as a DNA profile is exclusive to a person.

SENSING THESE ENERGY-EMANATIONS

In metaphysics, we accept that we all have this ability to pick up energy-signatures and translate them into impressions, sensations and feelings.

BUT WHAT DOES SCIENCE SAY?

The ability of animals to sense energy radiations[2] is well known to science. Sharks can pick up the radiated electrical waves of the muscle contractions of their prey; and others like the sea turtle and pigeons can even detect weak magnetic fields. Scientists believe that a light-detecting protein in the eyes of these animals functions as a magnetic field sensor and have found the same protein in our own bodies, which has some researchers wondering if *we too have a latent magnetic sense.* This begs the question as to whether we too may be able to sense the energy emanations of other persons or living beings. Actual scientific research is sketchy on this, but I believe that there are at least two real possibilities.

First, our largest sensory organ is *our skin* and it may well be sensitive to *energy emanations* from outside, channelling them through to our nervous system. We know that our skin has sensors which pick up heat and cold and it is quite possible that it responds to *electromagnetic impressions* in the same way as the sea turtles and pigeons do. I also know of many people who complain of headaches when in the region of a cell-phone tower and I personally remember when computers first came out in the early 1990s and how the radiation from the old-type monitors often made me sick. When in outer space, astronauts are protected against outside radiations by special space-suits.

The second possibility is that we pick up outside energy emanations through our 'auras'. There is quasi-scientific research into what is called the *human aura[3]*, an envelope of energy said to surround our bodies. Theoretically, this energy envelope could respond to any outside energies impinging on it, resulting in impressions, sensations and feelings. However, this research has not gained general acceptance in scientific circles and so it remains within the field of metaphysics linked to the phenomenon of synesthesia. I personally do not have a problem with this idea of an energy envelope surrounding our bodies. I believe it possible for the electromagnetic radiations of the body to come together and follow its shape more or less.

PAREIDOLIA

Another natural talent of the mind which helps us to form images from outside cues is *Pareidolia*[4]. This is when our minds form a familiar image such as an object or even a face from random cues, such as patterns in bushes or clouds. For example, children often play a game in which they try to see animals in the clouds. In this case, their minds use cues from partial forms in the clouds to shape what they see into animals. In psychology, this is called *Pareidolia* and it is very important to metaphysics.

These skills explain why it is so important to cultivate a clear and quiet mind for this kind of work, as what you see depends on your state of mind, as well as emotions, memories and beliefs. For example, if you were bitten by a vicious dog as a child, you may associate any barking or growling as a cue for danger and the picture memory of this nasty dog could pop into your mind.

During some of the processes I describe later, you will be working with impressions, sensations and feelings that you need to translate into images. However, you will find that to reach this stage of development takes time and training, but it is possible, as you will see in the real-life examples I present later in this book.

THE POWER OF OUR MINDS TO AUGMENT REALITY

SUPERIMPOSING IMAGINARY IMAGES ON REALITY

I am sure every one of you has had some experience when you believed that you saw something scary which later turned out to be only a shadow or a coat hanging on a rail. This is quite common. There also is a classic case study in psychology of a spectator calling a referee a clown and being convinced that he actually saw the referee's uniform change into a clown suit. In fact, research has shown that it is possible for us to superimpose visual images on reality. Remember that, even with our normal sense of sight, what we are seeing is only a view of reality formed in our minds from visual cues. We also know that we can have hallucinations, in that what we see can be influenced by illness and drugs as well as by our own imagination during certain mental illnesses. There is no reason why we should not be able to superimpose powerful subconscious images onto reality. In fact, I will prove this to be the case in later exercises.

SCHEMAS AND SCRIPTS

'All of that which we experience is processed in the mind.'

J. Henderson

I previously used the metaphor of a computer for our minds and mentioned briefly that our beliefs, expectations and past experiences are stored in mental programs called *schemas* and *scripts*. I mentioned how important they are in what we see and how we interpret the world. Let us now go deeper and see how these powerful programs actually work to affect our minds and thinking.

SCHEMAS

This power of our minds to select, shape, change or augment what we see (and understand) of the world out there is due to the *schemas* and *scripts* we have formed in our minds over the years. A script is also a schema, but I will deal with them separately to show you the differences between them.

In line with our computer metaphor, schemas would be like mini 'programs' having '*programming rules*' to guide us in our thinking, decisions and actions. Some schemas are simply inner speech (words) drawn up from the lessons or '*data*' we have gleaned from our past experiences, beliefs, attitudes and assumptions. Others are stored images which help us to recognise unfamiliar things. For example, using schemas, our minds can put together random cues which on their own do not make much sense to form a familiar image (Pareidolia). I mentioned the game played by children in which they see animals in the clouds. In this case, their minds are actually 'adding to' or shaping cues in the clouds to form the animals using the schemas of animals they have seen before.

Schemas actually have a positive role in that they are like 'programming macros' or *short-cuts* in our thinking which help to speed up our 'inner processing' and allow us to make quick decisions. The problem is that they use stereotyped judgments, assumptions and suppositions, which means that they *prime* our minds to see and process only that 'data' which fits in with, or is the same as, our present beliefs and ideas. So we will ignore anything which differs from our present thinking. The result is that we can make quick but impulsive decisions without really thinking at all.

DELUSIONS

For example, Fred sees his wife talking to another man at a party and assumes that she is flirting, as his schema for his wife includes the fact that she is popular with men. He will now choose to see only what suits his schema and will most likely accuse her of flirting, and she will accuse him of being delusional, as all her actions, (which were actually quite innocent), would be seen and interpreted (wrongly) in the light of his schema. The biggest problem is that many schemas work at a subconscious level and we are not even aware of them.

ILLUSIONS

Images from our *schemas of objects* can be superimposed on reality, resulting in optical illusions, such as the example of a spectator calling a referee a clown and seeing his uniform change into a clown-suit. I have personally had an experience when I misread a street signboard, but I will swear that I saw the right name on the board. We need to be careful, as what we see can be an illusion.

SCHEMAS FOR SELF AND REALITY

In metaphysics, the two most important schemas are those for *self* and *reality*. These are important to us as they contain the *rules* we have set as to what we are prepared to consider when it comes to ourselves and reality. If our self-schema is not flexible enough, it will stunt our personal growth by stopping us from searching for, and arriving at, new self-insights. And our schema for reality will influence what we consider to be 'real' in the world (or the universe).

THE IMPORTANCE OF THE WORDING IN OUR SCHEMAS

If we look at the wording in our schemas for *self and reality*, it all seems straightforward, but when working subconsciously, exactly what we have said to ourselves is very important. I will show you why with a real-life example;

JAMES' SELF-SCHEMA

Look at James' self-schema as an example. James has never had any spiritual experiences and is not a religious person. When it comes to himself (self), he believes in only what he can see, (in fact, this applies to many people in our society today).

This is the type of schema that kicks in when James looks at himself in the mirror.

'I am James Smith.'

Rule: 'I only believe in what I can see.'

'I can see my body in the mirror.'

'I don't see a soul in the mirror.'

Rule: 'Therefore I am (only) a body.'

See how his self-schema has *embedded rules* in its lines of thinking. In this case, '*I only believe in what I can see*' and '*I am only a body*'. As a result of this schema, James automatically removes any possibility of his having a soul when he thinks about himself. He has no expectations of an inner metaphysical experience and psychologically speaking, this schema will make it difficult for him to recognise or even understand one if it happened.

SCRIPTS

I am sure that most of you are familiar with a script for a play or a film which contains all the actors' lines and movements. Our scripts are similar, in that they have a series of steps or instructions on how to cope with different situations in life that we have put together over the years to make things easier for us. They give us simple prompts on what to do and when to do it, and in this way, they are also shortcuts in our thinking which shape how we act in different situations and also *how we interpret* what we see.

Let us now look at James' subconscious script for reality. I bet that you will see the problem here:

JAMES' SCRIPT FOR REALITY

'Reality is what I can see.'

'What I see are only material things.'

'Reality is made up of material things.'

Rule: 'I need not look further for another reality.'

James has a script for reality in which he automatically discounts any *spiritual* experiences as well as subtle feelings, sensations or impressions which are at the heart of metaphysical and spiritual experiences. This script will prompt him to overlook or ignore any such cues or 'clues' which point to a higher reality. This will happen without him even knowing it.

SUE'S SCRIPT FOR REALITY

Now let us look at Sue's script for reality. Her script is open-ended and actually prepares her mind for deeper experiences. Open-ended means that, in spite of our own beliefs, our minds are open and we are willing to consider that there may be other ways of looking at the world apart from our own. This is very important when working with metaphysical principles.

'When I think of reality I keep an open mind.'

'My open mind means that I am open to unexplained experiences.'

Rule: 'If I have an unexplained experience, this may point to a higher reality.'

The problem with schemas and scripts is that they are put together from *beliefs* and *experiences*. However, some of our beliefs could be wrong and some of our past experiences unpleasant, but right, wrong or downright unpleasant, they are still included in our schemas. This means that a few bad experiences could end up as a set of negative beliefs and form a script which now affects the way that we act in similar situations.

Let me give you an example of this:

TOM'S NEGATIVE SCRIPT

Tom is not very successful with the ladies. Unfortunately, he grew up in unpleasant surroundings where he was belittled by his father. As a result, he has low self-esteem and is prone to thinking that he is not popular with women. These thoughts have now been internalised and have formed a negative social script which affects the way that he behaves in social situations. Let's have a look at his script:

'My name is Tom.'

'I am not very popular with women.'

'Women tend to reject me in social situations.'

'I then feel humiliated.'

Rule: 'So it is better I if do not approach them at all.'

As a result of this script, over the past months, Tom has avoided parties, even though his friends did invite him. They have now grown tired of his excuses and no longer call him up. Also, because of his obvious insecurity, women do not take him seriously. Tom knows this and often makes the remark, 'See, I told you I was not popular'. The problem is that he cannot see that it is his own script and self-schema with his negative thoughts and beliefs about himself that are influencing his actions, which, in turn, are sending the message that he is not a fun fellow to be with. This means that people will avoid him even more. In this way, a negative script or self-schema can become *'a self-fulfilling prophecy'* which is certainly not helpful, especially for our metaphysical development.

While it is true that we can make conscious and carefully considered decisions and not all our thinking is controlled by schemas and scripts, most unthinking actions are. Without us taking the time to think and consider things more carefully and make these conscious decisions, schemas and scripts will affect our everyday thinking and actions and limit our potential for growth.

THE POWER OF WORDS

'Mere words have an extraordinary significance for us; they have a neurological effect whose sensations are more important than what is beyond the symbol.'

Krishnamurti: Indian philosopher, speaker and writer

Words and concepts have a magical quality in that they represent our thoughts. We think using words. When linked together by logical reasoning, they can help us to arrive at good conclusions. This is the process I use in my *multi-dimensional thinking* approach.

WORDS AND PERSPECTIVE

Words have the power to evoke emotions. For instance, look at the way news can be presented in different ways by the media. The following examples of news headlines highlight the problem of 'perspective' or diverse points of view.

'Vicious dog attacks defenceless man'

'Cruel owner bitten by abused dog'

Notice the different *feelings* that emerge as a result of the word-usage, even though the reporters are describing the same incident from different points of view or perspectives. Incidentally, if we understand the notion of *perspective* we will have a far better understanding of reality. But I will have more to say on this matter later.

THE EFFECT OF WORDS ON OUR MINDS AND THINKING

If we look at the previous sections on schemas and scripts, we can see how powerful words can be if they are working at a subconscious level. Even consciously, in everyday life people can be easily swayed or seduced by highly emotional or great-sounding words and ideas, which can have almost a hypnotic effect on those who are open to the message. The right words can have a powerful effect on our minds. For example, if someone tells you that there's a vicious dog just behind the next gate, you will know what this means and be extra careful to ensure the gate is closed when you pass by. And if your partner phones and tells you that you have just won a pile of money in that competition you entered, your state of mind will quickly change and you will be very excited. In fact, words can be so powerful that, if we don't understand a word-concept, we will struggle to understand any *inner experience* linked to that concept.

Our understanding and openness to new knowledge deepens with each new idea that we master and this is the reason why I encourage reading holistic books, so that our thoughts and vocabulary can expand and our perspectives become more universal.

SELF-TALK

Having the right thoughts (or words) are especially important for our *self-talk*. Self-talk is the inner 'conversations' we have with ourselves when we are put into any situation. Put simply, it is 'what we tell ourselves' when placed in these circumstances. Sometimes we may speak our self-talk out aloud (thinking out loud), but for the most part it takes place subconsciously without us even knowing what we are saying to ourselves. And this is where the danger lies. The reason for this is that the *wording* of our schemas and scripts affects our decisions and actions, as it becomes our self-talk.

WORDS AND EMOTIONS

As I have just shown in the example of the two news headlines of the 'vicious' or 'abused' dog, the wording of our self-talk can trigger *emotions* which, in turn, can affect our thinking and decisions. These words can be either positive and uplifting, or negative and disempowering, and come from our schemas and scripts. It can be a real problem if negative messages filter through to emerge in our self-talk. Let me give you another example:

REMEMBER THIS LINE FROM TOM'S SCRIPT?

'I am not very popular with women.'

This will most likely be *Tom's self-talk* when he is around women and will reinforce his already-low self-esteem. It is so important for our growth and even our metaphysical development that we are prepared to *challenge and change* this type of negative self-talk. How to do this will be shown in a later chapter.

THE EFFECT OF METAPHORS ON OUR MINDS

To close this theme on the power of words, look at the *metaphors* you use to describe yourself, your situations and the world itself. Metaphors have a special, powerful effect on our minds and thinking. Earlier I told you of the real-life example of the spectator who called a soccer referee a clown and was convinced that he saw the referee's uniform change into a clown suit. In other words, the *clown metaphor* filtered into his subconscious mind and acted as a cue to activate his schema for a clown suit which was then superimposed onto the referee's uniform. This is not an isolated case and there are many cases of people using cue words to alter another's perception. In fact, cue words are at the centre of the power of suggestion used by magic entertainers.

Metaphors also subconsciously affect the way we look at ourselves, at life and reality itself. For example, the metaphor *'living between a rock and a hard place'* leads us to the idea that life is all suffering. However, if we change this metaphor to a more open and universal one, such as *'life is the field of all possibilities'* and we really believe it to be so, we confirm to our subconscious mind that we are open and receptive to new possibilities and the kind of inner experiences that come with a study of metaphysics, and our subconscious minds will respond accordingly. This power of our subconscious minds to govern and even alter our perception will be shown in a later chapter.

RE-PROGRAMMING YOUR SCHEMAS AND SCRIPTS

'Our words change our perception and if we change our language, we change our reality'

Luigi Boscolo: Psychoanalyst

In the previous section, I introduced you to the activity of schemas and scripts within your minds. In this section, we go a lot deeper into how they work and how you can actively change and 'rewrite' them to clear the way for greater openness and clarity in your mind and thinking.

WATCH OUT FOR NEGATIVE SCRIPTS!

Many of us do things that we regret, often without thinking, and wonder later why we made such a silly decision, acted in such an unpleasant way, or avoided something that we should have done to achieve success in our lives. This kind of behaviour is often the result of the schemas and scripts which we have formed in our minds over the years.

As I showed in the previous section, our schemas and scripts shape our self-talk or inner speech. You can recognise your schemas in your self-talk, especially those '*ego-conversations*' which start with 'I can't', 'I ought' or 'I have to' and so on. We don't realise how powerful scripts are until we fall into the trap of negative scripts. Our scripts contribute to our success or failure in our lives or careers and negative scripts can affect our thinking, feelings and decisions and ultimately, our futures.

LET ME GIVE YOU AN EXAMPLE OF A NEGATIVE SCRIPT:

John has been given a challenging job but tells his supervisor that he does not feel up to it. This will now affect the way his supervisor looks at John and could prevent him from getting that promotion he wants. Let's unpack the process and see how this came about:

JOHN'S SELF-TALK: 'I CAN'T DO THIS TASK'

John's answer to his supervisor was influenced by negative self-talk included in a script he has built up from his feelings of self-doubt from his past. Emotions always play a role as well, and they can certainly add colour to a schema or script. If we were able to see John's script on a screen, this is probably what we would see:

'I failed in the past.'

'I always fail.'

'I will fail again.'

(Therefore) *'I can't /won't do this task.'*

Notice how one line of negative self-talk leads to the next and it gets progressively worse. This is typical of a bad script. It is likely that John has had a few failures in his career. I think we all have, but the problem is that he has generalised these past failures to tell himself that he will not be successful with this new task as well. Remember that a script contains the *guidelines we will follow* when faced with a similar challenge. So this script will cripple John's willingness to accept tough assignments and will certainly not help his career.

As you can imagine, this type of negative script is very disempowering. Unfortunately, we all tend to remember our bad experiences and failures more than our successes, and these make for very unhelpful schemas or scripts, something we need to deal with if we wish to clear our minds and make way for personal growth.

'REWRITING' YOUR SCRIPTS

Schemas and scripts are quite tough to change as they have to be challenged and dismantled line by line. In tackling a negative and disempowering script such as John's, we will have to commit to plenty of honest self-examination and reflection. For instance, we will have to dig deep and review our thinking, ideas and beliefs about ourselves, identify our lines of self-talk and challenge each line with new positive truths about ourselves based on our more recent successes.

The problem is that we are not normally aware of what we have 'written' in them, so we have to fool our subconscious minds into thinking that we are having the kind of experience that normally 'cues' this negative self-talk.

This points to an interesting fact about our subconscious minds that allows us some control over it. You may be able to remember a time when you woke up sweating with your heart pumping after having a bad dream or a nightmare. This means that our subconscious minds cannot really tell the difference between a real-life situation and an imaginary one. So we make use of this 'loophole' in its workings to get what we want.

A SELF-TEST

We all have the ability to form three-dimensional, moving images in our minds. This skill is called *imagery or visualisation*, and we will be using it frequently in this book.

- So what you need to do now is to sit down with a notepad and pen and create an imaginary scene in your mind which will fool your subconscious mind into believing that you are having a particular experience, such as facing a new, daunting challenge at work. Try to make it feel as real as possible. Add emotions if you can.

- If you are successful, this imagined scenario will cue and activate your schemas and scripts so that you can have a look at them. If you do this properly, you will feel the effects of the schema kicking in by having uncomfortable feelings during your visualisation.

- Write down the first words that come to mind when you have these feelings. This will be your inner dialogue or self-talk activated by the hidden script in your subconscious mind which helps you to decide how you deal with crises or tough situations in your home or working life. In cases where your self-talk is negative, you will have to challenge each line and change it to a positive new self-truth, as I have mentioned.

I will use John's script as an example:

'I failed in the past.'

'I always fail.'

'I will fail again.'

(Therefore) *'I can't do this task.'*

You will have to challenge each statement and replace it with positive affirmations. There is more information on affirmations in the next section if you don't know how to create and apply them.

FOR EXAMPLE: POSITIVE AFFIRMATIONS

'I failed at one thing, but I am not a failure.'

'I am a hardworking and dedicated person.'

'I am a very valuable asset to my family and company.'

'I can do any task I set my mind to.'

You have to say these affirmations out loud daily for at least two weeks. Using a mirror will also be a good idea. After a few weeks, you should notice a change in your feelings and attitude towards new challenges. Do your same visualisation exercise in three weeks' time again and re-examine your self-talk. Hopefully, it would have improved by then.

WHY ARE OUR SCHEMAS AND SCRIPTS SO IMPORTANT TO METAPHYSICAL DEVELOPMENT?

Remember that these are *mind-programs* which influence your thinking and what you are willing to do when given new challenges or tasks. In other words, if you have any doubts or concerns about metaphysical processes, this will be reflected in your scripts and self-talk and will hold you back, and you will, in all likelihood, not be successful in *'connecting'* to your authentic self or any higher level of consciousness. By 're-authoring' these negative scripts you will improve your chances of success with metaphysical practices as well as almost any field of endeavour.

LET ME GIVE YOU AN EXAMPLE OF THE POWER OF CHANGING NEGATIVE SCRIPTS.

Here is an example of a *negative script for self* which shows how it can limit performance. Just over fifty years ago we believed that a human being couldn't run a mile in under four minutes. This belief became a script in the minds of all runners and ended up as a psychological barrier to achievement in the sport of running. It could be said that Roger Bannister was the first person to successfully '*rewrite the script*' for what is humanly possible when it came to running this distance. What is interesting is that, immediately after his record-breaking feat of a sub-four-minute mile, a number of other runners also ran this time in quick succession. It seems that his effort had '*given permission*' for the others to also change their scripts about the possibility of a four-minute mile.

THERE ARE VERY GOOD REASONS FOR CHANGING NEGATIVE SCHEMAS AND SCRIPTS

- Weak scripts for *self* can limit our chances for success, as shown in the previous example.

- Some schemas for people can be biased and judgmental, and it is easy to judge or even misjudge another person based on the schemas or scripts you have of that 'type' of person.

- Even worse, if your *schemas and scripts for reality* are fixed and rigid, they will close your mind to important cues that point to a higher reality and ruin any chances you have for deep insights or metaphysical revelations.

- Finally, schemas and scripts control what you see and experience during meditations, as the images and experiences are shaped by the schemas and scripts that you already have for objects, people, and what *is possible* in this world. We will look at this important principle in greater detail in the next section.

SCHEMAS AND SCRIPTS SEEN IN THE LIGHT OF THE COMPUTER METAPHOR

What we think or experience about ourselves and reality depends to a large extent on our beliefs and assumptions. As shown earlier, these are housed in our schemas or scripts. If I had to explain this using our earlier 'computer' metaphor, it would be like having hidden programs running in the background. If they are very negative we could see them as 'viruses' as they limit our 'processing' and potential for understanding ourselves as well as reality. This will have to change if we wish to prepare our minds for new metaphysical experiences.

NEW SCRIPTS FOR SELF AND REALITY

Metaphorically, we have to reprogram our software and clean out the viruses or bad programming which are holding us back from what we could be in terms of metaphysical development. A simple beginning to this process of reconditioning would be to challenge our old ways of thinking about ourselves and reality, and a good way to do this is to start reading uplifting self-growth and holistic books and articles that will help us let go of our preconceived ideas and assumptions about 'self' and reality. We simply have to stop thinking of ourselves in such a poor light and look to our future possibilities.

LOOK AT WHAT WE HAVE STORED IN OUR SCHE-MAS AND SCRIPTS

MATERIALISTIC SCHEMAS

Many people still believe that the universe is only made up of material bits and pieces (substance). They do not understand or wish to understand the concepts of quantum physics or a *universe of energy* and the important implications this has for us and our experience of reality. As I showed earlier, their schemas and scripts would probably include rigid beliefs such as: 'Everything is made from solid substances'; Matter is all that exists'; 'Reality is that which can be seen', which are quite limiting. Their minds would simply not be open to any suggestion of energy or exercises involving energy-work.

RELIGIOUS SCHEMAS

Similarly, religious people see life and creation (reality) as the work of a transcendent Divine Being (God) and their schemas and scripts would probably be made up of words and concepts drawn from sacred scriptures. This limits any possible metaphysical experiences and insights, as these scriptures are not up to date with the latest metaphysical ideas, having arisen in totally different historical times, cultures and value systems. Atheists have a problem in that they do not believe in any higher reality at all and will most likely have schemas and scripts in their subconscious minds which deny any 'spiritual' experiences, and this will be just as restrictive.

COMMENT

The problem is that, when it comes to our growth and development, highly selective schemas such as these will only allow us to experience a very limited view of the world and range of experiences in line with these schemas. Such schemas and scripts place people in rigid frameworks or 'sealed boxes' and they are no longer able to think out of these boxes. If we are serious about growth, development and self-actualisation, whether or not we study metaphysics, we will need an open, flexible, enquiring mind and an ability to look beyond existing paradigms (outside of the box).

This does not mean that we have to give up our present beliefs, but rather just try to open them up to new possibilities and make them flexible enough to allow for new and deeper inner experiences.

The easiest way of doing this is to be prepared to change our existing scripts for *self* and *reality*. If we do not, we limit our chances of success with metaphysical practices.

Let us begin with the process of mentally reprogramming these unhelpful schemas and scripts in a step-by-step manner. The first tool we will use is affirmations, which I introduced into the previous section but I will now go into more detail.

AFFIRMATIONS

'Words are loaded pistols.'

Jean-Paul Sartre:
French existentialist philosopher

Reprogramming our subconscious minds is a *multi-stage process* which begins with *affirmations* and the setting of new intentions to challenge our outdated subliminal schemas and scripts.

WHAT ARE AFFIRMATIONS?

As seen in the previous section on schemas and scripts, their content has a powerful effect on our subconscious minds. However, when open to suggestion, they will eventually accept new ideas if we impress these upon them repeatedly with enough emotion and intent. Affirmations are *self-talk statements* which contain positive emotionally-charged words and ideas, and if they are taken up by our subconscious minds, they help to change our schemas and scripts for the better.

HOW DO AFFIRMATIONS WORK?

The well-known psychiatrist, Milton Eriksen, believed that *emotionally-charged words* have the power to affect our subconscious minds and even bring about enhanced or semi-trancelike states of consciousness which we can use for deep processing. This is why affirmations work best when our minds are relaxed and open to suggestion, such as during meditation.

HOW DO WE USE AFFIRMATIONS?

For those of you who do not wish to meditate, you can simply repeat the affirmations to yourselves over and over in front of a mirror *with feeling* and a *sense of expectation*. It will take a few weeks before they will infiltrate your schemas and scripts and your subconscious mind accepts them as new rules for thinking, feeling and acting. However, this will make it possible for you to change your self-talk and open your minds to new inner experiences relating to self and reality. Without these changes, your outdated schemas and scripts will block or filter out these experiences.

To open up our minds, we will be using affirmations to communicate to our subconscious minds our willingness and readiness to connect with the deeper parts of ourselves and with the energies of the universe itself.

THE METAPHOR OF THE 'LOVER'

It is important to build a good relationship with our subconscious minds if we want affirmations to work. In this case, we can see our subconscious minds as *separate personalities*, and it is actually possible to communicate with them as such.

In my previous books, I have suggested using the *metaphor of a new lover* to describe the process of building this relationship. And we need to 'woo' this lover. In this case, affirmations would be like first introducing ourselves to our new lover, from which 'he' or 'she' will gauge our confidence and sincerity. Metaphorically speaking, we will not make a good first impression if we show ourselves to be indecisive and lacking in confidence and self-worth. For this reason, our first affirmations should be aimed at starting the communication and convincing our 'lover' of our inner strength, our sincere intentions and our desire for an intimate relationship. This is done by whispering 'sweet words' of kindness, love and appreciation.

For example:

'I am open to a relationship with my lover (subconscious mind).'

'I ask for the love and protection of my lover.'

'I embrace my lover (subconscious mind).'

'I thank you, my lover, for your care and concern.'

In other words, ask nicely, as if your subconscious mind was a real 'person'.

If you are successful with your introduction and wooing, your 'lover' will learn to trust you and will soon open the doors for you to enter their inner chamber where you metaphorically 'embrace' him or her. This 'embrace' opens you up to deeply personal experiences, after which you must shower them with appreciation.

This relationship with your subconscious mind 'lover' is necessary for all later metaphysical work, and not only to change schemas and scripts. Once you have the trust and cooperation of your subconscious mind it is never lost and you will find that your experiences during meditations seem almost 'magical', as it provides the power for amazing shifts in consciousness.

Let us now return to the use of affirmations for changing schemas and scripts.

USING AFFIRMATIONS TO CHANGE OUTDATED SCHEMAS

Remember James's old self-schema from a previous section?

'I am James Smith.'

'I only believe in what I can see.'

'I can see my body in the mirror.'

'I don't see a soul in the mirror.'

'Therefore, I am (only) a body.'

This schema is certainly not going to allow James any deeper experiences, as he does not believe in a soul or higher spiritual side to self. If he wishes to have such experiences, he has to change this to a more open and inclusive self-schema using *new affirmations*.

For example:

JAMES' NEW AFFIRMATIONS AND VIEW OF SELF

'I am not this body.'

'This is not who I am.'

'I am a soul having a human experience.'

'I am a being of light and consciousness.'

James also had a script for viewing reality which was not much better, if you recall:

'Reality is what I can see.'

'I am now looking at the world.'

'What I see are only material things.'

'Reality is made up of material things.'

Rule: 'I need not look further for a hidden reality.'

In order to open himself up to new experiences of reality, James will have to try new affirmations:

JAMES'S NEW SCRIPT FOR REALITY

'Reality is not as I believe it to be.'

'Reality is put together in my mind.'

'I accept a new view of reality.'

Rule: 'I am open to new experiences of reality.'

AFFIRMATIONS ARE LIMITED IN THEIR EFFICACY

The problem with affirmations is that they are not the most effective way of changing schemas and scripts. But if you work with them diligently they can filter through into your subconscious mind and challenge the rigid beliefs holding you back, especially if you have built up a good relationship with your subconscious mind 'lover'. Over time you may see an improvement in your thinking and self-talk about yourself and reality.

Try different affirmations and find those which you feel are working best to change your schemas. Eventually, your mind will begin to question your current thinking. What you want to achieve at this early stage is a new understanding that all may not be as it appears to be, and to strive for a belief in a universe of infinite possibilities.

Let us now look at other more powerful methods of changing outdated schemas and scripts.

INTENTIONS

'Man is what he wills himself to be.'

Jean-Paul Sartre

WHAT ARE INTENTIONS?

A more effective way of changing subconscious schemas and scripts is by setting intentions. An intention is similar to an affirmation, but it is more powerful as it is a direct instruction to our subconscious minds ('lovers'). Unlike an affirmation, which is usually repeated over and over, an intention is set only once, but its ability to change your schemas stems from your willpower and the positive, confident state of mind that you will need to do this. This gives the intention much more authority than an affirmation, but it takes time to develop this powerful state of mind. In terms of our metaphor of the 'lover', this could be seen as showing her (or him) that you are willing to take responsibility for your decisions and coming across as strong, powerful and confident. The effect of your intention also depends on your relationship of *trust and cooperation* with your 'lover'.

HOW TO SET INTENTIONS

Intentions can be set when you are fully conscious, but work best during periods of meditation, as your subconscious mind is fully open and responsive to this type of instruction at those times.

To begin, utter your intentions out loud. Later, with practice, you can form the instructions in your mind. But to do this, your mind needs to be completely free of clutter, conflicting thoughts and be totally focused, as our subconscious minds ('lovers') do not respond to ambiguous or doubtful thoughts or uncertainty. As a result, do a quick self-examination before setting any intention to see if you have concerns or hidden fears which could cause you to hesitate or doubt the process and get rid of them.

Once you have set an intention, let it go with full confidence that it will work. It is this singular, focussed, powerful state of mind and the action of will-power that convinces your subconscious mind ('lover') of your seriousness and readiness and which will assure you of its cooperation for the changes to your schemas or scripts that you want. You will have to learn to cultivate and apply this confident and positive state of mind when later working with your subconscious mind 'lover' to engage with higher levels of reality.

The more radical your intentions the more likely they are to *shake up and reprogram* your outdated schemas and scripts about self and reality. Use them a few times each day and act on them. In other words, do something that will convince your subconscious 'lover' that you are serious, such as reading up on, or talking to your friends of like mind, about alternative views of self and reality.

Meeting up with free-thinking folk at holistic festivals will certainly help you change your mindset as well.

HERE ARE A FEW SUGGESTIONS FOR NEW, POWERFUL INTENTIONS:

> *'I now set the intention to change my schema of self to one of infinite possibilities.'*
> *'I now set the intention to see myself as an infinite being.'*
> *'I now set the intention to no longer be bound by my old beliefs about reality.'*
> *'I now set the intention to open my mind to reality as it IS.'*

If your new intentions and approach to self and reality are accepted by your 'lover' (subconscious mind), it will allow changes to take place in those outdated schemas and scripts which are limiting your growth and potential. You will then open up to wonderful, new inner experiences. More on setting intentions is shown in the real-life examples given in later sections.

MORE POWERFUL METHODS OF CHANGING SCHEMAS AND SCRIPTS

The most powerful method of changing schemas and scripts is by using *interactive visualisation*. This method is discussed and explained in a separate chapter.

ENDNOTE REFERENCES

1. Synesthesia – our minds ability to translate one sense mode into another https://www.healthline.com/health/synesthesia#examples

2. The ability of animals to sense energy radiations – This is self-explanatory https://www.brainfacts.org/thinking-sensing-and-behaving/vision/2017/what-can-animals-sense-that-we-cant-071317

3. Human aura –an unseen envelope of energy said to surround the body, created by the electrical activity in the body https://medicalxpress.com/news/2012-05-scientific-evidence-healers-aura-people.html

4. Pareidolia – The ability of our minds to form recognisable shapes and figures out of random cues https://dictionary.cambridge.org/dictionary/english/pareidolia

CHAPTER THREE

SELF-DEVELOPMENT

'And we're seeing a higher level of consciousness and
many more opportunities for people to challenge their present
ways of thinking and move into a grander and larger
experience of who they really are.'

Neale Donald Walsch:
Author of *Conversations with God*

THE PERSONAL GROWTH CURVE

Metaphysics is not a study of the 'supernatural'. In fact, I do not believe that this concept has any value at all in relation to metaphysics, as I believe the metaphysical path to be a natural process linked to our personal growth and development. In this chapter, I introduce you to the idea of an *upward curve* as a graph for the growth in consciousness, understanding and morality that should take place during our lives. As we learn different social and life-skills we move up the curve until we reach the top and the point of *self-actualisation*, a state in which we fulfil our true potential and become what we are capable of becoming.

I discuss the different stages and skills needed for progress up the curve, from the moment of our first becoming aware of our need to change, to making the necessary commitment and then taking action to simplify our lives, increase our mindfulness, quieten our thinking and eventually arrive at emotional and mental wellness.

Finally, I show you how and why metaphysical practices such as meditation and visualisation are found at the top end of the growth curve and how *spiritual wholeness* can be seen as the same as self-actualisation.

STAGES OF DEVELOPMENT

'Real change has to be preceded by a change in consciousness.'

Eckhart Tolle

STAGE ONE – THE REALISATION OF OUR NEED TO CHANGE

THE COMMITMENT

Our first step up the personal growth curve is that moment of realisation in which we can stop what we are doing and consciously realise our desperate *need* to change and grow. This is the time when we make the decision for personal empowerment and do a 180- degree turnabout to begin releasing the selfishness and pettiness of the ego that we have built up over all these years.

However, reaching this moment in consciousness by simply learning from our mistakes could take an entire lifetime. Unfortunately, this is the course taken by many, and there is no guarantee that a person will have enough insight to look carefully at the common problems in their day-to-day lives and identify and work to correct the bad patterns or trends in their thinking and actions. If this is the case, the same bitter experiences with life, relationships, or finances, will come back time and time again until they are *forced* to reconsider what they have done in the past and make better-informed choices. Unfortunately, many people do not even reach this point and so pass away into eternity blissfully unaware of their true potential.

STAGE TWO - 'CLEANING HOUSE'

The second stage along this path of personal growth is having to metaphorically '*clean house*' and sort through all the clutter in our minds and expose and peel away the layers of the ego with their muddied contents to make way for the later authentic experience of 'self'. Let me break this stage down into a series of smaller steps:

SIMPLIFY YOUR LIFE

If you are preparing to travel the metaphysical path to self-actualisation you will need to make changes in your present lifestyle. Simply put, this stage involves *creating the time and space for growth* by simplifying and balancing your life, reducing distractions and becoming more mindful of your thoughts and actions. You cannot expect to discover new depths to self and reality if you are distracted by constant partying, pleasure-seeking and bad habits from living excessively and being caught up in the glamour of the entertainment scene, media brainwashing and celebrity culture.

This does not mean that you now have to isolate yourselves from the world, but rather, just to shift your focus from the *outer world to the inner world of experience* that is within your reach. Learning this lesson of turning to look 'within' could also take a lifetime, but it can be speeded up by using metaphysical processes which I will introduce later.

BECOME MORE MINDFUL OF YOUR THOUGHTS AND ACTIONS

Increasing your mindfulness will give you the *clarity* of consciousness you need for your journey ahead.

SO WHAT EXACTLY IS MINDFULNESS?

Let me try to explain this simply. Most of us go through life making decisions using our past experiences as a guide without really thinking of all the issues involved. This can lead to the stereotyping of people and situations and not always taking the best course of action. Mindfulness is being fully aware or conscious of what is happening around you and what you are thinking and doing *in the moment*, in the '*now*' without the clutter and clamour of racing thoughts. If it is still not clear, let me try to explain mindfulness as a blend of openness, inner-observation and most importantly, *a pure realisation* of self, but without any real thinking taking place at all.

Being mindful means that you are aware of who you are, what you can be (your true potential), as well as what you want to do with your life. This *sense of direction* is important if you want to travel the curve of personal growth and reach your full mental, emotional and spiritual potential. If you don't have goals, or know where you are going, you are not likely to find your way.

THERE ARE SPECIFIC EXERCISES TO LESSEN THE CLUTTER AND CLAMOUR IN YOUR MINDS AND IMPROVE MINDFULNESS.

You may remember that I mentioned the Alpha brainwave state in a previous chapter. Tuning into this state regularly will lower the activity of your conscious mind and help it to quieten down which over time, increases your mindfulness.

Sit quietly and comfortably, close your eyes and begin to breathe to a count of one to five. Focus on nothing else but the counting (either aloud or in your mind). Breathe in 1,2,3,4,5, hold your breath 1,2,3,4, 5, breathe out 1,2,3,4,5, hold your breath 1,2,3,4,5, breathe in 1,2,3,4,5, and so on. Carry on with the counting and breathing until your mind is free of all thought, completely quiet and you feel totally relaxed. Now try to be fully aware, mindful and 'present' without actually thinking. With practise it can be done.

Try this a few times each day.

EMPTY YOUR EGO

On a deeper level, 'cleaning house' also means emptying our egos of all the negative programs and unhelpful beliefs that are feeding and sustaining it. This means challenging our schemas and scripts, self-talk and perceptions and replacing them with powerful new insights about 'self'. I have just shown how schemas and scripts can be challenged with new affirmations and intentions. More advanced exercises will also be given later.

STAGE THREE – EMOTIONAL WELLNESS

As we move further up the personal growth curve, we enter the stage in which we rid ourselves of blocked and repressed feelings and achieve *emotional wellness*. This can be explained as being emotionally stable and balanced to the point that we can feel, identify and deal with our own emotions and still have empathy for others. If we are weak emotionally, everything will upset us and we will not move forward, being held back by doubts, uncertainty and fear.

Any personal growth course should always deal with *festering emotions* before negative thoughts. The reason for this is that these emotions cloud our thinking and make it difficult later on to identify and challenge our negative schemas, scripts and self-talk. The emotions need to be resolved first. I personally don't believe that it is possible for us to get to the point of self-actualisation if we are caught in a web of fear, anger and resentment from bad experiences and memories from the past.

We also need to be reasonably settled and at peace to connect with our *authentic selves*. On a practical level, this means cutting out the *emotional drama* in our lives as much as possible. We can easily become entangled in this 'drama' and end up like a rat running around in a maze.

A PERIOD OF HEALING

Dealing with emotions in this stage is the same for metaphysics as for any programme of personal growth and includes a period of *healing or self-healing*. We all carry emotional scars from the past arising from our unresolved issues and pain. Anger and resentment from past traumas and failures are obstacles to our progress and it's not possible to move forward if we are held back by doubts, fears and guilt from the past. If we wish to move forward with our commitment to personal growth we need to deal with our pasts, however painful they may be.

FORGIVENESS AND SELF-FORGIVENESS

Letting go of powerful emotions such as anger and resentment is important. We need to learn to forgive others as well as ourselves for past mistakes. Sometimes we can't do this on our own and need help from psychologists, counsellors or life-coaches. This is fine. You are not expected to go it alone. There are also metaphysical teachers out there who can give you wonderful guidance. However, if you wish to work on your own, exercises to improve emotional wellness are included in my earlier book *Multi-Dimensional Thinking*.

CULTIVATE POSITIVE EMOTIONS SUCH AS LOVE

Also, work at exchanging feelings of fear and doubt for more positive emotions. Here is a useful tip. It is not possible to hold onto two opposite emotions at the same time, so if you learn to cultivate and radiate a *continuous feeling of love* towards all persons and all sentient beings, fear can't stay in your mind and it will be easier to find the balance and emotional wellness that you need for your long journey ahead.

Positive emotions such as love, compassion and gratitude are helpful to personal growth and the metaphysical path. Cultivating these emotions by *helping others* will be useful to prepare you for world-service to come. In metaphysics, there is an onus on any person who has been given gifts of a deeper understanding or other metaphysical skills to use them wisely in helping others. This also means that metaphysics strives to cultivate natural altruism.

STAGE FOUR – MENTAL WELLNESS – A CLEAR AND POWERFUL MIND

As we move up the developmental curve we pass into the next stage, that of having a clear, open and powerful mind. This means being willing to cultivate this state of mind by replacing outdated ideas and self-limiting beliefs, letting go of unwanted negative mental debris, and 'shifting gears' to a universal, open, holistic way of thinking. This stage is common to most types of counselling or personal growth courses but is absolutely necessary if you wish to follow the path of metaphysics.

WE SUFFER FROM A LOSS OF AUTHENTICITY

Our minds are really our connection to the outside world and to reality itself. It is also the place in which we create artistic beauty and inspirational thoughts. However, it can likewise be a quagmire of self-defeating beliefs and assumptions which pollute our thinking and muddy our experience of life. All around people are struggling to come to terms with their mortality, often experiencing their lives as fleeting, impermanent and meaningless, feeling disconnected from that unpolluted core which expresses their true humanity. This *loss of authenticity* is probably one of the main reasons for anxiety and feelings of hopelessness and meaninglessness.

This whole situation was eloquently summed up by the Eastern sage, Krishnamurti who spoke of an 'emptiness' that goes with the experience of being human, which he called the '*loneliness of self*'. We usually feel this as a type of sadness which seems to come from the realisation that we are falling short of our true potential. However, this feeling of loneliness is a good starting point, as it may prompt us to do something about it.

STRIVING FOR A CLEAR, BALANCED AND FOCUSSED MIND

You may remember that earlier I showed you how negative schemas and scripts, unhelpful self-talk and beliefs and other psychological debris and clutter are embedded in layers in our minds. This clutter has to be cleared to allow us to think more deeply and clearly and to open the path for the core of *pure consciousness*, the *authentic self* we are trying to reach, to emerge. Without this clearing process, self-actualisation also can't take place.

THE ANALOGY OF THE GOLDFISH BOWL

Let me use an analogy which may explain this problem better. Imagine that we are all like goldfish swimming around in a bowl. The water in the bowl represents our mind and present understanding of the world. Outside of the bowl is the universe and what we understand as reality. However, the water itself is murky as the result of our jumbled-up thoughts and perceptions, painful memories and limiting beliefs which so clog up our minds that we have only a dim view of what is out there and cannot see things as they really are. The saddest thought of all is that we have all become so conditioned and accustomed to living in this bowl of dirty water that we cannot even imagine a different or larger world or universe out there. And all we have to do is to clean the water.

QUIETING THE MIND

To bring peace and balance to our minds all we have to do is to quieten them by reducing drama in our lives and shifting gears to a relaxed state. The easiest way of doing this is by cultivating a more philosophical approach to life ('don't sweat the small stuff'), learning to consciously relax, reading self-help books and taking the time to be more mindful. Mindfulness can be developed by being aware of the little things, such as taking a walk in your garden and noticing and appreciating even the smallest plants and flowers.

REMOVING ALL DOUBTS

A powerful and focussed mind has no room for doubt and uncertainty and a positive state of mind is important for personal growth. Try to remove doubts and fears from your mind by discovering the inner strength that comes from the commitment you have made to personal growth. If you still have doubts, do some self-examination to find out what is the source of these doubts and fears. Once again, it could be those nasty schemas and scripts formed from your bad past experiences. If this is the case, I have shown you ways of challenging and resolving them.

The best way to remove doubts and improve your confidence is, of course, by having success in applying what you have learnt about metaphysics and know to be true. This means persevering along this path until you discover that sense of achievement.

OPENING YOUR MIND

When it comes to metaphysical development we are often held back by strongly-held beliefs about ourselves and the world, or if we are religious, what is regarded by the church as 'right' or 'wrong'.

And if we are not able to accept a new idea for whatever reason, we will tend to avoid or ignore it. Unfortunately, this is not good for our growth as it limits our openness to new experiences.

If we wish to move forward along this curve we will have to open our minds to other possibilities and become more flexible in our thinking. However, I do understand that the path of metaphysics may be scary for some, and can be compared to standing on the edge of a precipice which has on one side that which we know, the everyday world, and on the other side, an unknown reality.

It is also true that I will be introducing you to new ideas which could challenge your thinking and kick you out of your comfort zone. But this challenge occurs with any form of personal growth, not just metaphysics, so you have to just keep moving forward.

EXPANDING YOUR MIND AND THINKING – THE COMPUTER METAPHOR

In the case of this book, the idea is not that you must believe and accept everything that I offer, but simply be prepared to consider other possibilities. The problem is that, in terms of our computer metaphor, at present, our minds are all *hard-wired* to function on this level of thinking and to connect with our authentic selves, they have to be upgraded. They do improve gradually over time if we process our life-experiences correctly, as we are constantly redefining our views of self and reality. But the process can be speeded up if we are willing to use metaphysical processes.

At present we get our knowledge and insight from conversations, books, the media, or personal experience. However, deeper levels of understanding will remain hidden until we can use the full power of our minds together with the cooperation of our subconscious minds. This involves being willing to learn new metaphysical skills such as meditation, visualisation and subliminal programming to bypass the blocks we have set in place. Some of you may have ethical, moral or religious objections to these processes and may want to have a time of self-introspection and preparation before you reach the point where you feel free to move ahead with the inner work that is needed. That is fine. But I will encourage you to return to the path when you are ready.

STAGE FIVE – ACCESSING THE AUTHENTIC SELF

Once we have dealt with all, or at least most of the emotional and psychological issues holding us back, we clear the way for a realisation of the highest, most moral and spiritual side of ourselves. This is called the *authentic or true self* in psychology and is metaphysically the stage at which we transcend or empty our egos and fill them with positive feelings of unconditional love and powerful states of mind such as resilience, flexibility, altruism and purpose, to arrive at a new understanding of our role in the world. This realisation is brought about through self-reflection and good actions and could also be termed 'spirituality'. If we go back to the analogy of the goldfish in the bowl, this is where we metaphorically *'poke our heads out of the water'* to see a bigger world out there.

Metaphysical processes to access our authentic selves are given in the chapter on meditation.

STAGE SIX – SELF-ACTUALISATION

This final stage of personal growth on the personal growth curve is self-actualisation. This means that we have reached the point in our lives where we have unfolded our full potential and become what we are capable of becoming, intellectually, emotionally, morally and spiritually. We can reach this through inner work by conscientiously following and mastering the previous steps or stages, but there are deeper levels to our psyches which we may not be able to access using only these means. So this is the point at which metaphysics and your average personal growth course part ways. In metaphysics, we include an extra stage in which we reach through into our subconscious minds using new skills such as meditation and visualisation and work at these deeper levels. Building these skills is a chapter on its own, so I will deal with them later in the book. In terms of our goldfish analogy, this is the point of *real transformation* when we realise that we are not fish at all and simply climb out of the bowl.

ACCESSING THE SUBCONSCIOUS

Metaphysics includes developing the skills to access and work with the largely untapped regions of our psyche, those subconscious areas which govern our deepest inner experiences. This goes much further than your average personal growth course as it includes ongoing communication with our unconscious processes to unleash the full creative power of our minds. The kind of abilities that come with this work include a raised consciousness, heightened sense-perception, improved intuition, inner sight and the unfoldment of latent abilities lying dormant for decades.

These skills are addressed in the following chapters listed in the next theme of this book, that of 'The application of metaphysical principles'.

THE APPLICATION OF METAPHYSICAL PRINCIPLES

CHAPTER FOUR

NEW SKILLS IN UNFOLDMENT

'Our normal waking consciousness, rational consciousness as we call it, is but one special type of consciousness, whilst all about it, parted from it by the filmiest of screens, there lie potential forms of consciousness entirely different.'

William James:
American philosopher and psychologist

DEEP PROCESSING

In this theme, we move onto the more advanced work in the book during which we will be dealing with several important metaphysical practices. I first begin this chapter by looking at the concepts of the 'self' and the 'soul' as understood in metaphysics, as well as in science and psychology, and then point out the role of symbols and symbolic images when working within our subconscious minds.

I then move onto the idea of enhanced states of consciousness and discuss methods of accessing the power of our subconscious minds using metaphysical practices of meditation, visualisation and spontaneous visual imagery. These powerful skills, if mastered, can change our view of reality. I explain the steps and processes in detail and link them to scientific and psychological research.

By this time, you may be beginning to see the relationship between metaphysics and the human sciences, in that metaphysics uses psychology and biology for understanding human behaviour, but moves deeper into the subconscious psyche to discover and unpack its hidden secrets. This is what makes it so exciting!

A METAPHYSICAL VIEW OF SELF

'A man is what he thinks about all day long.'

Ralph Waldo Emerson:
Lecturer, philosopher, and poet

'MAN, KNOW THYSELF'

This phrase is said to have been written on the wall of the Temple of Apollo at Delphi in ancient Greece and was used by many scholars such as Socrates to instruct their students. The phrase itself can be linked to the metaphysical principle of '*As above, so below*', which, when applied to us, means that everything contained in the cosmos, all its laws, principles, relations and aspects, are mirrored in some way in our own bodies and minds. In other words, if we wish to understand the mysteries of the Universe, we only have to look to ourselves and our own minds and bodily processes to know them. So let us begin by looking at ourselves from a metaphysical standpoint, starting with our sense of self, or ego.

THE EGO

Most people believe that our *ego* is who we really are. However, in metaphysics this is not entirely true. In fact, we are not born with our egos as they are, as they are built up from a core of self-awareness which is *'populated'* over time with beliefs about ourselves and our experiences in the world. In modern metaphysics, the ego has had a bit of a bad rap, but, in fact, in pre-historic times it was necessary to have a strong sense of self and a simple memory bank in which past lessons, experiences and skills could be stored, as well as motivating emotions such as fear and anger and a lot of aggression, which was needed to survive in such a harsh and dangerous environment.

However, in this enlightened age, the evolutionary drives and instincts of the ego are a problem, as selfishness, greed and instinctual, violent actions are not acceptable in a modern, ethical society. Those attributes and skills which were once necessary for survival have now become an obstacle to our growth. We still store these early instincts and drives at a subconscious level, but we find that they do stick their heads out again from time to time when we lower our consciousness as a result of stress, alcohol or drugs.

It is essential to have an ego, as the sense of self or 'I' acts as a core or point of reference for all our experiences. The problem is what we store in them and the outdated way in which they still work. Assumptions and fixed beliefs which once saved the caveman, now simply limit or distort our ability to reason effectively, which is quite a recent development in our human evolution. The narrow insights and perceptions of the person ruled by this type of ego was also once enough to function in prehistoric and even ancient societies, but not in the modern world. In other words, the simple mental programs and ways of thinking of early man still remain in our DNA and through the ego are often projected into a world striving for moral and spiritual development and human rights. It is then necessary to evolve our egos using moral, spiritual or metaphysical practices.

THE EFFECT OF THE EGO

A big problem is that, being self-serving, our egos protect themselves against any form of change, prompting us to ignore, or even reject outright, anything that goes against the beliefs that support it. However, metaphysics offers us a path in which we can still recognise and acknowledge our egos but can empty them of much unnecessary baggage, allowing us to reach through to what is called in psychology, our authentic selves and even beyond that to a universal 'collective' state of mind, which I will describe more fully later. The metaphysical processes that will open us to our authentic selves are given in the section on meditation.

EMPTYING THE EGO

To begin with this task, we need to know and accept that, amid all the clamour and clutter of our over-active minds and imaginations, there is in each of us an oasis of pure consciousness filled with positive feelings and states of mind such as love, faith and trust, our *true 'authentic selves'* which have been trying to assert themselves since the moment when as small children, we first became self-aware. Knowing this, should be our motivation to begin the process of emptying our egos of all undesirable qualities and filling it with the light of this higher, authentic sense of self.

Some metaphysicians believe that we should simply release our egos altogether to discover our authentic selves, but as I said before, as a cognitive scientist, I do not think that this is possible or advisable. The ego with all its limitations is still the *core of our self-awareness* which we use for our decisions and actions. I believe that if we try to simply let go of them altogether we could end up very confused. As I said, a better option is to consciously empty our ego of negativity and pain and the bad thinking and emotional habits we have built up in our lives and refill its 'shell' with positive thoughts, emotions and new moral and spiritual values. The metaphysical processes to do this will be shown as we proceed with the book.

THE DARK NIGHT OF THE SOUL

However, sometimes life itself will empty our egos for us in one sudden, life-changing experience, which is often traumatic and involves terrible humiliation and a loss of identity. In religious terms, this is called the *'dark night of the soul'* as mentioned in Scriptures, and it could come as the end of a marriage, a long-term relationship, a promising career, or some other equally painful experience, those times when we feel shattered, empty and alone and are forced to let go of our old sense of self or ego. Sometimes we can get lost in this experience and never recover, but if we recognise it for what it is, it clears the way for the next stage of evolution, letting go of the undesirable parts of our ego which have led to this pain and seeking out our authentic selves.

Do not dispair if you have entered, or are still in this valley of darkness in your life. Keep going, as the light is on the other side. I have been there and have lived the truth expressed in the words 'this too will pass'.

THE SOUL

Having just introduced the idea of the 'dark night of the soul', I am now obliged to say something about this important concept which is said to be the *highest part of ourselves*, and is spoken of in so many different religions. The idea of the soul is used frequently in metaphors and sayings in everyday life. For example; 'the 'soul' of the matter', 'that poor soul', 'I put my heart and soul into my work', 'music sets my soul on fire', 'food for the soul'. I could go on and on. Once again I will begin with the scientific and psychological views and move onto metaphysical aspects of the soul.

THE SOUL AS SEEN BY THE SCIENCES

Science itself does not really give any consideration to that elusive entity which we call the 'soul'. The closest we come to any sort of scientific explanation is this idea of a *higher or authentic self* in psychology, said to represent those most moral and ethical values and aspects of ourselves. It is certainly not seen as separate from our bodies or minds.

THE THEOLOGICAL VIEW

But if we jump over the fence to theological studies, we will see that our *soul* is seen as 'from God' and our true 'spiritual' essence, perfect, whole and complete. According to sacred scriptures and other ancient texts, it is said that we all, at some stage, separated from this perfect state of *soul-being* and took on a lower state of existence. This is called the '*the fall*' in religious terminology.

COMMENT FROM A SCIENTIFIC PERSPECTIVE

So far, so good, but the problem I have with these theological teachings is that they would have us believe that 'the fall' was due to an act of disobedience and that the suffering of our bodies is a punishment. I do not wish to confuse anyone, so you are quite welcome to accept this line of theological dogma as it stands. However, in terms of evolutionary science, the 'fall' could very well have been a natural process. In other words, 'the fall' could simply be a *metaphor* for the entry of human souls into bodies, which by then, had evolved to the point of being able to sustain life and the level of self-awareness said to be brought by the soul. Why I say this is because the Scriptures do not indicate the amount of time it took for the body 'formed from the dust of the earth' to reach the time when the 'soul was breathed into it', and this allows for a period of evolution to take place.

THE METAPHYSICAL VIEW

In metaphysics, our souls are also seen as something intangible that are above and beyond the physical realm. However, they are also viewed as an expression of a far larger *Universal Soul*, an incorruptible higher *template* of the human being just waiting for the opportunity to express. When expressed or channelled through the body, the soul is the source of our consciousness or self-awareness which it loses to a large extent when passing through the biology of our bodies which still contain the DNA for the basic selfish drives and instincts from earlier stages of evolution. So, in terms of metaphysics, our main aim should be to allow our souls to fully express through our bodies and minds by emptying our egos, reforming our instinctual drives and returning to our original state of consciousness. Perhaps now you can see why I say that metaphysics is a natural and practical process.

INTRODUCING MEDITATION AND VISUALISATION

'To the mind that is still, the whole universe surrenders.'

Lao Tzu: Ancient Chinese philosopher

In this section, we will be considering the skills you will need to learn to engage with your subconscious mind. But before this, you should have done some preparation. Firstly, I mentioned how important it is that your thinking should be more open-ended to allow you to move beyond conventional ideas and prepare your minds for your metaphysical journey into your subconscious. Secondly, we looked at using affirmations and intentions to change the schemas and scripts which may be holding you back. Finally, I mentioned how powerful, new inner experiences can be even more effective in bringing about these changes.

While affirmations and intentions are somewhat effective in changing schemas and scripts, there is no substitute for powerful inner experiences. Novel experiences directly challenge and shake up fixed belief systems at their very core and can shatter any rigid schemas or scripts relating to self or reality.

ENHANCED STATES OF CONSCIOUSNESS

However, enhanced states of consciousness are necessary to access our subconscious minds. We have to learn to raise our consciousness without the use of drugs, and this can only be safely done using processes such as meditation, visualisation, contemplation and forms of self-hypnosis.

I know that some of you are apprehensive about meditation, as there are so many negative stories about it circulating. However, I use a scientific, balanced approach (including the 'pros' and 'cons') when introducing it, so that you can make an informed decision to either practise it or not.

But before we begin the steps to the proper practice of meditation and visualisation, I need to give you some background into what you may see and experience during these processes, which will most likely be symbolic, as our subconscious minds often use images as a form of communication.

SYMBOLS

A symbol can be an image, shape, pattern, or object which carries within itself a symbolic meaning. Symbols represent, or stand in for concepts or ideas but offer a deeper understanding, as, if you look closely, you will see metaphysical principles hidden in their design, form and structure, which, if understood, will take you closer to the truth of the matter. Great truths, knowledge and wisdom were often hidden by scholars in this way and the idea was that important metaphysical principles were disguised from those who might ridicule or defile them.

Once we unlock their levels of meaning and come to realise and understand the hidden principles, symbols lead to powerful inner experiences, as recognition comes via our subconscious minds, which respond well to symbolic images. Sometimes the symbols have connections to knowledge lying deep within our psyches, truths, which if understood, can bring about feelings of excitement. Later on, when you start visualising you may find that some symbols spontaneously pop into your heads, such as triangles, squares and circles, which I sometimes use to explain difficult concepts. Remember to look out for them.

PERSONAL SYMBOLS

Those of you who work with dreams, or have already done some meditation, will know that most of what we see is symbolic and we need to translate the symbolic images into the correct messages using our own *language* of personal symbols. These symbols are drawn from past experiences and are unique to each person, having a special significance which we need to uncover using our own frameworks of meaning. The power of symbols lies in their links to our personal memories, beliefs and emotions, some of which we may not even be consciously aware.

During a dream, someone may see an image which brings back painful memories, as the symbolic image has the original emotions (fears) hidden inside it. An early childhood experience such as a near-drowning can be relived simply by seeing a scene or symbol of the sea and this can make the person feel very uncomfortable or anxious.

Later on we will look at some universal symbols, so it will be a good idea if you try to learn as much as possible about your own set of personal symbols. Think about those metaphors, objects and diagrams which have a special meaning for you and remember them. It will also help if you try to interpret your dreams. Later on, as you work with visualisation you will eventually learn your own language of personal symbols, as dreams use the same symbols as visualisations. For more information on dream interpretation, read my book *How to Interpret your Dreams*.

THE POWER OF MEDITATION

'Meditation is like a gym in which you develop the
powerful mental muscles of calm and insight.'

Ajahn Brahm: Buddhist monk

Due to the fast pace of life, work stress and family demands, our minds are filled with constant mental chatter. This takes all our attention and occupies our consciousness to the point that we never really stop and take the time to notice subtle inner experiences and sensory cues around us. Meditation is a powerful exercise to stop the *chatter* and at the same time improve your mindfulness, and is one of the advanced skills you need to learn if you wish to engage with your subconscious mind and even beyond that.

I know that not everyone is happy with learning to meditate, believing that one will encounter 'dark and mysterious' forces while in this enhanced state. Suppose if you consider the contents of your own minds as 'dark and mysterious' - then it could be a bit of a problem, as it is true that meditation can uncover the deepest parts of your psyche as well as some painful memories, and I suppose that this could be distressing for some. However, this is not any worse than going for counselling, or in my case, going to the dentist.

A SCIENTIFIC VIEW OF MEDITATION

Meditation is based on sound psychological principles such as *mental relaxation* and *conscious mind-control,* and when combined with visualisation, *mental creation* as well. In fact, research has shown that simple meditative techniques help to reduce tension, and it has become a recognised practice in some forms of psychotherapy.

It is the more advanced forms of meditation, when *combined with visualisation and imagery* that takes you deeper into your psyche and allows for self-exploration, moving into the realms of our subconscious minds and even beyond that to explore the mysteries of the universe. Our whole view of reality can change after the experiences and insights gained from powerful meditations.

HOW TO MEDITATE

To connect to our authentic selves, we need to reach through to our subconscious minds, and for this reason, we need a relationship between our conscious and subconscious processes. Meditation brings about enhanced states of consciousness in which we become more aware of the subconscious content of our minds and if we practise regularly, we will build this good working relationship that we need.

Meditation lowers brainwave activity so that our mental chatter subsides and we are better able to relax. This means that we have to learn to lower our brainwave activity to the Alpha state of 8-12 cps, and later on, to the Theta state of 4-7 cps. This allows us to bypass our normal thinking and opens the doors to our subconscious minds.

However, there are a number of steps you need to follow to begin:

STARTING WITH THE MENTAL RELAXATION EXERCISE

- The first is to learn to relax your body and remove all distractions. Ensure that you are alone, dim any lights and play soft, background music. Then begin the mental relaxation exercise.

- Sit quietly, comfortably and then begin to notice your breathing. Keep it regular. Now close your eyes and imagine a wave of peace slowly moving up from your feet, through the muscles of your ankles and legs, into your hips, over your chest and up your back.

- At the same time, begin to empty your mind of all thoughts until it is completely quiet. Do not use your willpower to hold back or forcibly remove distracting thoughts, as this only creates a new set of inner tensions.

- Merely allow all your thoughts to gently pass in and out of your mind without giving them any attention. Simply allow your thinking to slow down until your brain is just 'ticking over' without any real conscious activity taking place.

- Now continue to focus on your breathing as well as the feeling as the 'wave' passes through each muscle, limb or organ. Finally, allow the feeling to pass up your neck and out the top of your head.

DO THIS THREE TIMES.

At the end of the exercise, your mind should be peaceful and you should experience a feeling of total relaxation.

GETTING INTO THE ALPHA BRAINWAVE STATE

The next stage is to consciously be able to induce this Alpha state of consciousness.

- Sit comfortably and set an intention to consciously enter the Alpha state. You state your intention only once, but with absolute confidence and a positive state of mind. This lets your subconscious mind know that you are serious and know exactly what you want. I explained how to set intentions in an earlier chapter, and you may need to refer back to this section if you are still unsure.

- After your intention to enter the Alpha state has been set, close your eyes again and begin to relax by focussing all your attention on your breathing. This takes your mind away from thinking and is the same exercise you did to improve your mindfulness.

- Breathe to a count of one to five. Focus on nothing else but the counting (either aloud or in your mind). Breathe in 1,2,3,4,5 hold your breath, 1,2,3,4, 5 breathe out, 1,2,3,4,5 hold your breath, 1,2,3,4,5 breathe in, 1,2,3,4,5 and so on.

- During this breathing try to keep your mind clear of thoughts, but do not try too hard. Meditation is a process of 'letting go' rather than forcing your mind to be quiet. Practise this exercise until you can keep your mind quiet for at least twenty seconds. This is the Alpha state of total mental relaxation.

ENTERING INTO MEDITATION

- Now with your eyes still closed, move your focus away from your body, especially from your hands and feet, until you are no longer consciously aware of them. If you feel stressed at all it means you are trying too hard. Begin again and start over. Meditation is a very gentle process.

- Next, with your eyes still closed, open your senses and try to be mindful of everything around you, but without actually thinking. Shift your attention to your sense of smell and try to detect scents in the room, such as flowers or burning candles. Now change your focus to your hearing and listen more acutely for any noises in the room and outside, such as insect or animal sounds. Do not focus on your body or open your eyes, as this will distract you. Above all, do not be afraid, as you are only working with your own mind.

- After a while, let go of all effort and become mindful of cues such as sensations, feelings or impressions. This state of mindfulness can be likened to a combination of 'openness', 'listening', and most importantly, 'feeling'. Meditation increases your sensory awareness.

- You will know that you have entered into meditation when everything becomes quiet and you are aware of strange feelings from deep within yourself. At first, they will not make any sense at all. Do not panic or doubt yourself. This is normal. Gratefully accept the new state of consciousness that you are being introduced to.

- When you have spent a few minutes in this new state, slowly start thinking again by setting an intention to exit from the meditation. Do not suddenly just open your eyes and return to normal consciousness, as this may disorientate you. Slowly and gently become more aware of your body and breathe more deeply, feel your hands and feet, move them around and slowly open your eyes.

- Another way of exiting a meditation is to count down from ten, and at different stages, tell yourself you are disconnecting. For example, 'disconnecting, ten, nine, eight, disconnecting, seven, six, five, disconnecting, four, three, two, one' - open your eyes.

Practise this regularly until you are familiar with the process. You will know that you have achieved a measure of success when you start to feel more relaxed, at ease and certainly more mindful.

BEGIN WITH SIMPLE MEDITATIONS

I think the time has come for you to have a taste of what I have been speaking about using a simple yet powerful meditation. Hopefully, this may even shatter your old schema of self.

A BRIEF MEDITATION TO ACCESS THE AUTHENTIC SELF

- Relax using the breathing exercise and set an intention to experience your higher or true self. The only requirement is that you have to believe, (or at least accept the possibility), that everyone, including you, has a deeper, more spiritual side to self.

- Enter into a light meditation using the breathing exercise that has just been given.

- Take your time. Once your body is relaxed and your mind is quiet, lift up your hands, look at your palms and move your fingers in front of you.

- Repeat the words, 'I'm alive' a few times.

- Now turn your hands towards your chest and focus on the area between your hands and chest.

- Change the words to 'I am' and repeat them slowly over and over again a few times.

- Now change the words 'I am' to the word, 'I'.

- Repeat the word 'I' a number of times, slowly and deliberately with intent.

- Surrender and abandon yourself to the full experience and realisation of what it is to be 'I'.

- Carry on repeating 'I' with emotion until you are suddenly moved to take an unexpected, deep breath.

Do not be alarmed, as this is normal.

You have now had a momentary connection to your true *authentic self*. Remain in this state as long as you can, enjoying each moment.

- Slowly end your meditation, become conscious of your body and return to normal awareness.

Now measure this experience with a new sense of wonder against what you originally believed yourself to be. Open your mind to the idea that this inner experience reveals what you truly are, a being of light and consciousness, not a body of pain or a mind filled with fear and suffering.

I hope you all enjoyed this experience.

Practise this meditation until you feel changes to your beliefs about yourself and are eager and willing to explore the depths of your own minds even further.

USING SOUND WITH YOUR MEDITATION

You may find meditation easier and pleasanter if you play soft, melodious music in the background to help ease you into a meditative state. Some practitioners use drumming or chant. That is fine, as long as it is soft and repetitive. Rhythmic sounds lull our thinking minds into the Alpha or Theta wave patterns which are great for opening our subconscious minds up to incoming impressions.

Traditional Native American tribes, the Australian Aborigines, as well as the tribes of Africa used drumming together with rhythmic dancing to induce slightly enhanced states of consciousness and many still do today. Some Eastern mystics also use sacred words or sounds to induce changes to their consciousness.

VISUALISATION

'The use of mental imagery is one of the strongest and most effective strategies for making something happen for you.'

Dr Wayne Dyer: American self-help author

The more advanced forms of meditation combine with *visualisation*[1] to give it more effect and to allow one to actually see the changes taking place. Obviously, this takes a long time to develop. But in the meantime, let us look at the scientific and psychological basis for visualisation and all of its 'ins' and 'outs.'

THE SCIENTIFIC EXPLANATION FOR VISUALISATION

As conscious beings, we all have the power to create three-dimensional colour images and even entire animated scenes in our imagination. I am sure you can remember back to the daydreams you used to create and enjoy as a child. I certainly can! As adults, most of us have forgotten how to daydream or simply no longer find it necessary, a childish escape from reality, or so we thought!

I would like to believe that these childhood experiences prepared us for the more powerful use of our minds in *mental creation*[2] (imagery), but as I said, many of us do not see the need at this time. The funny thing is that we are actually still using our imagery centres in our brains to create three-dimensional scenarios without even realising it. Here I am talking about our dreams. So we still have the faculty but it is just not used as often, or consciously.

Psychologically, the real power of *created imagery* is the effect it has on our subconscious minds. As children our daydreams would inspire us to want to be superheroes, doctors or astronauts, but how quickly we forgot these early dreams. However, the fact is that today, visualised scenarios are still used by the world's top motivators to inspire and motivate people into action. And you can use this power during your meditations to bring about amazing experiences. But how is this possible?

THE PSYCHOLOGICAL POWER OF VISUALISATION

The truth of the matter is that our subconscious minds have a weakness in that they cannot really tell the difference between a real and imagined experience and they will often respond to a mental scene as if it were real. An example of this is a nightmare. Our breathing and heart-rate increase and we wake up in a cold sweat. This means that an imaginary situation has brought about the same reactions in our bodies and minds as a real-life event would, and this is a very important tool that we can use to get its cooperation. Our subconscious mind is far more powerful than we think, as it is open to reality and has a variety of powerful roles and functions that I will discuss later.

My example of the nightmare shows that we can change our state of mind and our bodily reactions simply by fooling and inducing a reaction from our subconscious minds. For example, if we create an imaginary scenario in our minds in which we see ourselves as happy and successful, and do it with *emotion*, our subconscious mind cooperates and during that time we can actually experience feelings of optimism, excitement, anticipation and expectation. Psychologically, this all primes our minds for better, more positive decisions and actions that can lead to success. Once again, this is the basis of the *self-fulfilling prophecy*, but this time it induces a positive state of mind. You may argue that this is only our imagination, but if you learn this skill you will soon discover that during meditation, our imagination, when used for visualisation, is a powerful tool which allows us to harness the power of our subconscious minds.

THE ABILITY TO ALTER SCHEMAS AND SCRIPTS

Apart from affirmations and intentions, research shows that our schemas and scripts can be changed at a very deep level by exposing ourselves to *novel, new, unexpected experiences* which forces them to try to adapt. If they can't, they will implode and be replaced by a new schema that copes better with the experience.

THE CASE OF PETER AND THE DOG

For example, Peter had a schema for dogs in which he described them as '*loving and playful creatures*'. This came about as a result of his good experiences with dogs in early childhood. Peter is now an adult and was unfortunately recently attacked by a vicious dog and badly bitten. This put a huge strain on his schema of dogs as '*loving and playful creatures*' and he could well have adapted his schema to '*Not all dogs are loving and playful*'. However, being a sensitive soul, Peter took it particularly badly and was not able to reconcile his new experience with his existing schema at all, which, as a result, *shattered or imploded*, and he formed a new schema with the wording - '*Dogs are dangerous*'.

His script in dealing with dogs now also changed radically, from '*playing with dogs*' to '*avoiding dogs*'. As a result, his whole attitude to dogs has changed to the point where he has feelings of fear when seeing a large dog, which he never had before.

The important fact is that his schema and script changed radically due to this new, unexpected experience which altered his perceptions of dogs, his feelings towards them and his behaviour.

The point is that none of us wants to undergo bad experiences like this in order to change our schemas and scripts, especially of self and reality, and fortunately, due to the backdoor into our subconscious minds, we don't have to. If we consciously create and act out *fantastical imaginary scenes* about ourselves and reality in our imagination, our subconscious minds will react as if the experience is real and over time, change or abandon our old schemas or scripts with the result that we will be more open to new inner-self experiences and higher levels or dimensions of reality.

I will give you examples of these fantastical scenarios later once you fully understand the process of visualisation otherwise they will be of little effect.

COMBINING MEDITATION WITH VISUALISATION

'Meditation is the dissolution of thoughts in Eternal awareness or Pure consciousness without objectification, knowing without thinking, merging finitude in infinity.'

Voltaire: French writer, historian, and philosopher

Visualisation is most powerful when used during meditation, as our subconscious minds are open to influence, and by introducing changes to the visualised scene, we bring about corresponding changes to our consciousness and inner states. For example, if we see ourselves moving through a series of visualised doorways and stairways with the intention that these are passageways to deeper or higher views of reality, our subconscious minds will respond and we should notice shifts in our perception. If we again use the analogy of our mind as a computer, this would be like keying in different commands to pass from one level of the program to the next.

HOWEVER, WHEN WORKING AT THIS DEEP LEVEL OF THE MIND YOU MUST REMEMBER A NUMBER OF IMPORTANT RULES:

- It is better to keep your eyes closed until you are used to the advanced processes.

- First, once you begin, never stop suddenly, as this can confuse your subconscious mind and you may become disoriented.

- It is not a good idea to shift your consciousness rapidly between different scenes, as you are working at a very deep level of your mind and this could place a strain on your neural pathways.

- Secondly, the scenarios you create should always have a sort of 'storyline', a logical beginning and end. In other words, if you visualise yourself in a house passing through a door to another level, always see yourself coming back into the house through the same doorway before you return to normal consciousness. If you do not do this you could also become confused.

It takes quite a while for this skill to develop fully, as the imagery centres in our brains only develop slowly. As a result, many people complain of not having success with visualisation, but you will probably find that they have missed out important steps in the development of this skill. The twelve-step method given in my previous book '*Multi-Dimensional*

Perception' is ideal for learning to visualise and you should follow this guide to allow for proper growth in the different brain areas to take place.

LEARNING TO VISUALISE CORRECTLY

A brief summary of the correct process, which I have shortened to eight steps to make it easier, is given as follows:

The mastery of visualisation or imagery begins with the improvement of your memory and recall and your ability to create three-dimensional images in your mind. This process evolves over time into more powerful forms of *advanced spontaneous imagery*. The proper method involves at least nine steps and each one has to be mastered before you can proceed to the next. If you follow the process diligently, you will eventually be successful and open yourself to a new world of interactive imagery which allows you to see into the hidden dimensions of your subconscious minds and even beyond that to the wonders in the Universal Mind.

STEP ONE - PRACTISE YOUR RECALL

Cut out a colour picture of a household scene from a magazine showing furniture and different objects. Study the picture for about half a minute and close your eyes. Try to recall as many of the features of the room and the objects as possible. You will need to practise until you can recall most of the objects and the furniture setting in the room quite accurately. If you are able to do this the first time, it means that your recall is excellent and you can move onto step two.

STEP TWO - LEARN TO MENTALLY CREATE SCENES

Close your eyes and create a colour image of the same picture you used before in your mind without looking at it. Continue practising until you can create it clearly and hold it for at least ten seconds. It can still be two–dimensional.

STEP THREE – USE YOUR IMAGINATION TO CREATE NEW SCENES (Keep your eyes closed for all further steps)

Enter the relaxed and quiet state of mind required for meditation and set your intention to create a new scene in your mind. It can be a real scene such as a view of your garden or simply something put together in your imagination, such as being on the beach.

Piece it together and hold it in your mind for as long as possible. Once again, at this stage, you can still keep it two-dimensional. You may find holding the scene together somewhat tiring. As soon as you lose concentration, end the imagery. Do this in the same way as you would for meditation (moving your fingers and hands or counting-down). Continue with this exercise over a few days using the same scene, gradually filling in as much detail, form, colour and texture as you can.

STEP FOUR – ADD IN OTHER DIMENSIONS

Set your intention and recreate your scene as before, but this time, add more depth and try to see it in three dimensions. Also add sounds, scents and movement to your scene. In other words, imagine seeing the leaves moving, get the scent of flowers, and hear the birds singing.

STEP FIVE – PLACE LIVING THINGS IN YOUR SCENE

Now imagine an animal moving in your scene. In other words, see your cat or dog walking through the garden. Once you have done this and are successful, slowly end your imagery and meditation. Continue with this exercise for a few more days, until you can do these mental tasks with ease.

STEP SIX – PLACE YOURSELVES IN THE SCENE

Begin your imagery as before with relaxation and enter into a light meditation. Set your intention to create an image of yourself in the scene as a separate figure. In other words, see yourself walking through the garden. Remember to include all the previous steps of three-dimensionality, sounds, scent, movement and animals. Seeing yourself at a distance in this way is called the *third-person perspective*.

Exit your imagery in the proper manner. If you have woven your visualisation into a story, close the session as if you were bringing the story to an end. In other words, see yourself leaving the garden and closing the gate behind you. You have to get your subconscious mind used to this process, as, if you end the session abruptly, you could become disorientated or confused.

STEP SEVEN – THE FIRST-PERSON PERSPECTIVE

During your next meditation and visualisation, create your scene as before but now try to put yourself into the figure you have created for yourself in the scene. Look through your figures 'eyes' at the grass beneath you and the path in front of you. In other words, no longer see yourself as separate in the scene. You are now looking out from the figure and are actually inside the scene. This *'first-person perspective'* is difficult and takes practice. Continue with this for a few days until you actually 'feel' the ground beneath your feet, 'touch' the foliage with your visualised hands and experience some actual sensations. Once again, after finishing the exercise, exit slowly and gently by leaving the garden and closing the gate behind you.

STEP EIGHT – SPONTANEOUS IMAGERY- THE THRESHOLD OF INNER SIGHT

As this is the most important and advanced stage of visualisation, it is dealt with separately in the next section.

SPONTANEOUS IMAGERY

'Proper visualization by the exercise of concentration and willpower enables us to materialize thoughts, not only as dreams or visions in the mental realm but also as experiences in the material realm.'

Paramahansa Yogananda: Guru of Kriya Yoga and
founder of Self-Realization Fellowship

In this section, we look at the application of the skill of *spontaneous imagery*. This is one of the most powerful tools in metaphysical practice as it allows you to see the changes taking place in your consciousness, as well as allowing you to communicate with your own subconscious mind. Mastering this tool will change your life!

In psychology, spontaneous imagery is defined as the *'unintended emergence of mental images.'* This is very important in metaphysics. Spontaneous imagery usually occurs during meditation and normally only happens after you have diligently practised meditation and visualisation for quite a while. Spontaneous imagery means that symbolic images from your own subconscious minds begin to spontaneously present themselves to you during visualisation. This sounds incredible, but I assure you that it works, and is a wonderful experience which marks your passage to what I call, the *'Threshold of Inner Sight'*. This means that you have been successful in establishing a close working relationship with your subconscious mind and you are now able to create a flowing *visual field* in which sensations, impressions and images from your subconscious mind, as well as from outside of your own mind, will be able to present themselves.

This phenomenon is based on the psychological fact that your subconscious mind has the power to place its own impressions and images into your visualised scene during meditation, in the same way as it does when you dream. However, as is the case with dreams, sometimes their meaning is not clear and you have to interpret the images. How to do this is explained in the next section.

Spontaneous imagery is not the same as true clairvoyant sight, but it does prepare your mind for more advanced types of inner vision as it teaches you how to create an inner 'visual screen' for images to project onto and also helps to develop the centres in your brain you need for inner sight. Eventually, you will not even have to create a visualised scene at all, as images will spontaneously present themselves to you during your meditations.

Do not attempt spontaneous imagery unless you have mastered all the earlier steps, otherwise, you will be disappointed. This is a very exciting stage of your growth, as it means that you can actually see the changes taking place during your meditations, including contact with other personalities in the Universal (Collective) Mind.

LET ME SHOW YOU HOW THIS WORKS:

- Once again, begin visualising during meditation. Keep your mind quiet and your eyes closed. Set your intention for your subconscious mind to communicate freely with you in the form of flowing impressions and images. In other words, metaphorically ask your 'lover' to interact with you on a personal level.

- Put together a visualised three-dimensional scene as before, but keep it simple. Once again, just see yourself walking around in your visualised garden or some other beautiful scene you create in your imagination. Now use the first-person perspective. At this time you are still actively creating the scene and the images and holding it all together in your mind.

- Now, slowly *begin to release active control of the scene until* it sort of 'floats' lightly in your consciousness with minimal effort. This fluidity opens your imagery to outside influences and your visualised scene now becomes an inner visual screen on which incoming images and impressions can be projected. If you are successful, your scene will stay more or less the same, in spite of the fact that you are spending less effort on controlling it.

- As you move along in your visualised scene, look for something which you are not creating in your own mind. In other words, you may see an object such as a rock or an animal suddenly appear which you did not consciously place there. This is your subconscious mind beginning to communicate with you using *symbolic representations* (images). Once this happens, give thanks, gently take back control of the scene and end your imagery with the story-line as before.

- Now, remember what you saw and try to interpret the meaning of the object or animal using your own personal framework of symbols which I spoke of earlier. Your subconscious mind often works with images and symbols, but you may have to translate them to get to the hidden messages.

THE INTERPRETATION OF SYMBOLIC IMAGES

I have explained how to interpret symbolic images in great detail in my e-book *'How to Interpret your Dreams'* so I will only give a brief guideline here.

Like your dreams, some spontaneous images are symbolic and you will need to interpret them metaphorically, although this is not always the case, as you will see later during examples of *advanced spontaneous presentations*. You may remember that a metaphor is only a simple way of representing a far deeper idea by comparing the two, and you will have to learn to interpret your personal symbols metaphorically as well if you wish to be successful at this.

When it comes to symbolic objects, the message is hidden in its day-to-day characteristics. For example, a log or a large rock is something you could stumble over when walking along a path, so metaphorically, a large rock or a fence appearing in your visualisation which blocks the path you see yourself walking on, could metaphorically mean a stumbling block in your life. In the cases of humanlike or animal figures, they most likely represent *aspects of your own psyche*. For instance, a wounded animal or person appearing in your scene may suggest one of your personality traits needs healing.

Your schemas or scripts will determine what you see. For example, as a result of my habit of going to the gym, my schemas for 'strength' and 'power' are linked to a person's size and build. This means that, if I see a large, muscular person in my imagery, or even my dreams, I associate this figure with power. Based on your own background and beliefs, you may see 'power' differently, such as in terms of powerful animals or even the lightness or brightness of the figure.

AMAZING CHANGES TO YOUR SCENE

We have now come to the most exciting part of spontaneous imagery and possibly the beginning of all your spiritual experiences in the future. *This is truly the threshold of a new world of higher communication and meaning.*

Apart from objects, sometimes animals and humanlike figures can appear in your visualised scene (inner visual screen) and the en*tire scene may change or shift of its own accord.* This will normally happen in response to a question you have put to your subconscious mind or by setting a specific intention.

HERE IS A SIMPLE REAL-LIFE EXAMPLE. LOOK CAREFULLY AT THE STEPS THAT SUSAN FOLLOWS.

SUSAN ENTERS THE HALL OF HER MEMORIES

Susan is a widow and has been feeling sad about her late husband and would like to recall some fond memories of their time together. She decides to use meditation and visualisation to bring her some comfort.

During her meditation one night, Susan closes her eyes and begins visualising and sets an intention to enter her 'hall of memories.' A hall is a suitable metaphor as it suggests a large library with many shelves of books and much available knowledge. She uses this metaphor of a hall of memories as she knows that her subconscious mind responds well to symbols and figures of speech.

Using the first-person perspective, Susan visualises walking down a path with a gate at the end. She now *engages spontaneous imagery* by letting go of her rigid control of the scene. To her relief and excitement, the scene stays more or less the same, but now a building like a library appears in front of her on the other side of the gate in her scene. This happens spontaneously without any action on her part. During her meditation and imagery, Susan is able to make a decision to enter, which she does.

Susan is fortunate, as after many months of practice her subconscious mind has completely taken over the whole three-dimensional moving scene and she now feels as like an *'avatar figure' in a computer game,* as she now has to make choices as to which door to enter or passage to follow.

Susan picks and enters one of the rooms and sees an old man standing in front of her with a large book. He opens the book and clearly, in her mind, Susan hears him ask her what memories she wishes to see. She has studied metaphysics extensively and knows that the old man is only a *symbolic representation* of a part of her subconscious mind in which she has stored her memories. What is interesting though, is that she is actually able to communicate with this part of herself as if it were a real, separate person.

Susan asks him to allow her to recall some fond memories of her husband, who is deceased. The old man agrees and turns to a certain page. But there is no immediate effect, as Susan has not yet learnt how to *simultaneously keep two different scenarios* going in her mind, being in the room with the old man and at the same time seeing the memories that she so desperately wishes to relive. So she thanks the old man and takes back control of the scene, leaves the building, goes back through the gate, down the path and ends up once again in her meditation room. Obviously, this is all taking place in her mind.

However, once Susan opens her eyes she is suddenly overcome with emotion, as many wonderful images of her time with her husband begin to unfold like a daydream. It seems that once she had closed her visualisation, her subconscious was able to project memories spontaneously into her consciousness. She relaxes into these pleasant memories and feels grateful for this opportunity.

COMMENT

I will not go too deeply into the more advanced exercises at this early stage, as later examples will give you a better idea of the true power of spontaneous imagery. As I said, it is important to first build a good relationship with your subconscious mind ('lover'), otherwise, it will not cooperate with you in your set intentions or requests. You will know that this relationship has been cemented when spontaneous imagery takes place during your meditations and visualisations. After this, you can simply set intentions for visions, shifts in consciousness, states of mind or perception. If you are successful, you will actually see the changes taking place in your visualised scene, as was the case with the 'hall of memories' example just presented.

ENDNOTE REFERENCES

1. Visualisation – the ability to create three dimensional images and whole moving scenes in your mind https://www.google.com/search?q=visualisation&oq=v&aqs=chrome.0.69i59j69i57j35i39j0j69i60l2.1549j0j7&sourceid=chrome&ie=UTF-8

2. Mental creation (mental imagery) – the process of creating these visual images and scenes https://www.merriam-webster.com/dictionary/imagery

CHAPTER FIVE

A UNIVERSAL COLLECTIVE MIND

'Being is the eternal, ever-present One Life beyond the myriad forms of life that are subject to birth and death.'

Eckhart Tolle

Shifting away from processes, we now move onto an important concept which gives direction to the rest of the book. As I said previously, I have a psycho-spiritual approach and see metaphysics and metaphysical experiences from the point of view of the actions of the mind as described in science and psychology. However, I also need a useful framework which will allow me to answer important metaphysical questions such as 'who are we?', 'how and why are we here?', and 'what gives rise to reality?' In this case, it is the idea of a Universal Collective Mind.

As a cognitive scientist, I have an affinity for the philosophy of the mind and any ideas associated with consciousness, so I tend to see everything, including my idea of creation and the universe itself, in terms of the mind and consciousness. As a result, in this chapter I introduce the idea of a single, universal, collective consciousness or mind as the creative source which gives rise to the universe and indeed, reality itself. This is not something that I 'sucked out of my thumb'. In this chapter, I produce scientific evidence from several quantum scientists who believe that the Universe itself may be conscious and show how the idea of a Universal

Mind can explain many strange experiences in our lives. However, this idea of a single, Universal Mind is not new, and has been hidden in myths, analogies and metaphors through the ages. I also unpack a number of these analogies and metaphors to show that this is not the stuff of fairy tales, as we are able to relate them to modern scientific principles.

Apart from quantum physics, I introduce several scientifically-based theories to support this idea of an interconnected, single consciousness in the universe, for instance *'systems theory'* in psychology which shows how a balanced, universal 'system' of consciousness is able to explain the concept of global brotherhood, as well as notions of inclusiveness, action-consequence and 'evil' in the world. Then I bring in some research which compares our universe to a *hologram*. A holographic universe fits nicely with the idea of a Universal Mind which 'creates' the hologram.

Finally, in chapter five, I introduce another framework which is also important for metaphysics, that of *'archetypes'*, personality patterns which exist deep within our subconscious minds, as well as the universe itself. The existence of universal archetypes formed in a Universal Mind can explain the many different concepts of God, as well as peoples' experiences of 'spiritual' beings.

IS THERE A SINGLE, UNIVERSAL CONSCIOUSNESS OR MIND BEHIND IT ALL?

'Develop your senses - especially learn how to see.
Realize that everything connects to everything else.'

Leonardo da Vinci

This is not as far-fetched as it may sound, as there are many earlier historical discussions on the possibility of a *single, universal consciousness in which we all share* giving rise to the universe and reality as we know it, as well as recent research in quantum physics which adds credibility to this idea. Let us start by having a look at some of these earlier ideas.

THE IDEA OF A UNIVERSAL, COLLECTIVE MIND

THE EARLY THEOLOGICAL VIEW

This idea of a universal consciousness (mind), which gives rise to the universe as we know it, is not new. References to the all-powerful *Mind of God* can be found in many religious texts, most notably Buddhism and even the ancient Hindu Vedas. In Christian theology, the injunction '*Be still, and know that I am God*' and the name of God as '*I Am that I Am*' could also be re-interpreted as meaning that the self-realisation of 'I Am', the consciousness that lies behind all our experience, is, in fact, 'God'.

THIS IDEA AS SEEN BY THE FIRST PHILOSOPHERS

This idea has also been introduced in one way or another by philosophers going back to ancient times. For instance, as far back as 400 BC, the ancient Greek philosopher Plato spoke of a higher world of *ideal 'forms'*, which could be seen as 'templates' for reality produced by a Supreme Mind. According to Plato, we all have access to this 'real' world of forms through our minds and thinking, but we must have the necessary wisdom and insight to see into this reality.

The idea of a single source of consciousness (mind) linking us all together was also introduced by the philosopher Hegel who put forward the idea of a world-mind or Spirit (*Geist*) which he believed was the source of consciousness on the Earth. His belief was that what we see and experience of the world and reality is actually formed by this world-mind in which we all share. More recently, the philosopher and theologian *Pierre Teilhard de Chardin*[1] presented a view of the Earth as being in the process of unfolding an *interlinking system of consciousness* which he saw as a global net of developing self-awareness (The 'Noosphere'). I quote him as follows:

'We are faced with a harmonized collectivity of conscious-
nesses equivalent to a sort of super-consciousness. The
earth not only becoming covered by myriads of grains
of thought, but becoming enclosed in a single thinking
envelope, a single unanimous reflection.'

Some of these theories are quite interesting. However, in line with my approach, I will concentrate on psychological and scientific arguments for this idea of a universal consciousness or mind.

A PSYCHOLOGICAL VIEW

Sociologists such as Emile Durkheim see a *collective consciousness* only as a collection of shared beliefs, ideas, attitudes and knowledge held by most people in the world, but not a 'collective mind' or an 'independent entity' in a metaphysical sense.

However, this idea of a single collective mind or consciousness in the universe can be linked to the *'collective subconscious'* as proposed by the Swiss psychiatrist and psychoanalyst Carl Gustav Jung; a deep area of the mind (psyche) which he felt was shared by all of humanity. Have a look at the next quote by Jung:

'The collective subconscious - so far as we can say anything
about it at all - appears to consist of mythological motifs
or primordial images, for which reason the myths of
all nations are its real exponents. In fact, the whole of
mythology could be taken as a sort of projection of the
collective subconscious.'

In other words, Jung believed that we are all connected at a very deep subconscious level and this could be seen as some sort of collective mind.

SOME SUPPORT FROM SCIENCE

COMPUTER MODELS OF THE BRAIN

Although there are always critics of this idea, I mentioned earlier there is some recent support from neuroscientists working with computer models of the brain who also believe that the complexity of the Universe points to the possibility that it may, in some way be conscious. For example, in his *Integrated Information Theory* (IIT)[2] psychiatrist and neuroscientist, Giulio Tononi maintains that the universe is a giant *information-processing system* in which every sub-system shares information with other systems, a fully-interconnected information-processing highway. Tononi maintains that this ability to process data in such a complex interconnected system points to consciousness.

I use this idea of *interconnected systems* as an analogy for the Universal Mind later on.

THE VIEW OF QUANTUM PHYSICS

'This life of yours which you are living is not merely a piece of this entire existence, but in a certain sense the whole; only this whole is not so constituted that it can be surveyed in one single glance.'

Erwin Schrodinger: Theoretical physicist

CONSCIOUSNESS AS SOURCE

The Nobel-prize winning physicist, Erwin Schrödinger spoke of a unified, single consciousness in his books, *Mind and Matter* (1958) and *My View of the World* (1958). A quote of his reads; '*Consciousness is absolutely fundamental. It cannot be accounted for in terms of anything else*'. In other words, Schrödinger maintains that pure consciousness is monolithic in that it cannot be broken down into other smaller components.

His view is supported by the famous physicist Max Planck (another Nobel prize-winner) who quotes as follows: '*I regard consciousness as fundamental. I regard matter as derivative from consciousness. We cannot get behind consciousness. Everything that we talk about, everything that we regard as existing, postulates consciousness.*'

EVERYTHING IS CONNECTED

Later, another famous physicist, David Bohm, presented arguments in his book *Wholeness and the Implicate Order* (1980) for what he calls the '*Implicate Order*'[3], a condition in which everything in the universe can be scientifically proven to be connected to everything else. Obviously this is at a sub-atomic (energy) level, but if we look carefully at world ecological systems, we can see this interconnectedness mirrored in the interdependency of the different systems and life-forms.

More recent research by several quantum physicists has resulted in interesting data from '*String*' and '*Spin*'[4] theories, as well as the paradoxes of *Quantum entanglement*[5], *Non-locality and Resonance* in which they attempt to prove that the whole universe is a *quantum field* or *matrix* of inter-connected energy at a sub-atomic level. The quantum model of the universe leads to new and exciting ideas, such as this view that we are all interconnected at a very deep energy level and all form parts of a *single whole*. This idea of a 'single whole' of pure consciousness points once again to one, universal, collective consciousness or mind as being the source of the universe and reality as we know it.

As you can see, this idea of a universal field of consciousness, or a unified or Universal Collective Mind has been around for quite a while and has a lot of support, but we simply have not paid much attention to it until now when it has been highlighted again in metaphysics. I would like to believe that this is because it is quite a complicated idea, but now with a greater acceptance of quantum physics and metaphysics itself, we have the concepts and understanding to make more sense of it.

I want to finish this section with an appeal to your common sense logic. In a conscious universe, everything, every part, every cell, would naturally be conscious in some way, with living beings all sharing in this consciousness to varying degrees, including humans, animals, plants, microbes and minerals. The fact that our Earth sustains so many conscious (sentient) beings, from the largest mammal to the lowest microbe, indeed suggests that consciousness may be the underlying principle of the universe and linked to the *principle of life* itself.

A GREAT TRUTH HIDDEN AWAY IN MYTHS, ANALOGIES AND METAPHORS

'What, then, is truth? A mobile army of metaphors, metonyms, and anthropomorphisms.'

Neitzsche: German philosopher

In this section, we look at several metaphors and analogies which lend support to this idea of a Universal Mind or consciousness. You may find some of them quite interesting and surprising and ask yourself why you have never noticed this before.

MYTHS, METAPHORS AND ANALOGIES

Throughout the ages, scholars and thinkers have used myth, metaphors and analogies to explain complex matters. A myth is simply a traditional story which is usually linked to the early history of a nation or people. It tries to explain historical, natural or social events in a colourful, dramatic way with a plot full of heroes and villains, but often with important principles hidden in the narrative.

A metaphor is simply a well-known object or experience from everyday life which we compare to a more complicated event or universal principle. Although it is a weak comparison, the metaphor has some common characteristics with the real thing which helps to make it more understandable. For example, a common metaphor is *'life is a journey'*, in which the 'ups and downs' and difficulties of real life are likened to the kind of problems we would face on a long journey, such as hills, fatigue, dangers and obstacles along the way.

An analogy is similar to a metaphor, but it is usually not an object representing something else, but rather a simple process used to explain a more complicated one. You may remember the analogy I drew between the voracious caterpillar and the damage caused by our selfish, instinctual drives coming from early stages of our human evolution. The emergence of a butterfly from a chrysalis can also be seen as an analogy for the process of self-actualisation as described in psychology.

Metaphors and analogies help us make sense of the complexities of our world and the universe. Over the years, a few metaphors and analogies have been used by philosophers, psychologists, scientists and theologians to explain important truths and principles and in this case, to present an idea that fits my description of a Universal, Collective Mind. We just have to look more closely, and remember to keep an open mind.

Remember that although the following metaphors and analogies are only figures of speech, they have a powerful symbolic effect on the subconscious mind and you may find one which resonates with your own thoughts or beliefs on the nature of the universe. In this way, they may be useful to clarify your own thinking.

THE METAPHOR OF THE DREAM

*'Indeed, the whole world is imagination, while He is the
Real in Reality. Whoever understands this knows all the
secrets of the Spiritual Path.'*

Ibn Al-'Arabi: Sufi mystic and philosopher

We often use phrases in everyday life such as 'He really needs to wake up', when we believe someone does not really know what is going on, or what they are doing. However, this is not quite the same as being asleep in a metaphysical sense. In metaphysics, the metaphor of the dream suggests that our whole idea of perception is fundamentally flawed and what we are experiencing of the world, and indeed our whole sense of reality, can be compared to a dream. This implies that we are asleep to the true reality and in this dreamlike state, only see things dimly through a sort of misty, sleepy haze in our minds. This idea of life as a dream has been around for quite a while, circulating in different cultures such as the Hindu tradition, Persian, Greek (Plato) and French philosophy (Descartes), Buddhism, and even in modern times, in films such as the *'Matrix'* series. In fact, Gregg Braden, speaking to biologist, Bruce Lipton, commented that the film, *The Matrix* should be known as a documentary as it is based on truth.

The metaphor is based on the argument that we can't really prove that life is not a dream because a dream can be very real, especially a lucid dream, in which we have a level of awareness which is enough to make choices and simple decisions.

DOES THIS MEAN THAT REALITY IS PART OF A DREAM?

Aspects of dreams are very useful in explaining what is meant by some writers when they say that our sense of reality is an illusion, as there are many resemblances between dreams and real-life. On the positive side, this means that one day we will be able to awaken from the dream to true reality.

Let us look at this comparison, so that you will better understand how a dream can be a metaphor for what we regard as life or reality and how this links up with the idea of a Universal Mind. Remember the metaphysical principle of 'As above, so below'. This means that if we look at how our own minds work, we should get a glimmer of what goes on in a Universal Collective Mind.

Firstly, Carl Jung believed that our own dreams are attempts to resolve subconscious tensions. Like our bodies, our minds also seek balance and a healthy expression and growth, and this means dealing with any unpleasant issues in our subconscious minds that filter through into our lives. In other words, our dreams provide us with the opportunity to be aware of, and to release unbalanced or unhealthy patterns of thought. In this way, they help to integrate our personalities.

Real life is pretty much the same, as we daily deal with challenges and even unpleasant situations and if we handle them effectively, can grow and become stronger, wiser people. In other words, life itself provides opportunities for us to learn in the same way that lucid dreams provide us with scenarios in which we have to face challenges and make decisions to improve what is going on in our subconscious minds.

Secondly, a dream is a scenario constructed in our minds and choreographed by our subconscious mind. According to Jung, they are full of symbolic cues so that we do not have to face the full truth of the matter, which could be traumatic. Once we interpret and understand the messages and lessons given in our dreams, we should know how to deal with our issues and bring balance and healthy growth to our minds.

Let us compare this to the previous chapter where I pointed out how our minds construct a 'view' of reality from sensory cues, perceptions and ideas. What we see and experience in life may not be exactly as it really is. We 'invite' it in, so to speak. In other words, what we see in real-life could *also be symbolic of a higher reality.* As is the case with dreams, perhaps in this life, if we were exposed to the full light of this higher reality we would not cope, so truth is being introduced to us gradually in a shared lucid-dreamlike experience with images and situations we understand and can manage.

SO WHO OR WHAT IS DREAMING?

This metaphor of reality (life) as a dream now introduces the possibility of a 'dreamer', someone or 'something' who is creating the dream. In some metaphysical texts, it is said that it is our souls which are slumbering and dreaming while in our bodies, creating this dreamlike sense of reality until they fully awaken. This is quite interesting, because it implies that our souls are expressing and experiencing life through our bodies. This sounds fine and great from a viewpoint of theology and is certainly worth considering, but perhaps there is another possibility.

In the '*Matrix*' film series you may remember that intelligent machines were creating an artificial reality to enslave mankind. In our case, I do not for one moment believe that machines are involved in creating our sense of reality, but the idea that our reality is being formed outside of our own minds certainly cannot be discounted in the light of the idea of a Universal Collective Mind. Let us look at this again using the workings of our own minds as an analogy.

As humans we can consciously form images and entire three-dimensional scenes in our minds through our faculty of imagery. We are also able to dream as a result of the activity of our subconscious minds. There is, therefore, no reason why a collective mind could not be doing the same, as it is, by definition, the combined mind of us all. In other words, the collective or Universal Mind could be the dreamer, creating imagery which we, as part of the dream, experience as reality and everything else that goes with creation. These are all ideas for you to consider.

LIFE AS A DRAMATISED PLAY

'All the world's a stage and all the men and women merely players.'

Shakespeare

How would we explain the changing tides, events and scenes of life in our world and what would be the point of this illusion?

As an active universal consciousness, the Collective would also have its own inner dynamics and we would see its shifting tides mirrored in global events in the dream, filtering down to our level in the form of new changes, situations and challenges. If I may use a second metaphor of life as a dramatic play, any events and situations unfolding on the '*stage of life*' would be the scene-changes and actions necessary to help with inner adjustments to keep harmony in the Universal Mind, which will be shown later to be a *balanced system.*

In this way, it could be said that this 'balancing act' is our role as human beings, and the events shaping our history are only mirror images of more profound cosmic shifts and events taking place within the Universal Mind, which has a trickle-down effect on our personal lives.

A SCIENTIFIC CRITIQUE

Although at first glance, this whole idea of life as a dream may seem laughable and nonsensical, but this dream-metaphor can explain many scientific, psychological, philosophical and religious paradoxes in the world today. For example, it explains why science has, as yet, not been able to point to the true basis of reality, apart from the sub-atomic order indicated by quantum physicists. If this reality is a shared 'dream' generated by a Universal, Collective Mind, our bodies, minds, thoughts and perceptions would form an integral part of the dream, meaning that we would never be able to really stand back and objectively view (or measure) it from the outside.

WHAT ABOUT PSYCHOLOGY?

Psychologically speaking, the dream-metaphor would also explain why our subconscious minds create a veil of appearances to hide a reality which we, as yet, can't fully process. A lucid dream is so close to reality that we cannot, in all truth, tell the difference. So it seems we are stuck with this world of upside-down perceptions until we can 'wake up' and see with clarity. Seeing ourselves as actors in a 'dream-play' of a collective mind could actually be useful in explaining our own coming into being. On the positive side, if we are presently 'plugged into' a dream, there must be ways in which we can awaken. This '*awakening*' points to a whole new range of possible developments relating to consciousness and perception which are quite exciting.

The problem is that many of us want this 'dream' to be real, because it is comforting and often brings us pleasure, as was the case with the dreamers in the 'Matrix' film franchise. So convincing ourselves to awaken will not be easy.

WHAT DO THE PHILOSOPHERS SAY?

Philosophically speaking, if we ask the question why a single Universal Mind would create this illusion, we only have to look at the reasons for our own dreaming, which are *unresolved issues*. Perhaps during its initial coming into being and subsequent expansion, imbalances and tensions have arisen in the universe and its conscious part, the Universal Consciousness or Mind, and need to be resolved. If this dream-state indeed mirrors the higher reality and universal imbalances and shifts are reflected in the trials and tribulations we face in human history, by resolving them and bringing balance and order to the mind of the dreamer, in this case, the Universal Mind, we become active agents of change and our role is so much more important than we initially believed.

THE METAPHOR OF A 'DIVINE MIND'

'As you look upon creation, which appears so solid and real,
remember always to think of it as ideas in the mind of God,
frozen into physical forms.'

Sri Paramahansa Yogananda:
Founder of the Self-Realization Fellowship

This is a theological approach to reality and creation and asks the question of whether creation is merely a bundle of emanated thoughts and images from the Mind of God, and can be seen as a religious spin on the idea of an intangible Universal Mind creating and sustaining the universe. This idea goes back quite far into history to the time of the earliest theologians. For instance, the '*Mind of God*' is mentioned in the sacred scriptures of many religions. Some Buddhist teachings also describe 'Mind' as awareness, eternal and limitless, implying that its true essence is universal and beyond everyday experience.

Most sacred teachings speak of God creating the universe out of *chaos*, which seems to be the first state of existence before an *active principle* brought order from the chaos, which in terms of this metaphor, would be the Will and Intent of the Mind of God. However, this chaos still exists at a deep level of reality, as seen in the scientific law that, if left to themselves, all created things tend to break down into their basic components or lowest state. This further supports the ideas that the unfoldment of the universe is still incomplete.

This theological idea of a '*Divine Mind*' is similar to the metaphysical idea of a Universal Collective Mind, as they both imply a universal state of consciousness as the source of reality as we know it.

A PHILOSOPHICAL VIEW

Theoretically, in philosophical terms, thoughts or images emanating from a Universal Divine Mind could lead to the creation of *'active scenarios'* which to us, being part of this Mind, become reality as we know it. This is not unreasonable, as we can compare this to our own minds and thinking and see a similar, if not identical, process. For instance, we are able to create three-dimensional images in our minds and thoughts are also formed in our minds and follow on one after another by a process of association. In terms of Christian and Jewish mysticism, this flowing thought-process could be seen as the *hierarchic emanation of thought-forms* starting with the celestial hosts and ending with the souls of men (and women) created within a background context which we would see as the physical universe.

Following on from this, if a Divine Mind is the source of all consciousness, it stands to reason that the emanated thought-forms would also have the capacity for consciousness. These thought-forms would include all sentient beings and imply that the *principle of life* flows from the Divine Mind as well. In this case, life would be linked to the consciousness and activity of the Divine Mind.

This idea of an emanation of thought-forms also reminds me of *Plato's world of ideal forms*[6], said to be templates for all created things, as well as the notion of *universal archetypes* as described by Carl Jung. I would advise you to read up on this as it is very interesting.

THE METAPHOR OF A DIVINE MIND FROM A PSYCHOLOGICAL PERSPECTIVE

I understand that many of you may still be undecided as to the idea of one Universal Mind, so let me offer you a few more comparisons from psychology. To do this, I will have to go a bit deeper into this metaphysical principle of *'As above, so below'* by presenting it in more modern terms as the *'Macrocosm'* (the Universal Mind), represented in some way in its parts (the *'Microcosm'*), in this case, our own minds. This means that we should be able to infer some of the attributes of the Divine Mind from the faculties of our own minds. As I showed in previous sections, this appears to be the case, as we too, have consciousness, the ability to perceive, the power of thought, intent and imagery, which, it seems, would also exist within a Divine Mind.

A SCIENTIFIC APPROACH

'This life of yours which you are living is not merely a piece of this entire existence, but in a certain sense the whole; only this whole is not so constituted that it can be surveyed in one single glance.'

Erwin Schrodinger

In the following section, I discuss a few scientific models which also lend support to the idea of a Universal Collective Mind.

IS REALITY A HOLOGRAM CREATED IN OUR COLLECTIVE CONSCIOUSNESS?

WHAT IS A HOLOGRAM?

Recent scientific research can now give us new perspectives on this idea of a Universal Collective Mind by comparing any *thought-form creations to a hologram*. In physics, a hologram is a three-dimensional image or set of images formed by the interference pattern of light beams from lasers. It has a number of unique characteristics which we can use to compare with our physical universe. In this way, the universe (and our reality) could be likened to a hologram of three-dimensional images projected by a single, Universal Mind.

This idea of a 'holographic' universe was already included in my previous book *Multi-Dimensional Perception*, in which I presented information from another publication, *The Holographic Universe* (Talbot, 1996), listing scientists in the field of quantum physics who believe that the entire universe (and indeed, reality itself) behaves like a holographic projection at a sub-atomic level. Here I am specifically mentioning the famous physicist, David Bohm and the neurophysiologist, Karl Pribram. Their work is discussed fully in the book I have just mentioned.

But let us now look a bit deeper at this comparison:

As I said, a hologram is created by refracting different laser light beams, which are pure energy. Physicists have already shown that at a sub-atomic level, the universe itself is also pure energy, which could likewise be seen in terms of light. The source of a hologram is a powerfully focused beam and according to some quantum physicists I mentioned earlier, the origin of the universe is consciousness or conscious energy itself. In other words, the universe could have been formed with *holographic characteristics* by a Universal Mind with the power to create three-dimensional images with focused intent, which to us, appears as reality, when, in fact, it is merely patterns or 'templates' of energy. In this case, remember the psychological evidence I provided earlier which showed how we actually assemble our own view of reality in our minds.

LET US EXAMINE SOME SPECIFIC SIMILARITIES BETWEEN A HOLOGRAM AND THE CREATED UNIVERSE:

- To begin, we turn to the field of mathematics in which Prof Kostas Skenderis of the School of Mathematical Sciences at the University of Southampton points out that a hologram is similar to the created universe, in that what we presently see in three dimensions as reality is actually two-dimensional. This has been confirmed by psychological research which shows that each eye only sees in two-dimensions, but it is our *stereoscopic vision* combined with cues of the angle of view, light and shadow and relative size which give our vision 3-D depth and perspective. He points out that it is the same with holograms, in which three-dimensional images are encoded onto two-dimensional surfaces, for example, credit cards. In fact, he believes that the whole universe could, in some way, be 'encoded'.

- To continue, I am sure that most of you are familiar with the holograms on credit cards and in some cases, on decorative metal plates or ornaments. What is particularly interesting is that, if we break one of these ornaments with a hologram etched into it into different pieces, the same three-dimensional image can be seen in any of the parts. In other words, each part of the hologram contains the whole within itself.

- This sounds a bit crazy but just think about it a while. Our own bodies, and indeed every form and living thing created in nature, also reveals this holographic characteristic, in that its whole profile and physical characteristics can be seen in any one speck of its DNA.

- However, there is an important psychological dimension to this. A hologram changes as we look at it from different angles. It has many levels of imagery or inner dimensions. Think of the hologram on the credit card as an example. It changes as we tilt the card in different directions. It's all a matter of perspective. Is this not the same with our own minds when we view reality? We know that each of us sees and interprets the world differently in line with our past experiences and schemas, but we still believe the small fragment we see to be the whole truth.

THE SYSTEMS APPROACH TO REALITY

Science sees a '*system*' as an interconnected network of interacting working parts. In psychology, the brain is seen as a system, as it has a number of interrelated regions all carrying out different functions. If we look at this definition of a system, it will include the brain's by-products of mind and consciousness, as they show characteristics common to all 'systems'. This will become clearer as we explore this analogy further.

SCIENCE VIEWS THE UNIVERSE AS A SYSTEM

In terms of recent scientific research in *Integrated Information Theory* (ITT), as a result of its ability to process large amounts of information, (a key characteristic of systems), the universe can be seen as a giant mega-system, a fully-interconnected information-processing highway with many complex sub-systems. These sub-systems are the many galactic, solar and planetary systems which are all connected energy-wise, to become one giant universal system. This would certainly be supported by astronomers.

A UNIVERSAL MIND AS A 'SYSTEM' OF CONSCIOUSNESS

The ITT links the complexity of systems to different levels of consciousness and points to the universe itself as being conscious in some way in order to cope with the huge amount of information-processing that takes place. A conscious universe, in turn, implies a 'mind' to direct and act with that consciousness, which points to a Universal Collective Mind as being the conscious component of the universe, resulting in a self-regulating, balanced, mega-system of consciousness.

ASPECTS OF SYSTEMS

Let us now look at some of the main aspects of systems[7] and see how they all lend support to the idea of a single, Universal, Collective Mind.

- Systems are all interconnected. This means that all living systems are ultimately connected to the aspects of life and consciousness in the collective mind. In other words, each of us is a part of the whole, connected through the world (global) system to the universal mega-system of consciousness itself.

- Systems also strive to reach a point of *balance and equilibrium*, which allows them to work efficiently. Once they are balanced, even the tiniest imbalance in the system would be felt by all. A good analogy for this would be a spider's web, in which even a slight movement in the furthest corner is felt throughout the entire web. Keep this in mind when we later discuss the Universal, Collective Mind as a self-regulating, balanced system.

- Another important characteristic of systems is that they are 'self-regulating', reaching this state of balance or equilibrium only after sharing information and *adjusting* to each other. In other words, ongoing *communication* within the universal system is essential in order to find this balance. The importance of this sharing of information for our global system is that it seems that only by coming together and sharing ideas can we ever hope to discover a more complete and holistic view of reality.

CHANGES WITHIN THE UNIVERSAL COLLECTIVE MIND FROM A SYSTEMS PERSPECTIVE

Astronomers tell us that the Universe is expanding. And if we use the systems analogy to follow this line of thinking, accepting a collective mind as the conscious component of the universal system, this notion of 'expansion' will help to explain many of our current global changes. With the universal mega-system being *self-regulating*, what we see happening on Earth is often the effects of *ongoing expansion, correction and balance* as the mega-system grows (the universe expands), increasing the scope of its sub-systems. For example, shifts in the consciousness of the Universal Collective Mind would be felt by people in the world as new levels of social awareness, which we actually see happening today.

Why then do we find it so difficult to see this growth taking place in our societies, the world or even in the universe in real-time? With hindsight, glancing back on history, we do see major changes that have taken place in our thinking and value systems, especially on an ecological, moral and spiritual level. If we consider the '*analogy of the play*', the answer becomes clearer, in that we are active role-players in this unfolding drama and it is very difficult to step back and see from the point of view of the audience while we are still on the stage. What this means is that we cannot really ever know truth unless we learn to step outside of our present reality.

Another important result that comes from viewing the Universal Mind from a *systems perspective* is that, with human beings an integral part of the mega-system, we can never be separate from it, as it provides our very life and consciousness. Although we feel separated, this is not the case, and this means that it is possible for is to return to a realisation of our true relationship of oneness simply by letting go of those blocks in our minds that prevent us from realising our unity. So there's still plenty of work to be done.

COMMENT

We have reached the point in our history where we are starting to ask the right questions about ecological, human and animal rights and discussing important issues such as global warming and renewable energy sources, but still not finding any satisfactory answers. The problem is that we are dealing with many personal interests and agendas and solutions to these fundamental issues will not be found in day-to-day thinking. We have to go deeper, into the very principles that govern life and evolution. We need a fully inclusive and holistic picture of the world and universe and new insights into the path that we need to travel which can only come from metaphysics.

Seeing the Universal Collective Mind in terms of systems theory gives us a more fully inclusive and holistic picture, as it allows us to go deeper and find two important metaphysical principles, namely *inclusiveness* and *action-consequence*, both of which have a profound effect on the inner workings of our world and Universe. Paradoxically, in unpacking these two principles we will be able to clear up some religious confusion relating to the notions of evil and karma. Well, I suppose this is the point of multi-dimensional thinking, to cut across the borders of different fields and find solutions.

In the next sections, we examine these two principles in more detail.

INCLUSIVENESS

'The basic laws of the Universe are simple, but because our senses are limited, we can't grasp them. There is a pattern in creation.'

Albert Einstein

This *interconnectedness* within systems points to a metaphysical principle of *inclusiveness*. Once different subsystems are coupled and reach a point of balance, the entire mega-system becomes fully inclusive. The notion of a Universal Collective Mind also embodies this principle, as everything, all of reality, is said to be formed within its consciousness.

WHAT DOES THIS IDEA OF INCLUSIVENESS MEAN FOR US IN EVERYDAY LIFE?

First, 'inclusiveness' means that all sub-systems are of equal importance to the whole and none can be excluded. Within the global system, we have different social, cultural, religious and belief sub-systems, and in the light of inclusiveness, all these subsystems are, in essence, equal. We simply cannot judge one as closer to the truth, or as more important than another. Each is needed to complete the mosaic of our *global society*, the larger system.

Also, within all systems of society, inclusiveness points to a natural inter-connectedness between people, a brotherhood of mankind. The problem is that with our present limited perceptions and the ongoing narratives promoting separateness which we are exposed to daily in modern society, we don't see this inclusiveness, our brotherhood, inter-dependence, or the 'bigger picture' of humanity, and this leads to the intolerance and disagreements we see in the world today.

ACTION-CONSEQUENCE

'The mind is its own place and in itself, can make
a Heaven of Hell, a Hell of Heaven.'

John Milton; (1608-1674)
English poet and intellectual

This pull towards *adjustment, balance and harmony* in systems is very important. Systems remain balanced until something inside the system, or in the larger network of systems, changes, and they then work to correct the imbalance.

IMBALANCES IN THE UNIVERSAL AND GLOBAL SYSTEMS

In the previous section, I mentioned how natural adjustments taking place within the Universal Mind linked to the expanding universe and the 'adjustments' taking place between major astronomical sub-systems, may filter down to our global system and bring about massive changes to conditions like temperature and climate. We see this happening even today. These major changes could, in turn, result in natural disasters and even worldwide disease, but could be seen as *'balancing actions'*, all designed to keep the equilibrium of the universal mega-system during its process of expansion and unfoldment. This is the 'bigger picture' or more holistic view I spoke about.

However, there are other causes closer to home, the consequences of imbalances that we have brought about ourselves, which can spark global changes. For instance, if we apply the principle of balance and equilibrium to the world (global) system at large, it means that every action or change to the system will have its consequences aimed at correcting this imbalance. I have said that all systems, including global or universal systems, will act to correct themselves if anything threatens their inner balance and harmony. This explanation links up with the principle of 'Consequence' as introduced in my previous publication *Multi-Dimensional Thinking* as well as the idea of *karma* as taught in Eastern metaphysical philosophy.

In terms of systems theory, a system naturally moves to adjust to a disturbance to its equilibrium. In other words, any consequences arising from this 'adjustment' are *perfectly natural* and in tune with the principle of *action-consequence*, which is pretty much Newton's Third Law of Motion[8]; 'to every action, there is an equal and opposite reaction.'

Within the global system (everyday life) it is we, with our human short-sightedness, who judge the outcome of this adjustment as good or bad or right or wrong, whether it takes place at the level of a society, or as a global event. As we are integral parts of the global and mega-system, (in this case), the Universal Mind, we can't distance ourselves from them to see these consequences for what they are, natural adjustments to disturbances and threats that we have made to the inner balance and harmony of the systems themselves.

COMMENT

THE IMPARTIALITY OF THE UNIVERSAL MIND

However, what is important for metaphysics, as well as our everyday understanding, is that this 'natural adjustment' means that the Universal Collective Mind is *impartial and non-judgmental*. In fact, the whole idea of 'the wrath of God' does not fit well with the scientific systems analogy. This is a human concept that we have created.

This principle of action-consequence should then be a guiding light for growth and development. If we do not exercise common sense and reason in our decisions, we place ourselves in its path and it then appears as a judgment on us, an unpleasant consequence of something we have done or failed to do. As the whole mega-system is interconnected, this can be on a global scale, a natural outcome of actions or conditions which we as a global community have put into motion, or in our social and family systems, (our personal lives), as hateful thoughts and actions which are a threat to society or the harmony of our relationships with others. In each such case, we should expect the consequences.

As a result, we could say that nothing that happens to us is truly unfair. We simply fail to see how it is a consequence of our own actions or else part of a larger process of universal, global or personal development. We are talking here of a matrix of natural, metaphysical laws and principles which, as yet, we do not fully understand.

THE PRINCIPLE OF RANDOMNESS

However, I would agree that bad things can happen to people without their actions being involved. As it is still expanding, it is clear that the universe has not fully unfolded and this may be giving rise to an *element of imbalance or randomness* in the mega-system which enters our lives from time to time in the form of freak accidents or being an innocent victim of crime. This implies that some of the original chaotic energy which existed before the ordering of the universe can still be found in the deepest recesses of the Universal Collective Mind, and this is unfortunately embodied in some criminal minds.

As we now move away from the systems analogy, we see that the principle of action-consequence has a bearing on *our notion of evil* in the world. However, I will still refer to the systems analogy periodically as it can be quite useful to explain some otherwise baffling events taking place in the world.

THE NOTION OF EVIL OR 'THE DEVIL MADE ME DO IT'

'Evil is an extreme manifestation of human sub-consciousness.'

Eckhart Tolle

Ironically, the kind of questions we often ask ourselves when the wheels fall off is: 'Why did this have to happen to me?' or 'Why is there so much crime and suffering in the world?' Some of us come to the conclusion that this is due to the actions of some evil influence which exists in the world. But is this true? And exactly what is evil? Can we always shift the blame to someone else or something outside of ourselves?

Metaphorically, many people are still asleep. In the early stages of human social development, the un-awakened person will go about feeding only their basic drives and needs, (as shown in the metaphor of the caterpillar), and only later as they awaken more and more, begin to change their beliefs and actions. You may remember my discussion on the *four stages of consciousness*. So let us look a bit deeper at this issue of consciousness once again.

NATURAL CONSEQUENCES AND CONSCIOUSNESS

We have just discussed the principle of action-consequence, in which suffering is often simply the *natural consequence* of imbalances or destructive environmental, social or political actions that we introduce into the world, or else our failure to deal with threats to the balance of the global system. The Universal Mind, as a balanced system, is dealing out impersonal and impartial natural consequences and so 'evil' would be a concept which only has meaning for us as people.

For example, the aggressiveness and selfishness of wild animals are not regarded as evil, as we know that they are only acting out their instinctual drives and we accept that they do not have the free will and thinking skills to make what we call 'moral decisions'. A lion killing a rival in the animal kingdom is accepted as natural and normal. However, in human society, killing a rival would be regarded as wrong and therefore evil.

Evil is linked to human norms which state that when a person's behaviour is destructive to others, it is 'evil'. In other words, the person's consciousness has regressed to a point where the animal-like drives and instincts from our earlier stage of evolution cannot be managed or controlled. In this state of mind, slip-ups enter their thinking and they engage in selfish, aggressive and murderous acts, which, to our human norms and understanding, can be legitimately labelled as 'evil'.

THE NOTION OF KARMA

DO WE HAVE MORE THAN ONE CHANCE AT LIFE?

In metaphysics, 'bad stuff' happening to us is sometimes seen as our 'karma', or *'just desserts'*. This is a variation of the idea of someone *upsetting the balance* in the home, family, society, the nation, or the world as a whole, which results in a swing-back of the pendulum and unpleasant consequences for the person(s) who created the imbalance. This is similar to the principle of action-consequence and Newton's Third Law of Motion, but there are a few differences.

Firstly, it is believed that we create 'good' as well as 'bad' karma. In other words, if we do 'good' we will eventually reap the rewards. There is some truth in this from a social psychology point of view, as people who 'do good' are usually acknowledged and liked by others, although not always.

The main idea here is that by accepting the law of karma we can align ourselves with it, focus on doing good, and 'clean up our act'. However, if this is out of fear of what karma will do to us, it might not have so much value. Personally, I do not like doing anything out of fear.

REINCARNATION

This brings us to the second difference, whether we can actually complete this task of 'cleaning ourselves up' in only one lifetime. I recently saw a posting on social media by a blogger called 'Banter King' in which he says what if when we die (in hospital), the *'light at the end of the tunnel'* is actually the light in another hospital room in which we are immediately reborn and the reason we are crying is that we know we have to forget everything from our previous life. Although I do not believe that this is the case, as there should be a time of *'reconciling the books'* if we wish to reincarnate again, this allegory certainly delivers a powerful message.

In metaphysics, the principle of *reincarnation*[9] is accepted, which means that we can deal with our karma over many lifetimes and any shortcomings left over in this life will simply be faced again in another life under different circumstances until they are resolved. In other words, each person is given chances in different lives to deal with all their issues until they are totally free of karma, at which time they are ready to move on to a higher form of life.

COMMENT

The problem is that some metaphysicians explain every failure or unpleasant event in a person's life as 'bad karma' from a previous life and everyone living a privileged or successful life is just reaping their 'good karma' built up from previous lives. To me, this is a bit simplistic in light of the huge amount of possible reasons for success or failure, most of them related to the person's level of motivation, insight, understanding and decision-making skills.

However, I do accept karma as one of the possible causes of misfortune, but rather as the karmic short-term consequences of stupid decisions and not extended over many lives. The reason for this is because *I no longer personally subscribe to the notion of reincarnation*. Ancient texts I have studied, as well as what I have learnt by engaging the Universal Collective Mind, have led me to believe that reincarnation is a soul-choice linked to certain metaphysical and religious paradigms and that we have the *free will* and *power to decide* whether to deal with these issues after we have passed on, in another life on Earth, or in a higher form of life without being born again. In which case, at death, we would simply move onto this next state of being or level of the Universal Mind and deal with our outstanding issues there. Later on, I will present real-life experiences which show that *'reconciliation of the books'* can take place after death. This is essentially the religious notion of *'Purgatory'*.

Reincarnation may be real for those of us who are not yet aware of our *soul-power* to choose but falls away once we have insight into the true nature of our higher authentic selves or souls, and can make more conscious choices.

SOUL CONTRACTS AND 'UNFORTUNATE EVENTS'

Then there is a situation called a *soul-contract*. Some metaphysicians believe that relationships and interactions between people, whether good or bad, have been planned before they are born. I have personally experienced a soul-contract with regards to a relationship, souls agreeing to get together to work with each other as people and even have long-term relationships as part of a prior soul-agreement, but I have a problem accepting that every experience involving others has been pre-ordained by a soul-contract, as this will seriously threaten the universal principle of free will. It will also be difficult to understand and accept how every act of violence and even murder is part of an earlier soul-contract.

It is possible that some difficult interactions between people, even conflict, could be part of a soul-plan for each person's development, but as a counsellor, I maintain that with the human ego and lower aggressive drives involved, conflicts could easily exceed the scope of what will help in one's development, leading to irreparable damage to another person's psyche such as in severe trauma, and this would not be 'development' but rather the 'destruction' of the personality. In these cases, I would have to blame the element of randomness in which innocent persons are sometimes caught up in the self-destructive behaviour of others.

TAKING PERSONAL RESPONSIBILITY FOR OUR LIVES

'When you think everything is someone else's fault, you will suffer a lot. When you realize that everything springs only from yourself, you will learn both peace and joy.'

Dalai Lama

I understand that this may differ somewhat from traditional religious doctrines which tend to lay the blame for evil only at the door of entities such as the 'devil', fallen angels and demons, and see mankind as helpless and solely dependent on divine grace. I do feel that the time has come for us to start taking responsibility for our own thinking and actions and stop blaming tragedies on the 'judgment' or 'wrath' of God, or some unseen evil personality. At the end of the day, we are allowing this to happen in our minds, over which we have control, and I believe that, in most cases, as shown in the systems analogy, it is we who upset the balance of family, social, national or global systems, and it is the correction, or consequences, of these actions that filter through to become unpleasant experiences in our personal lives.

ARCHETYPAL PERSONALITIES

However, in metaphysics, we do acknowledge 'shadow beings' or 'dark companions', *archetypal personalities* in the lower realms of the Universal Collective Mind which try to find expression in the ignorance, ego and selfish instinctual drives of the undisciplined human mind. But it comes back to our own responsibility in understanding and properly managing our minds and the conscious choices that we make. In fact, I would not be far wrong in likening everyday life to a battle between *conscious thinking* and *rationality* on one hand, *and delusion, greed and selfishness* of mankind on the other. I will discuss the issue of 'archetypes' of the Universal Mind in the next section.

Finally, perhaps if seen as part of a broader plan or 'bigger picture', these negative influences and their challenges may reveal to us our own *shadow-side* and inadequacies. If we deal properly with them, we are able to develop virtues such as compassion, patience, resilience and trust in a higher power. In other words, our so-called battle with 'evil' may be an important part of our own soul-development and unfoldment, but we fail to notice that the battle is actually *within ourselves.*

HOW DOES ALL THIS MAKE SENSE?

'A human being is part of the whole, called by us 'universe',
a part limited in time and space. He experiences himself,
his thoughts and feelings, as something separate from the rest
▯ a kind of optical delusion of consciousness.'

Albert Einstein

If, by now, you are starting to open your mind to this idea of a Universal Collective Mind, (which you choose to call 'God', 'Spirit' or the 'Universe' as you wish), you are probably asking the question of how this all-powerful mind actually enters into the insignificant personality, mind and life that is in each of us? Once again, I will use analogies to explain these processes.

THE ANALOGY OF THE HUMAN BIOLOGICAL CELL

THE PROCESS OF UNFOLDMENT

First, I can offer you an explanation using an analogy from biology. Following conception, a single human cell reproduces and replicates itself many times. Eventually, we have a great many cells having the same genetic material as the original. After this, each cell develops on its own, eventually joining with other similar cells to form organs. Finally, the organs recombine to form one fully-functioning body. For life on this sphere, this process of *differentiation* and *reintegration* seems to be the simplest and most perfect form of growth and development, and this could very well be the template used by the Universal Mind for its own unfoldment and expression into a multitude of forms.

Let me pose a question:

Why is it so difficult for us to see ourselves as part of the Universal Collective Mind and why do we not experience it in everyday life?

In metaphysics, it is believed that the limitations we introduce into our own minds and personalities are due to an illusion of separation brought about by those parts of us that are still undeveloped or 'asleep'. Science tells us that we are only using a small portion of the true potential of our brains, so we are actually accessing very little of the Universal Collective Mind due to our biology, as well as those mental programs and subconscious blocks I showed you earlier. In other words, it can be said that we are presently 'hard-wired' for only a partial experience of reality. This filtering prevents us from knowing the full extent of the Universal Mind, as well as the thoughts and experiences of the many other persons to whom we are connected. This is probably for the best at this time, as our minds are quite fragile and we could easily be overwhelmed by too many new experiences. For this reason, our subconscious minds have to protect us from a complete overload which would happen if the 'sluice-gates' were fully opened.

In other words, until such time as we have evolved biologically and mentally, we will have to be satisfied with our present personal sense of self. However, with the right training, some of these limits can be bypassed and, for brief moments, we can discover a deeper and more powerful experience of a higher source of self and reality. It is only during these enhanced states that we realise our huge untapped potential for growth as an integral part of the Universal Mind.

THE IMPORTANCE OF ARCHETYPES

'The collective unconscious consists of the sum of the instincts and their correlates, the archetypes. Just as everybody possesses instincts, so he also possesses a stock of archetypal images.'

Carl Jung

In the previous section, I briefly mentioned other separate personalities or 'archetypes[10]' of the Universal Collective Mind. So what are they and how can they affect us? In this section, we look at this important aspect of ourselves and the Universal Collective Mind.

THE ORIGIN OF ARCHETYPES

Carl Jung showed us that through our human psyche we have access to a *collective mind*, (at a subconscious level), and he also pointed out that this collective mind hosts a number of universal '*archetypes*'. The term 'archetype' has its origins in ancient Greek. The root words are *archein*, which means 'original or old'; and *typos*, which means 'pattern, model or type'. In other words, archetypes could be seen as *early patterns or forms* created in the consciousness of the collective mind. In fact, the idea of universal archetypes points once again to a Universal Mind to form them.

In line with my earlier conclusions, being formed out of consciousness by a conscious Universal Mind would imply that these patterns are also, to a degree, conscious in some way, and in terms of the hologram analogy, will reflect at least some of the characteristics of the Universal Collective Mind. In other words, we could see them as 'sub-personality patterns'. However, in metaphysics, and especially in my *psycho-spiritual approach*, universal archetypes are far more than this, which you will clearly see as you progress through the book.

WE 'MIRROR' UNIVERSAL ARCHETYPES

As we are connected to the Universal Collective Mind at a subconscious level, universal archetypes are 'mirrored' in our subconscious minds as thought-structures or sub-personalities representing different aspects of ourselves. Carl Jung mentioned twelve universal archetypes that can be seen reflected in the human subconscious mind, but I will only point out a few important ones which you must have encountered in your everyday lives.

THE INNER CHILD

The first common archetype is the '*innocent*' or '*inner child*', which embodies our original childlike innocence and enthusiasm which is often suppressed during our adult lives. This is probably the most well-known archetype mentioned in articles and books. The personality pattern of our inner child will emerge in dreams in which we see memories of our childhood and feel the joy of those carefree days. And it will be felt in the excitement of doing something we used to do as children, such as riding a roller-coaster.

THE HERO

Then we have the '*hero*' archetype, which fills our minds with grandiose ideas of saving the world and is often brought out by our frustrated aspirations to be seen and acknowledged. If properly channelled, this archetype can fuel our drive to make a difference in the world and in this way it can be useful. However, if not channelled in a useful way, it will let us know of its frustrations in our dreams by regularly presenting us as some sort of super-hero, receiving accolades for battling the baddies. It seems to have a life or consciousness of its own, which is important for metaphysics.

THE CAREGIVER

We may also have within our psyche a '*nurturer*' or '*caregiver*' archetype, which usually comes out when we become parents. This archetype can also be useful in driving our actions in caring and nurturing other persons (and animals), and explains the crazy cat-lady in a better light as someone having a strong nurturer archetype with plenty of love and care to give, but does not have a family.

THE VICTIM ARCHETYPE

Finally, there is the '*orphan*' or '*victim*' archetype. This universal archetype becomes a *negative personality pattern* in the psyche of a person who houses their pain and unhappy emotions from the past and prompts them to blame others for their misfortune. In this way, they 'play the victim' and constantly seek attention or drama. This archetype also houses long-standing resentments resulting from intense dissatisfaction with their lives in general, or else resentments against people from the past. This can make a person very bitter. If the negativity is very bad, the affected person can become toxic to others, or have a *'cloud of drama'* surrounding them, drawing in more and more negativity. This is a nasty fellow, and in my opinion, it may even lead to violence, as persons with a strong victim archetype may try to recover their lost personal power by taking it from others.

WHY ARE ARCHETYPES SO IMPORTANT?

As they exist deep within our psyche, we need an enhanced state of consciousness for archetypes to present themselves directly to us. For this reason, they are often seen in our dreams and, as will be seen later, can also make an appearance during our meditations and spontaneous imagery. They appear as humanlike figures or even fictional characters shaped by our own personalities, schemas, expectations and beliefs. For example, a preoccupation with wealth and possessions could mean that one of our archetypes takes on the form of an opulent well-dressed dignitary, while a victim archetype may be seen as a pathetic, broken figure. These are not figments of my imagination. Archetypal emotional and thought patterns can be identified during psychotherapy by certified professionals.

In my earlier book, *In Search of the Oracle*, I described a powerful personal experience with my archetypes, in which several of them presented themselves to me during a meditation. *Each appeared to have its own consciousness and personality and was able to communicate its needs*. I will give you a summary of this meeting with my archetypes later in the book. However, you will need a background in meditation and spontaneous imagery to understand this experience. Without this, you may have trouble understanding what was really going on, and I don't want there to be any confusion later.

So, what is my preoccupation with archetypes? It is clear that we allow the universal archetypes to enter our subconscious minds as *sub-personality patterns* that are common to all of us, but my studies and experiences have also shown me that there are many other universal archetypes which do not normally enter our subconscious minds and they also appear to have an independent existence and separate personalities. But if they are not coming from us, where do they come from?

It is not far-fetched to consider that, in the light of own subconscious minds being able to house archetypes, that a far-superior, universal 'collective subconscious' or mind could do the same and even more, in this case, forming the universal archetypes listed by Carl Jung as well as billions of other archetypal *personality patterns* within itself. I mean, we are talking about a 'Universal' Mind.

During the meditation I mentioned in the previous section, which I will explain later, my archetypes were able to communicate with me and actually seemed to have a separate, conscious existence. This stands to reason because as I said earlier if the Universal Collective Mind is the source of all consciousness, it is quite reasonable to believe that any archetypal patterns it creates would have at least a degree of consciousness as well. And it turns out that this is the case.

LET US CONSIDER OTHER CRUCIAL ASPECTS:

Does the existence of archetypal patterns or 'personalities' within the Universal Collective Mind mean that *they are real, or are they only figments of the imagination*? The answer to this is quite complex, in that they are certainly not being created in our own imagination. They are already there, and in this way, can be seen as real. But they do take form in our minds and are, therefore, in some way, dependent on our mind-processing. This can be confusing, so let me explain further.

There are two separate parts to this question which I will answer one part at a time.

ARE ARCHETYPES 'REAL' PERSONALITIES OR NOT?

If we decide to engage the Universal Collective Mind during meditation, we actually have to pass through our subconscious mind and open a connection. This is called being in a 'connected state'. When connected in this way, our minds 'merge' with the Universal Collective Mind and we enter a new state of *enhanced consciousness*. While in this state, archetypes become very real to us, as our minds are now part of this consciousness, which we could also call a 'higher reality'. They can communicate with us, and we with them. Simply put, they are 'real' in their own realm but do not exist as independent beings in this one. I will explain this further in the *analogy of the veil* which follows.

This analogy will also help to answer the second part of the question, that is:

HOW DO THEY TAKE FORM IN OUR MINDS WHEN WE ARE IN A 'CONNECTED' STATE?

You may remember the abilities of our minds to translate impressions into images (Synesthesia) and to form complete figures from random cues (Pareidolia) that I discussed earlier. As a result of these faculties, we will see archetypes as separate, distinct personalities during a connected state, when, in fact, they all exist within one Universal, Collective Mind. Let me explain how this happens using another analogy.

THE ANALOGY OF THE VEIL

'In a universe of total consciousness, consciousness exists in all its parts and all its forms.'

Jimmy Henderson

I will use the idea of a veil in an analogy to explain how our minds isolate a specific archetype from the Universal Collective Mind and see it as separate, while it still remains an integral part of the collective.

Imagine a group of people standing behind a very large hanging veil. You cannot see anyone behind it. All you see is the white, flat surface of the veil. When his name is called one man steps forward and presses himself against the veil. The veil is soft and malleable and you now begin to see visual cues such as the outline of his body and possibly even some of his features, as the veil takes on the shape of his face. However, when he steps back away from the veil, it takes back its original flat form and it was as if he was never there.

COMMENT

The metaphor of a veil is often used in metaphysics to explain the separation between dimensions of consciousness, mostly that of our earthly plane and the next. During spontaneous imagery, which is the process of imagery that usually takes place during meditation, you are creating a 'veil' in the form of an inner visual screen onto which archetypes can project their characteristics and you see cues which allow you to form an image using your faculties of Pareidolia and Synesthesia.

At this time it's important to point out that using spontaneous imagery to communicate with an archetype in the realm of the Universal Collective Mind, is not the same as 'calling up' a spirit using occult board-games or rituals, as you are working only with a projected image, so there is no real problem from a religious point of view. What is interesting is that, later on, with further inner development, you may begin to see through the 'veil' of this reality, as it becomes thinner. In advanced meditations, we even use the analogy of 'parting of the veil' to pass through into higher levels of the Universal Collective Mind.

MEETING YOUR OWN ARCHETYPES

'The true sign of intelligence is not knowledge but imagination.'

Albert Einstein

THE POWER OF SPONTANEOUS IMAGERY

Let us look at the power of spontaneous imagery in entering the depths of our own psyches and exploring what lies hidden there. This is a powerful experience, as we will be metaphorically *'entering the dark cave of our own subconscious minds'* and what we find there could make us uncomfortable, or even bring some distress. This is why you need commitment and courage on the metaphysical path. The first challenge is always to face yourself and the depths of your own mind, in this case using the skills of visualisation and spontaneous imagery.

A MEETING WITH MY OWN ARCHETYPES

To help you understand the correct method of using spontaneous imagery and meditation to explore the depths of your own minds, I will share and unpack my first experience of using these tools step-by-step to meet with my own subconscious archetypes many years ago. I recorded this experience in great detail in my first book *In Search of the Oracle*.

However, before I show you how I entered the deepest, unknown part of myself, I need to point out some more important details about engaging archetypes:

- Although our own archetypes follow the patterns of universal archetypes in the collective mind, they are formed from our own *unresolved emotions* or past issues, emotional energy that needs to be *balanced, resolved or transmuted*. Transmutation is an advanced skill which will be shared later. This example only shows you how to resolve or balance them.

- We also need to remember that any names, words and messages from archetypes usually have to be interpreted symbolically and metaphorically, as they only get translated into concepts in your conscious parts of your minds. However, do not try to interpret anything while in this state. Do the interpretation later when you return to normal consciousness.

- Finally, it is also not advisable to think consciously when you are in this type of deep, enhanced state of consciousness. Just let it flow. I knew this, so I had prepared a manual on the table next to me in order to quickly write down brief notes without dropping out of the semi-trancelike state.

One evening, I relaxed and began with meditation and visualisation. I had been toying with the idea of using meditation and spontaneous imagery to enter my own subconscious mind but had to build up the courage as I did not know what to expect. After considering all the possibilities, I decided that the experience would be worth whatever I was going to see and set the intention to go within. So I entered into a particularly deep meditation in which my consciousness was just ticking over.

Using visualisation, I mentally created a three-dimensional garden with a pathway leading to a gate and beyond the gate was a large dark building with a metal door like a vault. In my visualisation, I used *first-person imagery* to pass through the gate and then engaged spontaneous imagery, letting go of the scene. I had had some previous experiences of the way that my subconscious mind took over the scene, but this time it was very quick, precise and real.

As I took the decision to open and enter through the vault door, (which was not locked), a darkened staircase immediately appeared in my visualised scene. It was dark, but I could see that it spiralled downwards. I was extremely happy that my subconscious mind had responded to my set intention and the scene was now unfolding of its own accord.

Moving down the steps, at the bottom I found another dark, but open doorway. I was apprehensive of what I might see, but not fearful, as I had had some experience of this practice by now. As I entered the room, which was empty of furniture and damp and chilly, it became a little lighter and I was now able to see the outline of a small figure. I was relieved and almost amused to see that the figure appeared to be a small, insignificant little man who appeared very frail and weak. This was unexpected, as I had prepared myself to meet my archetypes and was expecting a larger and scarier apparition. I found that I was able to communicate with him and asked him to speak to me. He responded and in a sad 'voice', (words which passed through my mind), told me that what I now see is only a shadow of what he should have been. He said that his name is *Ignorance* and said that, as a result of my unthinking behaviour over the years, he had been able to 'spawn' several other archetypes.

COMMENT

Note the personification of a state of mind, (ignorance), in the name of the archetype. I think you will find the same, or at least similar, figures of speech and symbols used if you engage with your own archetypes. As I said, our subconscious minds use more generalised images and symbols, as we interpret them in our own language and give them personal meaning in our own concepts.

The 'words' of the archetype said that my ignorance over the years had led to many subconscious issues, some forming other archetypes. I accepted this, knowing that he was not talking about education but rather mistakes being made as a result of my being young and inexperienced at the time. So I was not too concerned, as I felt that this would change with more maturity.

To continue with the visualisation

I did feel sorry for him, as the figure seemed very dejected and unhappy and so I asked him to forgive me, and told him I would commit to becoming a wiser and more considerate person. This seemed to be the answer that he wanted, as when I thanked him for his message, he seemed more confident, smiled and faded away into the background.

It became a bit lighter by that time, (as I grew used to the experience), and I then saw what I had initially been expecting much scarier-looking humanlike creatures, and for a moment, felt a bit uncomfortable. However, I knew that they were only *creations of my own mind* and the feeling quickly went away. I spoke to the largest figure which looked quite hateful and had a big, powerful-looking frame. These characteristics told me that this was a strong and angry emotional pattern in my subconscious mind which had given rise to this archetype.

His said his name was *Prejudice* (another personification). He accused me of being a hypocrite, pretending to love others and yet judging them. This was a revelation to me, as I had always thought of myself as a reasonable person. However, I did have feelings of guilt and regret and I acknowledged what he had to say. I told him I would try harder to be more 'authentic' and loving and thanked him for his message. He seemed satisfied and also faded away.

The light was becoming a little brighter and I then saw the figure of a naked woman cloaked in a long gown. In the beginning, I thought her body was quite alluring, but when she threw off her head cover I was shocked to see that her head was actually a skull. This gave me quite a fright, but I recovered quickly and challenged her as to who or what she was. She said her name was *Lust*; and that it is '*she who twists love into passion*'. The words came through quite clearly. I did not reply, as I felt a bit ashamed and did not yet understand the deeper side of her message. But I thanked her and she also faded away.

COMMENT

I had no real answer for this archetype as I was still young at the time and no doubt my material desires were an issue. But once again, the issue of love had come up. *It seems that love in one's heart can prevent the forming of unpleasant archetypes.* Something we need to keep in mind. When I thought of her appearance later, I interpreted the skull to mean that 'lust' (metaphorically), whether for money, possessions or power, would only lead to death (of the soul), as symbolised by the skull. This was a strong warning from my subconscious mind, which I took to heart.

To continue with the visualisation

The spontaneous imagery remained strong and more figures came out of the darkness. The next one seemed quite pleasant at first, well-dressed, in fact, a noble-looking male figure. I invited him to tell me who he was. He seemed upset and accused me of not recognising him in spite of my giving him so much attention. I wondered what this archetype could be. He then proudly stated that he was *Vanity* and was actually my favourite archetype. I did not know what to say, as being young and ambitious I had no doubt, a strong ego and was very confident in my work and career. Just when I thought this interaction was going to be quite pleasant, he called me a fool and suddenly opened his fine cloak to reveal a skeleton. This came as quite a shock, as he had seemed so well-mannered. My reply to this figure was that I will deny him further power, (I will make an effort to avoid vanity in the future), but thanked him for his message. After this, he also smiled and faded away into the dark background.

COMMENT

When I later looked at what had happened, I realised that his message meant that over the years I had cultivated a growing vanity at the success in my career and this had filled me with thoughts of self which had no real substance, (a skeleton has no body). This archetype was the embodiment of my ego, which had deceived me into focussing only on myself. The opening of his cloak to reveal a skeleton symbolically also meant that vanity leads to soul-death.

By now you should have noticed a number of key principles in working with any archetype, whether your own or others existing out there in the Universal Collective Mind.

- The first is humility and the second is respect. When you are working deep within your own subconscious mind this is not a time for arrogance or denial, otherwise, you will never be able to satisfy or 'balance' them.

- To balance or 'resolve' your archetypes, you first have to acknowledge them and their message, second, recommit yourself to positive change, and third, thank them for their cooperation.

- You can also ask them directly to release or transmute their pent-up emotional energy. This will allow your responses to events and situations to be less affected by them.

As I continued with the visualisation, the next archetype to present himself to me was large and fat and appeared quite affluent (well-dressed). He had with him a few chests which looked heavy and seemed to be full of treasure, but when he raised the lids there was nothing inside. He called me 'master' and told me that his name was *Greed* and explained that his task was to hoard and not allow the *natural flow of universal abundance* to pass onto others. I thanked him for his message but he stayed behind to point out and introduce other smaller figures to me. He was obviously not convinced of my sincerity.

COMMENT

I was quite shocked as I had been unaware of this vice at the time. I always thought that I had been satisfied with my lot in life and was not seeking wealth. But archetypes are formed from the thoughts and feelings that we ourselves regard as important enough to store at a subconscious level, and our own feelings cannot lie to us.

When I thought about it later, the symbolic meaning of the empty chests was that wealth is only an empty promise and cannot bring true fulfilment. Another important point was that abundance flows like a river, and hoarding (metaphorically building a dam), will not allow crops to grow. Water has to flow from the river into the fields (of life) where it can help others to grow as well.

To continue with the visualisation

In my spontaneous imagery, the scene was now unfolding completely of its own accord and more figures were coming out of the shadows. The archetype called *Greed* introduced them to me. He pointed out this one little figure huddled in the corner whom he said should have been a prince called *Will* (will-power), but said that I had denied him his rightful place and he was now only a humble archetype of *Apathy*. In this way, he was telling me that I had not nurtured the gift of will-power and intention that had been given to me. I took this to heart and recommitted myself to develop this strength and the little figure seemed much happier.

Greed then told me that another archetype was approaching whose job it was to show me the '*dark side*' of life. I felt a bit apprehensive (one can have strong feelings during visualisation), as *Greed* introduced him as the first 'son' of the archetype of *Ignorance*. This latest figure seemed strange to me, as he had a noble bearing and was radiating quite a lot of light. I could not believe that he was the one to show me the 'dark side' of life at all. I greeted him and asked him to show me where all the light came from.

But once again, I had been deceived, as the new archetypal figure cast off his rich clothes to reveal only a mass of rotting bones. He laughed and then told me that his name was *Deception*, the first born of *Ignorance* and it is he who twisted my thinking and understanding to make them only shadows of what they should be. I was shocked by this revelation and immediately committed myself to finding truth and authenticity in all I do and not allow myself to be fooled again. After I thanked him he also smiled and faded away into the background.

COMMENT

I think it was at that moment I realised how easily we can be deceived by fine-sounding words, ideologies and empty promises, but the only truth is what we ourselves personally know to be true.

I had always thought of myself as a person with a balanced outlook, but this archetype made it quite clear that his actions are able to affect our beliefs, thinking and understanding of the world and we must be very careful when working with so-called 'facts' to always look below the surface for hidden contradictions, or when dealing with people, to hidden agendas and motives, as we can easily be fooled by what we see on the surface.

Finally, the fact that the archetype of *Deception* introduced himself as the 'son' of the archetype of *Ignorance* told me that archetypes can be associated with one another or even flow from one another, forming a sort of hierarchy. This was an important insight, which was very useful when it later came to working with universal archetypes within the Universal Mind.

To continue with the visualisation

After that, I was starting to feel tired and set an intention to finish the meditation. This spontaneous imagery had taken a few hours, the presentation of archetypes seemed to be over and I was quite drained but very grateful for the profound insights. So I again took control of my visualisation and moved out of the vault, back up the stairs and out the doorway, past the gate and returned slowly to normal waking consciousness. I then wrote down my review of the whole experience as it appears in my book *In Search of the Oracle*.

FINAL REVIEW

If I had to interpret the symbolism of what had happened and what I had seen in my mind's eye during the meditation and spontaneous imagery, I would say that the journey down the stairs into the vault was symbolic of my descent into the depths of my own mind. This was being made possible with the cooperation of my subconscious mind which was bringing about all the shifts in consciousness and imagery in response to my original request (intention). The light slowly coming on in the vault symbolised my adjusting to the situation and the greater insight and understanding I was being given.

As you have seen, during this experience I was exposed to vivid and often fearful humanlike figures, which I, fortunately, knew to be my own archetypes, personifications of my drives and vices as well as doubts, fears and other unresolved aspects of my personality. These were archetypes that I had created and hidden deep in my subconscious during my early years. They were being introduced to me one at a time as they emerged from my inner 'Pandora's box'. With each meeting, I had felt intense and contradictory emotions such as fear, joy and even arousal. I was not really afraid, because I knew that they were all part of me and that I had to deal with each of them in turn, not by using force, but rather by accepting them and the lessons they brought.

I also believe that much of what I was confronted with was rather a warning and not necessarily my actual emotional state at the time. In other words, I was being accused by my own *inner self* of having negative tendencies or weak areas in my subconscious makeup which would later become a problem if not addressed. My attention was being drawn to attitudes, beliefs or character traits that needed work or improvement. It was an extremely powerful experience, one which will remain with me forever.

I understand that this type of experience may appear frightening and possibly unnecessary, and this is probably why most people are put off meditation or warned against meditation by religious institutions. But these are not demons, as is generally thought, but simply aspects of our own deep psyches which have taken on visible symbolic forms due to Synesthesia and Pareidolia, the power of our own minds to translate emotions, feelings and tensions into images, as I showed earlier.

The fact of the matter is that we can choose to simply enjoy life blissfully unaware of the depths of our consciousness and those self-created demons in our minds. In other words, we can stay with the knowledge and understanding which we now have, lead a relatively peaceful life and pass, untroubled by undue guilt and confusion, into eternity, or we can embark on our journey into self, searching for the treasure of our true inner being and our source in the Universal Mind.

I, for one, have always been restless, believing that there is so much more to life out there, or in this case, the life and experiences to be found within, and I am sure that there are many of you who will also not settle for anything less than truth and authenticity. And the truth is to be found deep within ourselves. It takes courage and commitment, but it is very rewarding.

ARCHETYPES THROUGH THE AGES

'To know thyself is the beginning of wisdom.'

Socrates

I believe that we have already interacted with universal archetypes in many ways in our lives, most of the time as the personal archetypes that exist within our own psyche. However, the existence of archetypes can explain many religious and spiritual paradoxes as well. For example, it is quite possible that many early philosophers, priests and holy persons came into contact with archetypal personalities during prayers and meditations, classifying and treating them as mythological gods, deities, or celestial personalities (angels). According to popular historical and cultural beliefs and traditions, they are part of the Universal Collective Mind and *will all reflect its aspects* to various degrees. In fact, I believe that many religious and metaphysical experiences can be explained in this way. As just shown in the analogy of the veil, they can be simultaneously very real to us during enhanced states of consciousness, but are at the same time, part of the Universal Mind.

IS A THEOLOGICALLY ACCEPTABLE VIEW OF ARCHETYPES POSSIBLE?

This is possible if the religion is not too dogmatic or fear-based. An important aspect of archetypes is that they explain the metaphysical concept of the *emanation of a hierarchy of celestial beings* as described in many religious texts. From a theological viewpoint, these archetypes can also be seen as 'parts' of God reflecting 'His' aspects in various ways and this is probably why they may have been worshipped as God (or gods) in ancient times.

OUR OWN CREATION

Remaining with theology, the idea of archetypes can also cast some light on our own creation and purpose as human beings.

And now the big question:

ARE WE OURSELVES NOT ACTUALLY CONSCIOUS ARCHETYPES OF THE UNIVERSAL COLLECTIVE MIND?

A THEOLOGICAL VIEW

To answer this, I will have to link up with some early theological ideas. Remember that archetypes are personality patterns formed in the Universal Collective Mind, which, as seen in the definition of 'archetypes', are models or templates for later forms. Theologically, our souls could very well be *'archetypes of God'* (if God is accepted as a Universal Mind), as they meet the criteria of being *'part of God'* and yet have a conscious, independent existence through our bodies on this plane of existence.

This idea that we ourselves could also be archetypal forms emanated by the Universal Mind answers many religious paradoxes. For example, it could explain the word-play in sacred scriptures around the idea of our being created in the 'image' (imagery) of God, and the mythology of the 'fall from grace' can be explained as a loss of consciousness resulting from our pseudo-separation (not actual) from the Universal Collective Mind. This is truly an exciting idea, as from a theological viewpoint, being an archetype means that we are never separate from God.

COMMENT

COMBINING BIOLOGY WITH THEOLOGY

If our souls are archetypes or sub-personalities of God, it would explain how the consciousness of the soul has to be adapted to 'fit' the neurological structures of the body, accounting for our loss of consciousness during physical embodiment. And the aspects of the Universal Mind we express would be at the level of our soul and higher authentic self and not our bodies, which are actually formed from the same substance as the Earth and are designed and shaped to cope with the conditions on this sphere of reality.

ARCHETYPES EXPLAIN OUR TRUE ROLE AND PURPOSE

Carl Jung believed that archetypes help to organise and give form to his 'collective subconscious.' In other words, if we accept our role as archetypes, we play an important role in the unfoldment of the Universal Mind, channelling it and its aspects until it reaches full expression (this 'channelling' would be like live streaming in current technological terms). As a result, our thoughts, lives, actions and experiences throughout human history, become like a choreographed play or drama acting out the intentions of the collective mind.

THE ANALOGY OF THE DRAMATISED PLAY

Like the producer of a dramatised play, the Universal Mind provides the backdrop, props and scenes and then we act out the *'script'* representing the changes associated with its inner unfoldment. Its changing inner dynamics as it unfolds is mirrored on a lower level in global events, filtering down to our level in the form of new cycles, changes, situations and challenges. The events and situations unfolding on the stage of life represent the scene-changes and props necessary for the inner adjustments of the Universal Mind as a system. As I said before, in this way it could be said that events that shape our global history, both positive and turbulent, are only reflections of more profound cosmic shifts and changes taking place within the Universal Mind. Global events have a trickle-down effect in our personal lives as we have to adapt and change, bringing us more inner growth and development.

To some people this may sound like we do not have a choice in the matter, but we have the power of free will to change 'roles' or deviate from the script from time to time. However, I am sure you will agree with me that things seem to go smoother when we listen to the promptings of our heart (soul) as to what decision to make and which direction to go. Eventually we will come back to the role or path that is right for us, guided by reason and the principle of action-consequence.

I believe that one day we will all come to realise that we have to follow the script to the letter, as this is the chosen path of unfoldment of the Universal Mind, and any decisions we make on our own to serve our own egos, will only delay our growth.

ENDNOTE REFERENCES

1. Pierre Teilhard de Chardin – a modern philosopher who believed that the world has an interconnected matrix of consciousness https://www.wired.com/1995/06/teilhard/

2. Integrated Information Theory (IIT) – a recent scientific view that the universe is like a giant information processing system and its complexity may suggest a type of (AI) consciousness https://www.psychologytoday.com/us/blog/mind-in-the-machine/201512/neurosciences-new-consciousness-theory-is-spiritual

3. Implicate order –a theory that everything is connected (and balanced) at an energy level (a single whole) http://quantum-mind.co.uk/theories/david-bohm/the-implicate-order/

4. String and spin (theories) – Quantum theories on the behaviour of sub-atomic particles https://en.wikipedia.org/wiki/Relationship_between_string_theory_and_quantum_field_theory

5. Quantum entanglement –when sub-atomic particles are linked together and the action of one affects the otherhttps://www.google.com/search?q=quantum+entanglement&rlz=1C1LENP_enZA870ZA870&oq=qunatum+entanglement&aqs=chrome.1.69i57j0l5.8987j0j4&sourceid=chrome&ie=UTF-8

6. Plato's world of ideal forms – the philosopher Plato's belief that there exists a higher world of perfect forms or templates which give rise to reality as we know it. https://study.com/academy/lesson/the-theory-of-forms-by-plato-definition-lesson-quiz.html

7. Main aspects of systems –the main characteristics of scientific systems. This is particularly important for the operation of the brain and mind systems https://www.alliedacademies.org/articles/the-brain-and-mind-as-a-system-7681.html

8. Newton's Third Law of Motion – Newton's law of cause and effect - for every action, there is an equal and opposite reaction. https://www.google.com/search?q=newton%E2%80%99s+third+law+of+motion+definition&oq=Newton%E2%80%99s+Third+Law+of+Motion%2C&aqs=chrome.3.69i57j0l5.2684j0j7&sourceid=chrome&ie=UTF-8

9. Reincarnation – the belief that we come back in another body after we die https://www.google.com/search?q=reincarnation+definition&rlz=1C1LENP_enZA870ZA870&oq=reincar&aqs=chrome.4.69i57j0l5.20692j1j7&sourceid=chrome&ie=UTF-8

10. Archetypes- According to Carl Jung, these are universal personality patterns are said to exist in the universe and also within our own subconscious minds http://www.soulcraft.co/essays/the_12_common_archetypes.html

ADVANCED
METAPHYSICAL WORK

CHAPTER SIX

THE SUBCONSCIOUS MIND

'You were born with wings, why prefer to crawl through life?'

Rumi: Persian poet

HARNESSING THE POWER OF YOUR SUBCONSCIOUS MIND

Normally, our subconscious minds are only thought of in terms of regulating body functions such as digestion, breathing and heartbeat. However, it actually does a lot more than this and plays an important role in our metaphysical growth and development. However, to gain its cooperation for the metaphysical practices to come, we need to build a relationship of trust and this takes time and commitment.

In this chapter, I explore three main powers or roles of our subconscious minds; first, as protectors of our consciousness; second, as mechanisms to feed us information; and finally, as providers of the underlying power for enhanced states of mind, the creation of thought-forms and the projection of our senses and consciousness.

Our subconscious minds give rise to our dreams and we also explore ways of interpreting dreams in this chapter. They are likewise very active during meditation, able to bring on enhanced states of consciousness without the use of drugs. The psychiatrist, Milton Erickson believed that these trancelike states are actually quite common, but we don't recognise or even think about them. For instance, I am sure that many of you have had the experience that, when driving long distances, you simply 'clock out' for a few minutes. And when you start noticing things again, you have driven quite a few kilometres using only your subconscious mind. This is called 'road-hypnosis'.

Imagine being able to call upon this ability of your subconscious minds, as well as other powers, at will, and consider what it can do for you when properly managed and controlled. In this section, you will learn how to do this to bring about amazing inner experiences.

THE POWERS OF OUR SUBCONSCIOUS MINDS

'The conscious mind may be compared to a fountain playing in the sun and falling back into the great subterranean pool of subconscious from which it rises.'

Sigmund Freud

A HUGE PROCESSING ABILITY

THE COMPUTER METAPHOR

Earlier I used the metaphor that our conscious, thinking minds are like entry-level-computers which can easily become overloaded by too much data or confusing data which it can't 'process'. However, things are different with our subconscious minds, which are like '*Quantum computers*', able to process huge amounts of information. As a result, they are our '*interfaces*' with a vast world of 'data' out there which we could use to our benefit. However, to tap into this data we need to build a *channel* for information to flow freely between our conscious and subconscious minds. This channel will enable us to make full use of its immense processing capabilities and is established with the help of meditation and spontaneous imagery.

THE PROTECTIVE POWER OF OUR SUBCONSCIOUS MINDS

I mentioned earlier that our minds are selective in what they allow in and can block anything which does not fit well with our existing beliefs or views. This is because our subconscious minds act as *filters* for what we allow into our consciousness. In line with our computer metaphor, it could be said that they act as *buffers* which filter out anything they deem harmful to our minds. This will cause us to disregard anything which may be unduly stressful, or simply *too much data* and allow in only that which we need for our everyday use. You can see this clearly in a person who has had a *traumatic experience*. They quickly 'close up' as a measure to protect their fragile state of mind.

You can also experience this filtering in a crowded supermarket. You do not really hear much of the conversations going on around you, and for good reason. If this filtering action did not take place, our minds (which are actually quite fragile), would be totally overloaded by all this activity and the massive amounts of information coming in. However, we still hear that which is important to us. For example, if we move through a crowded, noisy room at a party we won't hear anything specific unless we stop to focus on it, but we will pick it up if someone calls our name, even above the din. In other words, our subconscious minds filter out unnecessary 'data' but allow us to hear that which is personal and important, such as someone calling our name.

THE METAPHOR OF THE SPHINX

Metaphorically we could say that our subconscious minds are the *guardians* or *protectors* of our consciousness, as they can regulate our inner experiences, according to states of emotional or psychological readiness. This reminds me of the legend of the Sphinx, a giant mythical creature with the body of a lion and the head of a woman which acted as a guardian of the ancient city of Thebes in Greece. To pass by and enter the city, a traveller had to show a 'readiness' in terms of courage and belief in oneself, otherwise they would be devoured.

Fortunately, we will no longer be eaten, but rather only prevented from having the experience. Our readiness will depend on how open our thinking is, our level of understanding, and the beliefs and values housed in our schemas and scripts. In other words, are they rigid, or flexible enough to allow us to take in *new ideas and experiences?* If our minds are not open to the inner experience, the processes will simply not work.

A typical example of this subconscious protective mechanism can be seen in those people who do not believe in ghosts. These persons tend to subconsciously ignore or deny anything suggesting that ghosts exist and their subconscious minds will help them by blocking any cues suggesting otherwise (unless it is forced upon them). This implies that we often lose out on an experience which could change our perspective on life or reality just because we have a closed mind, or do not believe that it is possible.

A FEEDBACK MECHANISM

Our subconscious minds are storehouses for painful memories, unresolved drives and many of the schemas and scripts I mentioned earlier. It houses most of our hidden personality patterns as well as archetypes, which, as mentioned, are like sub-personalities formed from our unfulfilled desires and needs. Although it happens mostly in dreams when our conscious minds are quiet, sometimes these schemas, memories and drives can emerge in our everyday consciousness. This is because we, ourselves, are psychobiological 'systems', with ongoing communication taking place between our subconscious and conscious mind processes.

This communication can be in words, as *self-talk*, as well as impressions, sensations, feelings and symbolic images, as we see in our dreams. In this way, our subconscious constantly feeds back information to us about unresolved issues, personality weaknesses and obstacles to our growth and development. This is very useful. We also get this information directly during enhanced states of consciousness (meditation and spontaneous imagery).

BIOFEEDBACK

Our bodies have a natural subconscious intelligence with which it communicates its needs in the form of feelings or cues which, as subconscious communications, act as early warning systems for preserving our lives and health. For example, feeling ill after a meal could mean that we have eaten something poisonous or disagreeable. And every one of us has, at some time or another, had hunger pains or uncomfortable feelings and sensations which have told us that we need to eat or drink. This power of our subconscious minds to communicate our bodily needs can also be seen in diagnostic and holistic treatments that use *biofeedback*.

What is not so well known is that our ability to respond to impressions, sensations, feelings and other cues can be enhanced, improved and used to warn us of emotional or psychological as well as physical threats. Once again, this is probably a natural instinctual ability going back to the time of early man which was necessary to warn him and keep him safe, a skill which we have simply neglected. For instance, many people will admit to feeling uncomfortable in strange situations, but do not give it a second thought. In most cases, these feelings are overlooked or simply ignored. But our subconscious minds are far more open to outside cues than our normal senses, and under the right conditions, they can certainly warn us of possible threats to our physical, emotional or psychological well-being. We simply have to acknowledge, accept and interpret these warnings. This protective system develops together with the relationship of trust and cooperation between us and our subconscious 'lovers' and is experienced as intuitive messages and promptings.

DREAMS

Dreams are the most common method by which our subconscious minds warn us of an unhealthy inner state or a threat to our emotional or psychological health. When we are sleeping our thinking mind is naturally quiet and these messages are given in the form of dreams. While some dreams are only a replay of the day's experiences, others that emerge from our subconscious minds take on a more complex symbolic nature and have important hidden messages.

A RETURN TO THE METAPHOR OF THE DRAMATIC PLAY

You may remember that earlier I used the metaphor of life as a dramatic play. This also applies to our dreams. We dream because, in the same way as our bodies heal, our minds also want to heal, and dreams are a non-threatening way of warning us of an unhealthy inner state.

Think of dreams as Shakespearian-like plays or dramatisations in which unresolved archetypes, inner conflicts, unfulfilled drives, needs and concerns become embodied in characters in complex scripts, with each setting, prop, character, object or activity sending a powerful symbolic message regarding issues hidden deep within your psyche.

The problem is that most of the time our dreams are made up of images and metaphors which are not literal and have a personal symbolic meaning coming from our own thinking paradigms, belief systems and schemas. For instance, if you are religious, you will most likely see your dream characters and the story-line in terms of religious ideas and values, while another person who is more scientifically-minded will probably see things in a more clinical light. Interpreting dreams is a complicated process, and unless you can do this, they are not of much use as feedback.

The detailed process of unpacking dreams can be found in my earlier book, How to Interpret your Dreams. In this chapter I only give a basic outline.

HOW TO INTERPRET YOUR DREAMS

Keep a dream journal next to your bed for making quick notes when you wake up, as the dream fades quickly, and have ready-made headings for the different dimensions of the dream so that you do not waste time writing it down. Try to remember any *feelings* you experience as well, as they can also be a clue to the meaning of the dream.

STEP ONE

There are several different dimensions or levels in your dreams, each having its own set of symbols and meanings. For instance, the background always suggests the *context or theme* of the message. Try to recall if your dream was light or dark and involved a natural scene or buildings of some sort. What you see as the background is only a clue to the underlying theme of the dream and should not be taken literally.

For instance, the sea is often considered a metaphor for the ebb and flow of everyday life, with tides flowing in and out as events unfold. A dream playing out against the backdrop of the sea would probably suggest a problem or situation arising in your normal day-to-day life which requires attention. Likewise, a dream-scene in a desert (which is usually desolate), may suggest a situation in which you feel isolated and alone and are seeking assistance. Search your feelings as well.

A dream playing out in semi-darkness may mean that you are experiencing a crisis and at a loss as to what to do (having trouble seeing your way forward). Notice the metaphors. The idea is find a connection between the background of the dream and your present circumstances, needs or state of mind by looking at the symbolism involved.

STEP TWO

Once you have jotted down the details of the background, the next step is to recall the immediate surroundings in your dream. This will give you more information on your *present situation* and state of mind as well as your *outlook* on the world. For instance, in 'looking out' onto the world, you would normally use the windows of your home or office. In your dream, any building in which you find yourself is a metaphor for 'where you are' at the moment.

Try to recall the characteristics of the structure, as this could point out your present life-situation or world-view. For example, a 'small' window could suggest your having a limited outlook on life. A dark and damp building could relate to your mind being in an unpleasant state (place), or you could be having a very negative view of the world. A building or house in shambles could suggest that your present situation, state of mind or outlook, is chaotic.

Perhaps a real-life example will help you understand these steps better.

EXAMPLE

THE OLD HOUSE

Peter had a lucid dream in which he saw himself in a huge old house. Everything was dark and dusty and really needed cleaning. He was also struggling to put the lights on. The dream was quite lucid, as he remembers himself feeling around for the light-switch and thinking that something must have caused the power failure. He could not find the switch and his dream ended suddenly.

COMMENT

This kind of lucid dream is not unusual after one has committed oneself to the metaphysical path. In this case, this was feedback from Peter's subconscious mind letting him know where he was in this task and what lay ahead on his path. The house was a vision of his present view of the world, meaning that at that time it was quite cluttered and neglected. The only positive part was the size of the house, which meant that his views were big (broad) enough to see more of the 'big picture'.

In other words, his first task is to clean up his thoughts and thinking processes (clean the house), making way for a clearer view of reality. His impression of a power failure meant that his energy is being taken up with unnecessary concerns. The metaphysical path is best travelled when we simplify our lives, as this allows for fewer distractions and obstacles.

STEP THREE

Moving away from the surroundings in your dream, your next step is to focus on the activity which took place. The type of drama, scenario or situation that is being played out, reveals the *content* of the message, which as I said, could point to an unfulfilled desire in your life, or to some other issue which needs attention. Ask yourself how the activity in your dream can be applied (metaphorically), or related (symbolically), to your present situation.

For instance, a scene which involves travel could be a call for change, or the broadening of your boundaries and the opening of your mind. A battle or conflict in your dream could be referring to a similar situation within yourself. Any threatening situation in your dream may be a warning of a matter that urgently needs to be resolved, something which is a real problem for your mental well-being or inner peace.

STEP FOUR

The next dimension involves the actual images, characters and objects that you see. In terms of Gestalt psychology, every object or person (character) in your dream represents a certain aspect of *yourself* and you will need to ask yourself what aspect of your personality the figure represents. Look at the characteristics of your dream-characters. Were they big or small, aggressive or loving, threatening or supportive? For example, a poor, abused, helpless child could be your archetypal wounded 'inner child' bringing you a message, while a richly-dressed figure could symbolically represent your unfulfilled desire for wealth.

What is also important is what the characters are actually doing. Also, interpret this metaphorically. For example, a fight with another figure in your dream could be pointing to a conflict within yourself that needs attention. Try to remember how you interpreted the different aspects and the actions of your archetypes when you first entered your subconscious mind during visualisation in a previous chapter.

STEP FIVE

Look at the objects in your dream. Each has a particular symbolic meaning and adds something to the final interpretation of your dream. Dream-objects can be understood in terms of their *practical uses or effects* in everyday life and applied (metaphorically) to your present situation or path in life. For example, seeing a large boulder on your path would suggest an obstacle to be overcome and a crossroads, a decision to be made. The guideline is to think of what you would do if you came across this situation or object in real-life and see this as a metaphor for what you are facing now.

STEP SIX

To unlock the final meaning and message of your dream, link together everything you have written down for each dimension of symbols and look for a *common thread or message*. Interpreting your dreams will help you to make sense of your scene changes in your spontaneous imagery as well, as your subconscious mind uses the same set of personal symbols and the method is the same.

LUCID DREAMS

Lucid dreams feel vividly real and are different from normal dreams in that we have some degree of awareness, enough to make choices and simple decisions. These dreams are very powerful, as our subconscious minds are wide open, and if we reach through and figuratively grab hold of it, we can change the dream in such a way so as to give direct instructions to our subconscious minds and bring about amazing inner experiences.

The experience of lucid dreaming is well known in older cultures and is recorded in tradition as the 'dream-world' of the Australian aborigines and the North-American Indians. Recent anthropological research has suggested that the Bushmen of Africa also had lucid dreams and induced alternate (dreamlike) states of reality, enough to give content to their spiritual practices and their paintings.

Lucid dreams sometimes occur spontaneously, but you can also learn to consciously call up and control them. Once again, keep in mind that what you see during lucid dreaming is put together in your mind using your symbolic processes of interpretation and will depend largely on your beliefs and way of thinking and past experiences.

I have personally had many lucid dreams, possible the most powerful may have been a glimpse into my own past, one which links up with the legend of Atlantis and should prove quite interesting for those of you interested in this subject.

REAL-LIFE EXAMPLE OF A LUCID DREAM:

THE SUBMERGING OF ATLANTIS

This revelation took the form of a powerful lucid dream, possibly the most important I have ever had. I awoke in the dream to find myself running along a road from what appeared to be intense heat and radiation. I noticed small meteorites, like chunks of debris, raining from the sky which had turned quite red. There was also smoke all around. I stopped, turned and looked behind to my left and saw the most amazing sight I have ever seen, a giant, flaming, red planet coming up slowly over the left horizon. It was huge, taking up at least half of the sky and seemed to be turning slowly. I then turned away and felt myself running towards what seemed to be a pyramid-like mound or temple on a hill. Inside the temple were several people in Egyptian-like dress.

By that time the red planet had almost completely taken over the left sky and I could see it rising slowly like the sun coming up. At that time, whole sections of the ground seemed to be moving and when I looked back to where I had come from, I saw a wall of water about five meters high coming towards me. It was not a wave, but it seemed like the whole earth was tilting on its axis as a result of the gravity of the nearby planet and the continent was simply moving down into the sea. The water was coming towards the temple and we tried to find shelter inside. After that the dream stopped and I woke up and recorded the details of this profound experience.

COMMENT

From a psychological viewpoint there are many possibilities here. Remember that a lucid dream is not the same as a normal dream, which simply reflects what is in our subconscious mind. A lucid dream is extremely vivid and real and appears to come from an even deeper level of sub-consciousness. As a result, it can be a warning from our subconscious minds about conditions that are building up around us, or, as seen in this case, a flashback of times gone by. This idea of previous lives is a difficult problem for psychology and needs to be explained further.

A flashback is a vivid memory which is normally stored in our subconscious mind. Assuming that it was not a silly fabrication of my own mind, the fact that it seemed to be from a very ancient time, implies that I was accessing memories from a deeper level of mind, possibly the memory banks of the larger collective, Universal Mind. This is not far-fetched if we accept that our own individual minds share the same faculties as the collective and no one will deny that we can store memories.

This experience opens us up to the possibility that we can tune into events from our pasts which are stored in the *collective memory of the Universal Mind* and it may not have been my own memory from a previous life at all. This experience, in fact, supports the idea of a collective mind. You will have to decide for yourselves on this matter. Personally, I felt I was the person in the lucid dream, as I could actually feel emotions brought on by the catastrophic event.

THE AKASHIC RECORDS

It seems that the Universal Mind has large memory banks and can, by analogy, even act as a sort of *'internet cloud'* to store vast amounts of past information. This has already been suggested by systems theory and is not a new idea, as in metaphysical philosophy, images and information from the past are said to be stored in this way in what is called the *'Akashic records'*.

Taking into account the architecture of the temple and clothing of the people I saw, this could very well have been a vision of the submersion of Atlantis, caused by the close passing of a rogue planetoid which caused the Earth to tilt and submerge half of civilisation. This was not properly recorded in ancient texts at the time as it could have happened some 10 000 years ago, although some ancient writings suggest it was much earlier. It seems that during the lucid dream I may have stumbled upon the story of the submersion of Atlantis.

THE 5 STEPS TO LUCID DREAMING

There is a proper process in preparing for lucid dreaming which I will discuss with you in 5 steps.

STEP ONE

Prepare for lucid dreaming by setting intentions immediately before you sleep and try to be aware of moments in the dream in which you have some degree of consciousness.

STEP TWO

If you have a fleet moment of awareness, try to quickly introduce a single conscious thought. For instance: 'I am dreaming', or 'I am aware', to lengthen the moment of awareness, and then try to make a conscious decision to take over the dream.

STEP THREE

Once you gain control of a lucid dream you will experience it as subtle, flowing and flexible. Any new thoughts, ideas or emotions you have will immediately take on some form and produce vivid images. However, a lucid dream works on a deeper level of mind than meditation and from this point you can give instructions directly to your subconscious mind. You can either decide to set an intention to move through to a deeper level of consciousness, or use a round-about manner by changing the setup or the 'script' in your dream.

STEP FOUR

For example, once you have control, set an intention to create a flight of steps leading upwards with the idea that this will lead to a higher level of consciousness. You could also create a doorway and hold the thought that this is the threshold to a new dimension of reality and see yourself entering. If you use this method correctly, your subconscious mind will respond to your instructions and actions and open your perception to these profound inner experiences.

Working within a lucid dream is not at all easy, and, in fact, it is very demanding in terms of energy. You will notice your energy waning fairly quickly as you begin to lose focus in the dream. However, with practice, you can lengthen the control-time of your lucid dream. This is also a useful exercise for increasing mental stamina and will-power.

STEP FIVE

All lucid dreams should be ended by consciously setting an intention to wake up, as this sets the tone and pattern for all future trips into other dimensions of the Universal Mind. More details on how to achieve lucid dreaming are fully described in my other book, *Multi-Dimensional Perception*.

THE POWER TO AUGMENT REALITY

One of the greatest feats performed by our subconscious minds is its power to augment our sense of reality. During advanced meditations our perception is complemented by the actions of our subconscious minds, which retain a memory of all that we know, as well as data we have not yet consciously processed. In other words, during slightly enhanced or relaxed states of mind, our subconscious minds can become very active and be able to superimpose their superior perception onto our everyday reality.

This means that whenever an ambiguous situation arises, such as those which challenge and change our schemas and scripts for self and reality, our subconscious mind steps in and creates forms which augment what we actually see (*Pareidolia*). Simple typical examples of this are faces being seen in the bushes and the illusion of an intruder that can be created by a simple coat hanging on a hook in semi-darkness. More complex cases, such as that of the football fan seeing the referee wearing the clothes of a clown have also been recorded. In all these cases, the 'gaps' were simply filled in by the persons' subconscious minds using their existing schemas and scripts.

THE MISREADING OF 'SMITH STREET'

I have personally experienced this phenomenon myself. I cannot remember the actual name of the road as it was many years ago, so I will simply call it 'Smith' Street, but the experience itself is still burnt into my memory and was very real. There was a company I wanted to visit in Smith Street and while I was driving along I kept in my mind an image of a signpost with this name so that I would recognise it when I saw it. I soon saw the signpost and turned into the road. However, I could not find the shop I was looking for and when I got to the end of the road, saw that it was 'Smit' street and not 'Smith' (it was a close match to the actual street name). To this day, I would swear that the signboard said 'Smith' street, and it probably did, at least to my augmented sense of sight, as this is what I was *expecting to see*. The illusion was created by my *expectation* and an image of the correct road sign had actually superimposed itself on my field of vision.

This augmentation has an even higher level. Once you have mastered spontaneous imagery you will find that even in everyday life you begin to see a *'fourth dimension'* to everything. For instance, you will be looking at an object, plant, flower, or even an animal or person and begin to see patterns or 'energy auras' forming around it, or them. What is happening is that your spontaneous imagery is kicking in automatically and superimposing *thought-forms* around the object or person you are looking at. For example, when looking at a plant or flower it may suddenly take on a new depth and deeper dimension and it is almost as if you are seeing through to its essence, as 'energy fields' and patterns. The superimposed images are coming from your own storehouse of memories and schemas as before and will differ from person to person, depending on their past experiences.

Once again, many people will say that this view of surrounding 'fields' is just our imagination, but the fact that it happens spontaneously and surprisingly without any conscious effort on our part, leads me to believe that there is actually 'something' surrounding or infusing the object which is cueing our subconscious minds, which, in turn, is interpreting it as best as it can. We do not know exactly what it is, but it most likely has a basis in energy, as we cannot see it with the naked eye. But it is definitely not just our imagination.

Once you experience this, reality begins to take on a new depth and this becomes another useful tool in your service as well as your everyday life. I know of many metaphysical practitioners who use this skill to diagnose or work with the energy field of patients with great success. As I said, the augmentation is taking place in your own mind and 'imagination' and others may not see anything, but something 'real' is causing it to happen spontaneously, after which it takes shape and form in your mind. In fact, you will often find that skilled practitioners will often agree on what they are 'seeing' as their past experiences and internal schemas are more or less the same.

This power of our minds to augment what we see in line with our convictions, beliefs and schemas and superimpose this on our normal sense of sight, could also account for the many sightings of so-called mythical monsters on land and in the sea over the centuries. Although this does not mean that all these sightings are made up or fake. We see what we expect to see in line with our schemas and scripts and there could well be some truth to them. In other words, 'something' is there, but we may not be seeing it as it really is. We must always keep in mind how powerful our minds really are, especially our subconscious minds, in creating what we see, as it helps to put together our whole view of reality.

THE SUBCONSCIOUS MIND AS A 'POWER PACK'

SUPPLYING THE POWER FOR THE PROJECTION OF CONSCIOUSNESS

'The key to growth is the introduction of higher dimensions of consciousness into our awareness.'

Lao Tzu

Your subconscious mind has an all-important role to play during meditation. It is like a computer power pack which provides the power for spontaneous imagery and your shifts in consciousness in line with your intentions.

Metaphysical processes involving the projection of consciousness need huge amounts of mental and etheric energy. Your earlier visualisations, in which you took on a first-person perspective and 'projected' yourself into a created scene, are only the beginning. There are far more advanced uses for the projection of consciousness that demand the active role of your subconscious mind.

Let us look at a few real-life examples:

CREATING DIFFERENT SCENARIOS

SPACE TRAVEL

A step up from the first person perspective and normal visualisation is to set an intention to 'travel', (project your consciousness), using spontaneous imagery. I have found that the easiest way to do this is to create a scene of *outer space* and see, (and feel), yourself flying through space using only your consciousness. As I said before, the more three-dimensional and realistic you can make your visualised scenario, the more powerful will be the experience when your subconscious mind takes over.

THE FOLLOWING METHOD IS QUITE SIMPLE:

- Enter into meditation and create a scene of outer space. Include planets, the Sun and in the far distance, other galaxies. Set your intention to 'travel' and see yourself moving out into space using the first-person perspective.

- Engage spontaneous imagery. If you have used the method correctly, your subconscious mind will take over the scene, which will now shift of its own accord and it will appear as if you are accelerating through space, passing many planets at great speed. Eventually, you will see entire solar systems and galaxies receding into the background.

- You need to continue to apply will-power and sustained intention to keep yourself moving forward and if you become tired, exit the visualisation slowly by ending the 'storyline'.

With this type of inner experience, it will actually seem as if you are moving, although this is due to your rapidly changing position relative to the planets and star systems that you see 'passing you'. Everything will seem so real, beautiful and peaceful. As I said before, this is only happening in your mind, but to your subconscious you are really projecting your consciousness through space.

Amazingly, on a quantum (energy) level, this would be the same thing, as there is a metaphysical principle called the *Law of Affinity*, or *sympathetic connection*, which states that an accurate image or picture of something, (in this case, the cosmos), has an actual energy-affinity with the real thing. Keep this principle in mind the next time you look at a photograph of a loved one and seem to feel their presence.

SUPPLYING THE POWER FOR THE CREATION OF THOUGHT-FORMS

There are even more advanced methods of projecting your consciousness which involve creating *thought-forms* to house your consciousness and senses and sending this thought-body out deep into the Universal Mind. Once again, this is not possible without the power of our subconscious minds. I will deal with this in a later section as it is very advanced work.

In the meantime, let me give you a real-life example of how to actually project your consciousness and senses over a short distance in a very simple way.

THE ROSE

I remember entering my yard one day and looking at one of my rose bushes about fifteen meters away. One had a beautiful rose in full bloom. Under normal circumstances I would not have been able to smell this rose as I was sitting too far away. However, I thought this would be a good time to try to extend my consciousness (senses) outwards to smell the scent of the rose.

I sat down and cleared my mind completely of all thoughts, relaxed and set an intention to extend my consciousness to pick up the scent of the flower. I closed my eyes, turned my head slightly away so as not to focus intently on the actual rose, and opened and closed my eyes intermittently, and at the same time began to visualise the flower in my mind. My aim was to reproduce an image which resembled the real rose as closely as possible to use the Law of Affinity I have just described.

Whist holding the image in my mind, I begin to sniff intermittently, searching for its scent. Initially there was nothing, so I tried again. I took my time, keeping the image of the flower in my mind and from time to time opening my eyes to ensure my image closely resembled the actual rose. To bring about this expansion of the senses, I realised that I had to let go and allow my subconscious mind to take over. After a few attempts this happened and I distinctly got a quick whiff of the scent of the rose. It was fleeting, so I had to remain very mindful and perceptive.

COMMENT

Some people might say that I created the scent in my imagination. So after this experience, I went up to the rose and made sure that the scent was the same. Remember, I had not previously smelt the rose, so its scent was unknown to me. Being able to pick up a faint scent at such a distance convinced me that I had actually been successful in extending my senses (consciousness) with the power of my subconscious mind using intention and working through my mental imagery. More advanced exercises on projecting consciousness are presented in the next chapter.

MAKING AN ALLY OF YOUR SUBCONSCIOUS MIND

'Your vision will become clear when you look into your heart. Who looks outside, dreams. Who looks inside, awakens.'

Carl Jung

Our subconscious minds can be seen as our allies in our process of inner development, as they can be persuaded to soften or release some of the blocks or barriers to our perceptions, enabling amazing shifts in consciousness and insight, as well as access to the Universal Collective Mind. This section describes the steps that you will need to follow to engage this Universal Mind.

STEP 1 – BUILDING A RELATIONSHIP OF TRUST

If you are really concerned about obtaining the full co-operation of your subconscious mind, it will be absolutely necessary for you to build a close relationship of trust. This relationship is also essential for engaging the Universal Mind, as to get there we have to pass through the subconscious parts of our minds, which are protected, as I showed earlier.

THE METAPHOR OF THE 'LOVER' (CONTINUED)

You may remember my earlier suggestion of 'wooing' your subconscious mind as a metaphoric lover. I mentioned that it helps to see your subconscious mind as a separate personality in order to build this relationship of trust and cooperation. You will know when this relationship is established by a radical improvement in your spontaneous imagery. You will find that you can bring about immediate changes to your consciousness or state of mind simply by setting intentions during your meditations. You will also find that your intuition improves and you have more powerful lucid dreams.

STEP 2 – OPENING A PATH THROUGH YOUR SUB-CONSCIOUS MIND

Our subconscious minds are also the interface between our conscious minds and the Universal Collective Mind. In line with its role as our guardian and protector, we must pass through our subconscious mind if we are to engage the Universal Mind. This *no-man's land* of the subconscious is very important for our day-to-day functioning. Without it we would be overcome by communications from all levels of reality. I showed you earlier how we have tangled up our subconscious minds with emotional and psychological issues and said they have to be cleared. In this case we have to ensure the path through our subconscious minds is open so that nothing hinders our passage to the Universal Mind.

Earlier in this book, I showed you methods of clearing your subconscious minds by changing or replacing unhelpful schemas or scripts blocking your way using affirmations and intentions. Now that you have (hopefully) mastered meditation and spontaneous visualisation, you can use more advanced methods of clearing the path through your subconscious mind using an *altered state* of *enhanced consciousness*. Apply these techniques regularly if you wish to keep the passage open.

The following examples show how meditation and spontaneous imagery can be used to do this.

THE ANALOGY OF CLEARING THE 'CAVE'

One evening, David started his usual meditation and set an intention to see his subconscious mind in terms of a deep cave. In many ways this is an accurate comparison, as our subconscious minds are indeed hidden, deep and can be dark and mysterious and filled with collapsed debris (bad memories and unhappy archetypes).

David then set an intention that he wished to clear his mind of all his unwanted psychological and emotional baggage and began spontaneous imagery. He used the first person perspective and imagined himself moving down into the cave. When he engaged spontaneous imagery, he saw it was filled with boulders and other debris on the floor. To David, this debris represented all the negative conditioning, thoughts and emotions that had clogged up his mind over the years.

David then imagined a big stream of water crashing down into the cave and washing away all the sediment. The water was a metaphor for the power of his intent to release the debris and clean out his subconscious mind. He noticed that his imagery shifted of its own accord under the power of his subconscious mind and how the floor and walls of the cave became cleaner and lighter as the water washed the sediment and debris out on the other side.

David noticed that some debris remained after the first wash, so he re-did the exercise until the cave was clean. When he was satisfied, he left the cave and ended his visualisation.

When David first did this exercise, he reported that the amazing thing was the sense of freedom of consciousness that it brought. His mind felt clearer and he was more mindful. His subconscious mind had responded to the imagery and 'washed out', or released, a number of his old schemas and patterns of thinking.

CLEANING THE 'GOGGLES'

One evening during a meditation I decided to try to again use spontaneous imagery to clean up my view of the world, so that my pathways to and from my subconscious mind would be clear.

I first set the intention that I wished to see what it is that prevents me from seeing things as they really are, engaged spontaneous imagery and opened my inner visual screen to new impressions. I immediately saw a pair of goggles take form over my eyes. Everyone's personal symbols are different so you may not see goggles, but some other symbolic object that *metaphorically* suggests a distortion of your (in-) sight, such as dirty glasses, a filter, blinkers or a cracked mirror.

I could see that I had trouble seeing out of the goggles, as they were clogged up with something. This meant that the pathway to my subconscious mind was not clear. In the visualisation, I redirected my focus and turned my attention to the substance on the goggles and looked at its colour, texture, shape and form. To me it was brown and tacky like mud, (all metaphorical of course). I contemplated its meaning for a while, and then made a new commitment to deal with what I believed to be *negativity symbolised* by the mud, as falling into mud is not an enjoyable experience, (unless you are a small child).

I then set out to clearing the path, (cleaning the goggles), using hand gestures as well as my breath to blow slowly to support my sustained focus and intention. Using a blowing action is also metaphorical (blowing something away), but being symbolic, it is understood and accepted by our subconscious minds. In other words, as I blew out slowly I kept the intention of clearing the goggles by this action, much like a gust of wind would blow away leaves and dirt, and it actually happened. I saw the debris on the goggles clearing a little. I noticed that I had to do this a few times. I now knew that the first part of my journey to the Universal Mind, that of the path from my conscious to my subconscious mind, was clear.

COMMENT

Negativity distracts us from the harmony and clarity needed for engaging the Universal Mind. In this example, my subconscious mind had provided the power for the imagery and created a pair of goggles to symbolise my outlook on the world. It had filled them with a dark sludge or muck, representing negativity. This was true, because at that time in my life things had not been going well and I was struggling to remain positive.

To digress a bit, I believe that many people think that those of us with a metaphysical view of the world cope wonderfully and do not have any problems or pain in life. Everything should go smoothly because we have some insight into the principles that govern our lives. In fact, it is often worse. Many metaphysicians are *empaths*, and *we* are very sensitive to the pain of the world as well as our own, with the only difference being that by exploring our subconscious minds, we can identify the real issues we have and do something about them.

STEP 3 – ENGAGING THE UNIVERSAL COLLECTIVE MIND

Apart from all the research, descriptions, metaphors and analogies I have used in this book to try to explain the idea of a Universal Mind, my many years of practical metaphysical experience have led me to the same conclusion. A universal system of inter-connected consciousness with many realms, dimensions or spheres exists at a very deep level of our minds. When connecting with these realms, we see and experience reality in a very different way.

Engaging the Universal Collective Mind involves communicating with archetypal personalities as well as other so-called 'spiritual' beings within its many dimensions. This is a very advanced skill and so I have devoted the whole of the next chapter to explaining it. This is a very powerful section for which you need to have mastered meditation and spontaneous imagery for it to be effective.

CHAPTER SEVEN

ENGAGEMENT

'We can see that we all dance to a mysterious tune, and the piper who plays this melody from an inscrutable distance - whatever name we give him - Creative Force, or God - escapes all book knowledge.'

Albert Einstein

ENGAGING THE UNIVERSAL MIND

I take you back to when I first introduced the idea of a universe of conscious energy and explain how this represents the activity of a Universal Mind. I then unpack this idea once again using more analogies as well as scientific and psychological research.

We move onto methods of exploring the depths of this collective level of mind, communicating with archetypal personalities within its many dimensions, some of which can be classified as 'celestials' and others as 'cosmic' personalities. Once again, I attribute these experiences to the activities of our minds and sound scientific principles relating to the characteristics of energy.

Finally, I invite a bit of controversy by introducing some ideas about a so-called 'hidden realm' or world of elemental archetypal forms on this sphere of reality that we normally call 'nature spirits'. This particular section may clash with some of your own beliefs, but as I said, all I ask is that you keep an open mind and allow me to show you how these experiences take place in our minds and are due to how we can sense and interpret the characteristics of energy. At the end of the chapter, you can arrive at your own conclusions and form your own opinions on the matter.

THE METAPHOR OF THE OCEAN

'Without this playing with fantasy no creative work has ever yet come to birth. The debt we owe to the play of the imagination is incalculable.'

Carl Gustav Jung

Let me once again try to explain the nature of what I believe to be a Universal Collective Mind in which we all share. I know that I have already given you several metaphors and analogies, but let me offer you another which may explain this in a way that I have personally experienced.

You could say that engaging the collective mind is like diving into the depths of the deep blue sea. In this case, it is not an ocean of water but rather of consciousness, one we still have to navigate carefully, watching out for signs or warnings of 'bad weather', as in this ocean we can get lost in the experience, or worse still, end up in the squalls of the *shadow realms*. And so we have to proceed slowly and carefully. I suppose it is for this reason these realms are hidden from us until we develop the navigational skills to sail on this 'sea'. I will now unpack this metaphor of the ocean to show you its similarities to the Universal Collective Mind as well as aspects and characteristics that you may experience when you engage.

Our present level of reality can be compared to its surface, and what we see in the world today is only a reflection of what is happening in its depths. As for the 'ocean' itself, there are many layers, the lightest of which is at the surface, (the sunlight layer), and the darkest in the far-off depths of this vast sea of consciousness, (the abyss and trench layers). It is quite interesting that the heavier layers of the Universal Collective Mind are also sometimes called the '*Abyss*'[1].

In this metaphoric ocean life abounds and reveals itself, according to its degree of consciousness. The changing tides of this great sea of consciousness reach us in waves, at times breaking on the shores of conscious experience and at other times remaining below the surface at a subconscious level. Like the ocean, the Universal Collective Mind has powerful currents and tides and an ebb and flow through which it creates changing patterns which form our lives and human history.

RULES FOR ENGAGING THE UNIVERSAL MIND

As is the case with the real ocean, if we wish to navigate the Universal Mind, we have to know the rules (and learn to swim).

I just mentioned that we have to move slowly and carefully when seeking to engage as there are '*rules*' for engagement. Fortunately, we have the protection of our subconscious minds, as well as archetypal personalities (*celestial helpers*) within the collective, to warn us when we 'step off the path', so to speak, and for this reason, it is a good idea to always seek and follow the guidance and directions given during your meditations.

As I pointed out before, celestial helpers are archetypes ('thoughts') formed out of the collective mind representing its different aspects, (like sub-personalities), and they can project onto the *inner visual screen* we create during visualisation. They interact with us through our spontaneous imagery, (changes induced by our subconscious minds). To understand this, I would advise you to refer back to the analogy of 'the veil'.

- Firstly, when it comes to the '*rules of engagement*' for engaging the collective mind during meditation, the best guideline I can give you is that it is always best to *ask* before doing something, or entering a new realm or sphere. If you are ready for the experience, you will hear or sense an intuitive 'yes', or just have a feeling that it is fine. If you have any sense of foreboding, it is best not to follow your course of action. Rather wait for another time, or find a different line of approach.

- Secondly, all archetypal personalities within the collective from the lowest elemental to the highest celestial power, should be treated with respect (but not worship).

- Thirdly, always acknowledge and give thanks for any help, guidance or warnings that you receive. This gratitude shows your humility, which is important when working with powerful archetypes.

- Finally, and most importantly, always enter the collective mind with a fearless, positive, confident, but humble state of mind. There is simply no place for ego, arrogance, doubt or fear when engaging the collective mind

MEDITATING TO ENGAGE THE COLLECTIVE MIND

'An attempt at visualizing the Fourth Dimension: Take a point, stretch it into a line, curl it into a circle, twist it into a sphere, and punch through the sphere.'

Albert Einstein

The method you will use to engage the collective mind is with a deep meditation combined with spontaneous imagery and the use of sustained intention. All these skills have been dealt with in previous sections. To bring about this engagement you have to find a suitable path through your subconscious, which acts as your bridge to the collective mind. In this case, the first step would be to merge with your true or authentic self. This is brought about with the 'I' meditation as shown below. The use of your hands should no longer be necessary.

THE PRELUDE:

STEP ONE: CONNECTING TO YOUR HIGHER SELF

- Enter into a light meditation

- Once your body is relaxed and your mind is quiet, repeat the words, 'I'm alive' a few times.

- Change the words to 'I am' and repeat them slowly over and over again a few times.

- Now change the words 'I am' to the word, 'I'.

- Repeat the word 'I' several times, slowly and deliberately with intent.

- Surrender and abandon yourself to the full experience and realisation of what it is to be 'I'.

- This is called being in a 'connected' state (connected to the higher self).

'Connecting' to your higher self is only a prelude to engagement with the Universal Mind, and the entire meditation needs to be one process, becoming more complex and powerful as you proceed. Also, create a storyline to allow for guidance along the way and follow this guidance.

THE PROCESS

Instead of giving you step-by-step explicit guidelines as I did in the case of the 'I' meditation (which could be long and boring), I will rather use a real-life example of a metaphysical student 'Jane' engaging the collective mind and point out the necessary steps along the way. Remember that each person's experience will be different.

JANE

Jane enters into meditation and sets an intention to pass through her subconscious mind with the idea of engaging the collective mind. Using spontaneous imagery and first-person perspective, she creates a storyline in which she is walking up a steep hill which has a beautiful palace on top. Out of respect, she personifies the collective mind as a *metaphorical prince* who lives there.

COMMENT

You can create any scene you like. The important point is to see yourself figuratively 'moving up', suggesting to your subconscious mind that you wish to *raise your consciousness* to connect with your higher self and later to engage with the Universal Collective Mind.

To continue with the visualisation

Letting go of the scene, it begins to unfold of its own accord and Jane sees an old man walking towards her. He asks her where she is going and she answers; to engage with the collective mind. The old man asks her if she is ready to complete this journey, to which she answers firmly and with conviction, 'yes' The old man then continues on his way without further concern.

COMMENT

As Jane had already cleared out and resolved her subconscious mind during earlier meditations, the old man is most likely a symbolic creation of her own mind, checking whether she has the necessary commitment and emotional state to successfully complete this task, as it is physically and mentally demanding. If she shows any doubt or hesitation, the old man, who represents the protective power of her subconscious mind (remember the metaphor of the Sphinx?), may have prevented her from going any further.

To continue with the visualisation

STEP TWO: RAISING YOUR CONSCIOUSNESS

As Jane moves upwards towards the palace, she realises that she is not really metaphorically 'dressed for the occasion' and remembers that to engage the collective mind, (viewed by Jane as the 'prince' in the palace), she has to be in a 'connected' state. This means connecting to her higher self and taking on the raised consciousness that comes with this enhanced state of self. Pausing briefly during the visualisation, she raises her hands up to the heavens, and quietly voices the phrase; '*I am that I am*', which she changes to '*I am*', and finally to '*I*'. As a result of her previous development, Jane's realisation of 'I' is enough to bring on a conditioned response and an immediate connection to her higher self which she experiences as a quick, deep breath. However, this does not break her focus or concentration.

COMMENT

It is necessary to enter the collective mind in a *connected state* using meditation and visualisation. However, there is no fixed rule when it comes to the scenario you create to enter as long as you set the correct intention, use the right etiquette to petition for a connection, and create a scenario which will symbolise your entering a higher state of consciousness. In this case, you saw Jane use the example of climbing up a hill. You can also use other simple metaphors such as climbing a golden ladder or going up a stairway to a higher level of consciousness, or a more complex one with membranes or veils symbolically supposed to hide the mystery of the collective mind. Your aim is simply to get the cooperation of your subconscious mind to raise your consciousness to a point which matches the consciousness of the collective, at which time you will be able to engage.

To continue with the visualisation

It took Jane many months of preparation before she felt ready to engage the Universal Collective Mind. In step one she took on the *connected state*, she now engages spontaneous imagery and asks for a glimpse of the true nature of the Collective Mind employing a solemn petition, using the words:

'Lend me your mind, Father.'

(Different words can be used, but they should preferably arise spontaneously in your mind.)

Jane immediately feels a bit disorientated as her consciousness rises dramatically to meet the consciousness of the collective mind. After a few seconds of excitement and expectation, she is spontaneously presented with a vision of a large veil. Moments later, the veil falls away and Jane sees behind it a *brilliant white light* which seems to fill her entire being. She knows that this is not of her own making, as she is no longer actively creating the scene.

Jane suddenly becomes aware of the true power of the consciousness within the collective mind. It is a remarkable experience but short-lived. She can't hold it for long as her energy is depleted. She returns to normal consciousness via the veil and gives sincere thanks.

COMMENT

Once again, the symbolism of the imagery is important. In terms of her beliefs, (schemas), Jane's symbolic processes translated the amount of energy present into degrees of light. The white light she saw was representative of extremely high energy, (undifferentiated in terms of colour), in other words, a pure form of energy. The veil represents that which masks the true nature of the collective from our everyday sight, pretty much in the same way that a veil hides the features of a woman in certain cultures. The spontaneous parting of the veil was a clear indication of permission for her to enter the hidden mystery of the collective mind. Notice how Jane's reaction is mirrored in her body. This often happens, due to the effect of our subconscious minds on our bodies during powerful, realistic visualisations.

During this brief engagement with the collective mind, Jane did not see any other images or figures apart from the veil and the light, but this was her first time so it was not unexpected.

If you have problems entering this connected state you need to examine your earlier preparations. As I said before, our subconscious minds will prevent us from having deeper experiences, if it feels we are not able to process them safely. Having little or no success at this meditation could mean that you still have unresolved fears, issues, doubts and concerns holding you back.

COMMUNICATING WITH ARCHETYPAL PERSONALITIES WITHIN THE COLLECTIVE MIND

'Angels are thoughts of God--to pray to an angel is to look to a level of pure thinking, divine thinking, and to ask that it replace our thoughts of fear.'

Marianne Williamson:
American author, spiritual leader.

The Collective Mind, by its very name, is a *community of minds,* a field of consciousness which links all human minds with celestial and archetypal personalities. In fact, celestial and archetypal sub-personalities are actually formed, and remain in the collective, and are not separate from it as are our minds and personalities. However, separation is only due to the limits of our conscious minds. So I suppose we could say that we are, in essence, also an integral part of the collective at all times. Using an altered state of consciousness brought on by meditation, we can bypass the confines of our conscious minds, access our authentic self, and communicate with the whole community of minds, as well as all sub-personalities within the collective. In this way, we can gather knowledge and insight into the true nature of reality. In this section, I discuss the proper method of engaging the universal archetypes in the collective mind as well as showing the different hierarchic levels of archetypes you are likely to encounter.

THE CORRECT METHOD

The process to engage with archetypal personalities is advanced and you must have mastered meditation and spontaneous imagery to provide a visual screen for them to project onto. The way you do this is, during meditation, create a *visualised first-person perspective* of the room where you are sitting, together with all the furniture and other items and allow the scene to superimpose itself around you. In psychological terms, you are creating an extended field of consciousness or perception surrounding you. And it is into this field which the other personalities will project. Remember, once again, that you are not actually 'calling up entities' using so-called '*magical rituals*', but merely creating a space in your field of consciousness to communicate with other conscious personalities in the collective community of minds. And it is possible to stop this communication at any time simply by changing your state of mind. In other words, this is a mental exercise and not an esoteric one, so it should not be a problem for you in terms of your religious or metaphysical ethics.

SO WHAT ARE THE DIFFERENT TYPES OR LEVELS OF ARCHETYPAL PERSONALITIES?

In an earlier metaphor, I described the collective mind as an 'ocean' of consciousness with different 'layers' or 'depths'. When engaging the collective I will speak of 'dimensions' or 'realms', as it is more in line with modern metaphysical terminology. In this case, I present the different classes of archetypal personalities based on my own experiences, which may differ from other metaphysical practitioners, as we each experience the collective in our own way.

You may remember that when you first entered your own subconscious mind you were challenged by your personal archetypes. Similarly, when entering the collective mind for the first time you will most likely be approached by *universal archetypes* in the form of 'celestial beings'.

CELESTIALS AND DEITIES

In terms of theology, this one universal collective consciousness would be viewed as 'God'. And in the higher realms of this collective mind, we can engage with personality patterns which will either present themselves as beings of light, which I choose to call celestials, (which we know as *angels and archangels, thrones, powers and principalities*), or other expressions of the collective mind which I will call *deities*. Like ourselves, these personalities all express the principles of life and consciousness of the collective mind to various degrees. As I showed you earlier in the analogy of 'the veil', they are all part of one consciousness, but when isolated by our thought and put together in our minds, they appear as separate personalities. These deities could very well be the so-called 'gods' of ancient Egypt, Greece, Rome, India and the Norsemen, all universal archetypes within the Collective Mind which revealed themselves to prophets and priests during sacred rituals when they were in enhanced states of consciousness.

THE MASTERS

The higher realms of the Universal Collective Mind also house the personality patterns of *masters*, enlightened personalities who once lived as we do, but who have ascended to these high levels having kept their consciousness through the veil of death. These illumined souls are also willing to assist in our growth and unfoldment. The consciousness of these souls, as well as the universal archetypes, is far higher and of a superior quality to our own and if we engage with them they are prepared to share their knowledge and guidance with us. This could come as visions, revelations or direct instructions.

SAINTS AND HOLY PERSONS

I have also communicated with other wonderful personalities within the collective mind and always found them willing to help, as long as we are dedicated, committed and sincere. In this case, I am referring to the personalities of saints and holy persons that have passed on but still exist within the realms of the collective mind. It seems that they have chosen to remain close to this realm to give guidance and support to those of us who are still finding our way. In metaphysical practice, they are usually called 'guides' as they usually give guidance to us as to day-to-day issues.

WHAT YOU ARE MOST LIKELY TO EXPERIENCE?

To engage with archetypal personalities, you must have mastered meditation, spontaneous imagery and *synesthesia*. Without these skills, you will most likely only feel a 'presence' in the form of sensations, impressions and emotions and possibly see some two-dimensional images. However, those with the gift of inner sight, (or spontaneous imagery), will actually be able to have real-time, two-way interactions with them. In other words, if you visualise a scene of the room in which you are sitting, (your surroundings) and engage first-person spontaneous imagery, you may see humanlike figures appearing in this visualised scene.

What you see in these projections will depend on your background, religious beliefs and cultures as housed in your schemas and scripts. They can take on different forms as celestials (angels), strange-looking 'deities', or other symbolic figures representing different aspects of the Universal Mind, possibly even including mythological creatures. It is probable that at first, you will see only light and colours, but later, as your mind gets used to the experience and your faculty of Pareidolia improves, you will begin to see transparent outlines, shapes and even forms and movement, especially to the left in your peripheral vision.

At first, these figures and images may seem like a daydream impinging on your consciousness, or projected images in a mist-filled room, and you will ask yourself if they are only figments of your imagination. However, they are appearing without your conscious thought and it makes sense that if this is happening without your own efforts, their origin is elsewhere.

What you see is only a *representation* put together in your mind from impressions, sensations and feelings you picked up while in a connected state of consciousness. And this will differ from person to person, as the sensations, impressions and feelings will be translated into images by your minds (Synesthesia), 'audited' by your schemas and scripts, and assembled by your faculty of imagery (Pareidolia). You can see now how this can be a problem if you have any existing beliefs or preconceptions about spiritual entities which are negative or fearful in any way, as your fears will shape what you see. This is also the reason why you have to continually upgrade your schemas to remove any doubts, fears, or outdated programs which will affect your seeing clearly and accurately.

WHAT WILL YOU SEE?

When it comes to the translation of impressions, sensations and feelings into images, exactly what you see is linked to your present framework of beliefs and thinking. For example, religious people may see a celestial figure as a traditional image of an angel as shown in old paintings and books, while a more scientifically-minded person may see the image as patterns of light and energy.

As it is only a representation, what you see will be symbolic and metaphorical, the same as in your dreams. In other words, aspects of holiness, strength, power or other characteristics will leave you with impressions which will translate into recognisable concepts such as light, colour, dress and physical aspect. For instance, the power of celestials can be represented by size or the concentration of light they emit and personality attributes by their facial expressions or demeanour.

Attributes will also be represented by objects they carry or their clothing. For example, a protective celestial may be seen as carrying a sword or even wearing armour, such as the common depiction of Archangel Michael, where these metaphorically point to aspects of power and protection.

Remember that although their existence within the collective mind is very real, what you actually see is only a symbolic representation of their *attributes and energy-signatures* being put together in your mind after the impressions have passed through your brain processes.

Generally, powerful celestial beings which we call angels and archangels seem larger and more luminous than saints or guides and have bands of light and energy entering their spinal area, giving rise to the idea of wings. With practise, you will eventually begin to sense and interpret the characteristics of their energy and be able to clearly tell the difference between celestials and other archetypes of a different order, such as deities, masters, devas, elementals or even 'shadow-beings', as they all have characteristic energy-signatures. Remember that after you have engaged with these personalities always voice your gratitude and appreciation for the lessons they bring and their role in your inner development.

CAN THIS BE EXPLAINED IN TERMS OF SCIENCE?

'Archetypes do not have a well-defined content but from
the moment they become conscious, namely nurtured with the
stuff of conscious experience...'

Carl Jung

Let us now discuss this important question in the light of scientific
and psychological research. Are these experiences all mere figments of
our imagination or can we prove scientifically that these personalities
actually exist?

THE PSYCHOLOGICAL VIEW

In terms of the phenomenon of *Synesthesia*, our minds can translate
sensory cues into colours and images through our senses working in
combination with imagery centres in our brains. It is possible that when
in a 'connected' meditative state, we are picking up patterns of energy
(energy-signatures) and using them as cues to form humanlike figures
using our 'person-schemas' and faculty of *Pareidolia*.

We already know that our minds are *selective* and that by using
our focus and concentration, we can isolate specific patterns in our
immediate surroundings and put them together again in our minds.
This is how our perception works in real life, by using colours, shapes
and shades to form a picture of reality in our consciousness. It is only
the *outside cues* that can be seen as real, so there is no reason why it
could also not happen during meditation. These archetypal figures are
forming without our conscious control out of cues in a similar manner to
our normal sense of sight, so it makes sense to believe that they also have
some sort of existence independent of our own minds.

By now you should be familiar with the archetypes deep within your own subconscious mind, the sub-personalities that embody and express different aspects of your psyche. As I mentioned earlier, our archetypes are accumulations of conscious (emotional) energy which we experience as separate personalities due to the way in which our minds work to separate and isolate them. And if you have experienced your own archetypes in some way in your life and accepted them as real, then there is no reason why you should not accept the archetypes within the collective mind as real as well, at least when you are consciously connected to the collective during meditation or some other altered state of consciousness.

Finally, on an emotional level, can we simply discount the emotions we have when interacting with archetypes and can we really regard them as imaginary when they arise spontaneously? The experience itself is very real.

A PHILOSOPHICAL VIEW

To answer this question from another direction using logic and reason, we would have to approach the question of whether an 'inner' experience can be considered as real as an 'outer' experience in the so-called real world. Be careful before you answer, as you need to keep in mind that all our experiences are processed in our minds, in our consciousness, without which we would have no self-realisation at all.

Many metaphysical practitioners have similar experiences when engaging personalities within the collective mind. If these experiences were imaginary, why would they have so much in common?

WHAT DOES THEOLOGY SAY?

During the centuries, people have prayed to or asked for help from these deities, celestials, saints and spiritual masters and many have claimed to have had mystical or metaphysical experiences during these times of prayer. Can all these recorded experiences be discounted as imaginary? The famous psychologist Eric Eriksen said that emotionally-charged words have the power to bring about semi-trancelike states of consciousness and I can well believe that this can happen during religious and mystical rituals when emotionally-loaded words and prayers are chanted. This could explain how priests and disciples in ancient times called upon and had visions of archetypal 'deities'.

A SCIENTIFIC EXPLANATION

I have left the scientific approach to this question until last, as it is the most difficult to explain.

First, quantum physics and IIT (Integrated Information Theory), already states that the complexity of the universe as a system points to some sort of consciousness. So the main issue remains if you can accept the universe as supporting consciousness in some way. If you can, then there is no reason why each part of the universe, each archetypal figure, in terms of the metaphor of the hologram, should not express this consciousness as well.

Second, I accept that the archetypal forms express through our minds and may not have a real existence on this plane of reality, at least not that I have personally experienced. When it comes to picking up their presence in a state of collective consciousness, it is not unreasonable to believe that this happens as a result of the sensitivity of our body's electromagnetic field or aura, or simply our skin, which has neural receptors able to produce sensations.

Third, I admit that it is unlikely that these archetypal personalities are making real incursions into our reality and what we see are most likely projections in the inner visual screen we create using spontaneous imagery. But there is definitely *something out there* giving rise to these projections.

The real issue here is how archetypes in a collective mind can be seen as separate personalities. Remember the *selectivity of our minds* which I showed you earlier, and how information is sorted by our minds at a subconscious level. In other words, what we are experiencing are actually 'cues' for personality characteristics in the form of conscious energy patterns taking the shape of humanlike figures in line with our people-schemas.

Let me try to explain this further using the metaphor of a prism.

THE METAPHOR OF THE PRISM

When light passes from one medium to a denser medium, it can be refracted in the same way that a rainbow is produced by the rays of the sun being refracted by droplets of moisture. Our minds are much the same, in that one, unified Universal Consciousness, (represented by white light), can be refracted into different aspects and attributes, (colours), by the action of our minds. In other words, when passing through our neural circuitry, our limited processing abilities separate this single consciousness into different aspects or attributes, which we then re-combine and see in terms of separate, conscious personalities. A psychological term for this is '*abstracting*' something from the whole, in other words, extracting from a collective consciousness only that which we need to make sense of it. We could also see this action as 'giving form' to what are essentially only patterns of thought.

COMMENT

I am sure that some of these explanations could be scientifically proven with the proper research and instrumentation, but because it borders on metaphysics so few scientists are prepared to undertake it.

CAN WE CALL UPON A SPECIFIC ARCHETYPE?

When it comes to seeking out and engaging with archetypal figures within the collective mind, we can actually *'tune in'* to a specific energy signature. You may remember that I said that, in metaphysics, names, symbols, images, or *energy signatures*, are seen as cues associated directly with a particular personality or archetype. An experienced practitioner can tune into a particular personality using intention and one or more of these cues.

THE ANALOGY OF A TUNING FORK

This association can be explained using the analogy of a tuning fork. When one strikes it and it is placed close to another fork of the same size and composition, it produces a resonant response in the other. Earlier I mentioned the metaphysical principle of *'affinity'* or *'sympathetic connection'*. We could then say that we call them up them during prayer or meditation using their names, symbols or images, and once we have a connection, we can get guidance or support.

Interaction and communication with higher archetypes and spiritual masters is very useful, as being closer to the source of the Universal Collective Mind and superior in terms of consciousness, they provide valuable guidance for our further progress. However, passing through to the more elevated regions of the Collective Mind needs more commitment, knowledge and effort, as you will find that your symbolic processes have difficulty working at such high levels of conscious activity.

The following are a few interesting real-life examples of interactions with archetypes that should give you more insight into the processes.

THE HISTORY OF ATLANTIS GIVEN BY A SPIRIT-GUIDE

One evening, while in a 'connected' state during meditation, I engaged in spontaneous imagery and created a visualised image of the room in which I was sitting. A bearded figure in white super-imposed himself on my visualisation and actually seemed to be standing in the room. He gave me more information on the lucid dream I previously had regarding the destruction of Atlantis. It was interesting that he actually knew about my previous lucid dream, so it shows once again how all our minds are connected.

He confirmed that I had been there but was a young man at the time and had not been involved in the corruption which had led to the destruction. The global shift I saw in my dream had indeed been caused by a passing planetoid and had led to the demise of Atlantis as a means of correction, (the principle of action-consequence). He told me that I had actually survived the flood by hiding in the temple which had sealed itself before the water reached it. This was a very interesting experience.

During this interaction, I took the opportunity to ask him a question on the origin of Atlantis. The old man, who was a spiritual guide, (a holy man who has lived previously), informed me that they had been a far earlier race of men and women who had lived a few hundred thousand years ago. This throws our accounts of history out a bit but links up with ancient Hindu teachings of *seven races of mankind*[2]. He said that we are all part of natural evolutionary creation and development, but modern man has been 'seeded' by superior intelligences from higher levels of the Universal Collective Mind to open the way for our souls to express. I was not sure what 'seeded' meant, but I assume there was some sort of intervention in the early history of mankind. But I will leave you to make your own conclusions, as I am not really happy with the idea of 'alien' involvement. In fact, this could just as easily be the theological idea of the *'early embodiment'* of the soul bringing about self-awareness.

He continued by saying that just before the time of Atlantis, the brutish early races of mankind who had regressed, were 're-started' with this *seeding of souls*[3]. This brought about a rapid growth of consciousness, morality and ethics, culminating in the glorious age of Atlantis. Unfortunately, corruption once again set in, with this race abusing the powers of the mind to control others. This caused a global imbalance leading to the destruction of Atlantis, although some had survived to form the basis of the later (Egyptian and Aryan) dynasties.

What was particularly interesting, was that he said that this 'seeding' of mankind to return to the original, pure and unpolluted earlier Atlantian consciousness, is still available to those who ask sincerely and are prepared to accept the responsibilities of this higher consciousness, for it will certainly bring about changes to your life.

I was extremely grateful for this information and ended my meditation in the normal way.

THE SPIRITUAL MASTERS

One night during meditation, Sue connected with her higher self and set an intention to engage the higher realms of the collective mind. After employing spontaneous imagery she said that the whole scene changed and she immediately found himself in the presence of illumined beings she could only describe as spiritual masters, some of whom she intuitively recognised. These masters, or 'avatars', have been born into this world throughout history and given rise to the great religions of the world. They now exist in the highest sphere available to us, the 'Christ Consciousness[4]'.

Sue was very grateful for their presence, but they did not stay long, as the moment she began thinking, they faded into the light and Sue ended her meditation.

THE CHRIST CONSCIOUSNESS

Although I am proudly a Christian mystic, it is actually important to view *Christ Consciousness* in a non-religious sense, otherwise, we will bind ourselves to messages given by the interpretation of historical texts when there is so much more to this. In metaphysics, the Christ is not seen as a single personality, but rather as a collective state of being, or a community of 'souls', minds and consciousnesses also known as 'the Son of God', the Divine 'White Light', the 'Presence of God', (as well as other names). By analogy, if we were to speak of imagery generated by the collective mind, this '*Christ community of souls*' would be the '*first thought*', '*first wave*' or '*first emanation*' of this Universal Mind.

Contrary to religious dogma, this sphere of consciousness is not owned by any particular religion but is open to any of us who strive for union or re-integration with our original source. I am also of the opinion that our souls originate in a flow from this Universal Soul and we can express its power and characteristics to varying degrees once we align ourselves with it. This could be interpreted in religious terms as 'becoming one' with the Christ.

Many spiritual teachers and masters throughout history have either embodied, or else attained, this state of consciousness, and even today, are prepared to assist those of us who are committed and sincere in the final steps of our unfoldment. We should try to think of these teachers as our elder brothers and sisters, metaphorically standing beside our beds as we slumber, giving us wake-up calls and even a 'shake-up' from time to time. In fact, we may have felt their presence and heard their voices during deep meditation, those few times when we have been close to 'awakening' to the truth. I will discuss this later again in the analogy of 'waking from a coma'.

Their teachings have been recorded and written in many holy books and scriptures throughout the ages, but these are open to selective misinterpretation, so I would advise you to also seek personal forms of revelation by working directly with these masters during your prayers or meditations. I would also encourage you to commit yourselves to them, as they have our best interests at heart. However, it is unlikely that we will meet them during our day-to-day meditations, as to enter their sphere is quite demanding and our minds will need to be totally clear, responsive and balanced.

COMMENT

THE ANALOGY OF 'THE FALL'

Sue's experience also sheds some more light on the religious metaphor of the *'fall from grace'*. It seems that any type of thinking, apart from pure realisation and contemplation during meditation, *breaks our alignment and connection with our source* in the Universal Mind, and in a religious sense this could be why our consciousness 'took a fall' when we started *thinking independently* and making our own decisions in a metaphorical 'Garden of Eden'. A natural process? Something to think about!

To continue with the visualisation

WHAT TO DO IF APPROACHED BY A 'DEITY'?

When engaging the collective mind on another occasion, David was approached by a large female archetypal figure who he suspected may have been worshipped as a deity in times gone by, as her features and form were strange and she was larger than most of the other archetypes. These deity-personalities have strong culturally-specific energy-signatures and are often linked to specific historical periods in ancient Egypt, India, Greece and Rome. In some religions, deities have been worshipped as gods and their help is called upon in times of sickness or misfortune.

This whole idea of many deities may be unacceptable to those of you who, in theological terms, believe in a single God. But you need to remember that all concepts of God are formed in the mind and will naturally differ, according to cultural beliefs. *Deities are simply universal archetypes which embody certain aspects of the Universal Mind,* which is ONE universal source, so all sincere petitions and prayers will eventually find their way home.

However, in this case, David received a warning from another figure who spontaneously appeared, (a celestial), to be careful not to commit himself to this 'deity', or any other archetypal personality, as this will unnecessarily bind him and his mind to this level, which he said, was not a good idea. I understand this to mean that our consciousness needs to remain free so that it can rise and journey through the many realms of the Collective Mind without being bound by commitments.

CAN THEY ENTER OUR SPHERE OF REALITY?

Many people swear that they have had contacts with 'spiritual' beings in their lives. These contacts have been recorded in ancient writings going back thousands of years, so it is not unreasonable to believe that archetypal beings can encroach on our own reality from time to time. However, as I have said before, these incursions into our earth plane would only be *projections* we see during enhanced states of consciousness. I believe that the true energy of a powerful archetype is hidden from us, or 'masked', so that it does not affect us, as our bodies are not made to confront such high levels of energy. Just think of the way that the energy of atomic radiation destroys a human body, and remember that the Universal Mind is the underlying source of all these energies.

Due to this problem, any visions or encounters with archetypes, whether as deities or celestials, are simply projections of archetypal energies within the collective mind which enter the inner visual fields we create for imagery, (visualisation), and then superimposed on our vision during enhanced or meditative states of mind. In saying that, the 'collective subconscious' could, to some extent, impinge on our everyday sense of reality. It is clear that Carl Jung supported this idea.

Archetypes influence us in different ways, usually through our minds, thinking and emotions, but I have seen how a powerful archetype can raise my energy-level and consciousness, while on the other hand, unfriendly elementals can tap our etheric energy and make us ill. So it is clear that we do respond to their energies even though it comes from a higher level, (see the section on *How to tap into the energy of the Cosmos*).

EXPLORING DIFFERENT DIMENSIONS OF THE UNIVERSAL COLLECTIVE MIND

'Evolution has ensured that our brains just aren't equipped to visualise 11 dimensions directly. However, from a purely mathematical point of view it's just as easy to think in 11 dimensions, as it is to think in three or four.'

Stephen Hawking

When we are moving around in the collective mind, archetypal personalities seem to be in different dimensions, but this is how we see the situation due to the structure imposed by our minds. In fact, these so-called 'planes', 'dimensions', or 'realms', are probably representations of lesser or greater degrees of consciousness (of the whole), using an earlier metaphor, different depths of the same ocean. To continue with this metaphor, diving deep into this sea with commitment and sincerity will allow us to find and bring to the surface the underwater treasures of knowledge and inner experience that exist within its depths. This should be one of the goals of the true metaphysician.

The many realms, or dimensions, of the collective mind, bring about different inner experiences and it's possible to move from one to another simply by creating visualised portals, membranes or veils through which we see ourselves passing during meditation and spontaneous imagery. In response to our visualised movement through these gateways, our subconscious minds will bring about the shifts in consciousness and perception that are necessary to process the new level of experience.

This section describes some important real-life examples.

THE METAPHORS OF THE TORNADO AND THE WHIRLPOOL

One evening after a deep meditation, I had a lucid dream in which I saw symbolic representations of both the height and depth of the many levels of the collective mind. At first, I found myself looking up into the eye of a tornado, which I took to represent its higher realms. Immediately after that, the tornado disappeared and I found myself looking down into the middle of a giant whirlpool in the sea. To me, this represented the depth of its lower realms.

COMMENT

This dream showed the different layers of reality or dimensions as formed in the collective mind. We live in a *multiverse* rather than a universe. We just don't know it. I saw the higher dimensions, signified by looking up from the base of a tornado, and looking down I could see other dimensions below, as represented by the whirlpool going down into the depths of the ocean. We are normally not aware of these other inner universes or other realities until we consciously commit to the metaphysical path, at which time, with effort and commitment we will hopefully be given glimpses of the true extent and depth of reality as created by the Universal Collective Mind.

The following is an example of one of the more interesting dimensions.

THE SILVER DIMENSION

When meditating one night, John set an intention to enter the higher dimensions of the collective mind and had an interesting experience. While moving from visualised 'room' to 'room' he soon passed into a 'technological' dimension that exists just beyond our own. However, instead of the colours we normally see on this plane, everything on this 'dimension' had a silver hue. Translated and moulded by his symbolic processes, to John this colour suggested a higher, (more noble), form of energy and consciousness, (metaphorically, as silver is a 'noble' metal).

During further excursions into this inner realm of the Collective Mind, John reported seeing figures which appeared to him as small, thin and silvery, although during other visits he saw some which were tall and very much like us. In some cases, after the meditation, John found that some images began to spontaneously superimpose on his surroundings and the silver hue filled the entire room.

COMMENT

In line with Jung's work on the collective unconscious, it is quite possible that this 'world', or silver 'dimension' of the collective mind, impinges on ours under the right circumstances and may be one explanation for the silver spheres seen in our skies from time to time.

To continue with the visualisation

THE SILVER PROTECTIVE 'SUIT'

To add to this example, I personally had a similar experience in which, in deep meditation and using spontaneous imagery, I once passed through a portal with the set intention of entering a higher realm of the collective mind. This time I felt no movement but actually experienced a feeling of discomfort and was surprised to note that my surroundings had also assumed a silver hue. As I glanced around in the visualised scene, everything seemed to have taken on this silver coating, including the walls of the room and even my own body.

This reminded me of a protective spacesuit, and this *single thought was enough to start a chain* reaction in my mind during which the silver environment began to change into what now looked like the inside of a 'flying saucer', complete with silver walls, portholes and strange-looking machines. Later, after returning to normal consciousness, I noticed that the silver hue remained in the room for a short while after the meditation.

COMMENT

To explain this experience in psychological terms, I have always been interested in science-fiction and would say that the simple idea of a silver colour surrounding my body resembling a space-suit could have activated my subliminal schemas or programs, releasing all my past images and ideas relating to space-travel gathered from books and films.

I also believe that the strange feelings and impressions during my enhanced state of mind were spontaneously translated by synesthesia into images and ideas of objects and structures that were familiar to my 'space' paradigm. In other words, the silver hue was symbolically re-interpreted by my mental processes as the walls, coating or envelope within a spaceship circling above the Earth, which in this case, could simply be a metaphor for a higher level of consciousness.

The silver residue in the room after the meditation indicates a possible connection between the energy of thought and other forms of energy. In other words, the point was made that there may, in fact, be very little difference between the energy of the mind, (consciousness), and that which provides the underlying structure of reality (colour and form).

This interesting case study could also explain some of the experiences of persons who claim to have been taken up into spaceships. Without casting any judgment on the truthfulness of any of these claims, my view offers another explanation in which introspective states of mind combined with a powerful desire and belief in alien visitors, coupled with the phenomenon of Pareidolia, which is our mind's ability to augment and put together a pattern (image) of something familiar, could also result in colours and shapes being translated into 'space vessels' such as that which I experienced during this meditation. Our minds are very powerful in this regard.

COMING TO NEW EVOLUTIONARY INSIGHTS AS A RESULT OF THIS EXPERIENCE

This experience of 'alien vessels' being formed in our minds led to me having new insights about our early evolution. As a scientific naturalist, I can't accept the theory of the creation of mankind from genetic manipulations by an advanced alien race from another planet. I believe this idea to be based on 'dodgy' interpretations of a few ancient tablets or artefacts with no real scientific basis or evidence. This 'all-at-once' top-down approach to human evolution also does not make sense if we look at the slow evolution of species still going on around us. Gradual evolution is accepted by scientists as the simplest and most valid explanation for our development from early to modern man.

I personally combine the metaphysical view of a universal pre-existing consciousness, (Collective Consciousness), with a bottoms-up natural evolutionary process in which early man evolved to a point of complexity where he was able to successfully channel the Collective Consciousness and reach a point of self-awareness. This does not mean that I am against the idea of the existence of beings from other dimensions, systems or planets. I have had experiences when I interacted with '*cosmic personalities*' in a connected state within different realms of the collective mind, but they are in a different energy-state than our own, possibly being fully-unfolded races who evolved long before us over many millennia and have already passed through the Earth 'school'.

Some of these intelligences on higher levels still appear quite human in many ways, which leads to the possibility that they may be descendants of earlier human races who have evolved to higher spheres of existence. The energy-signature of these *cosmic intelligences* is similar to celestials, but they have a more 'clinical' or scientific 'feel' about them. As I have just explained, it is quite possible that through natural development and evolution they are currently far more scientifically and morally advanced than ourselves. As a result of this moral superiority, they act as guides for their younger brothers and sisters (us) who are still in the process of 'growing up'.

IS A SCIENTIFIC VIEW OF HIGHER LIFE-FORMS POSSIBLE?

'Being is not only beyond but also deep within every form as its innermost invisible and indestructible essence.'

Eckhart Tolle

I will try to explain this in scientific terms. I believe that a point will eventually be reached in human evolution when physical bodies will no longer be able to sustain the high levels of consciousness they are channelling and the 'soul' and consciousness of the being will begin to incarnate in higher forms of life. In metaphysics, this is called *ascension*. This suggests that the human race, (or races), may have been around for much longer than we initially thought. As a scientific naturalist, I can accept this explanation, but you may well have other ideas and that is fine.

LOWER REALMS OF THE COLLECTIVE MIND

After connecting with the Universal Collective Mind a few times, you may find yourself more open to experiences on its *outer fringes*. However, these outer fringes also include the lower realms or astral levels. In metaphysics, it is believed that on this plane these astral levels surround the Earth with a dense etheric cloud which we can't see, but can certainly feel, especially during meditation, and I will need to include some words of warning about them.

ASTRAL DIMENSIONS

Imagine the whole atmosphere of the Earth being polluted by smog and poisonous gases. This would be to us like the lower astral realm, which is home to scattered wraithlike forms which are like cast-off residue from those who have passed on, as well as the personalities of those who are still struggling to reach the higher dimensions due to their being too 'attached' to the Earth sphere. Unfoldment continues after death but it is necessary to clear away your unfinished business and baggage to pass through to the higher spheres, otherwise it 'weighs you down'.

THE SHADOW LAYERS

The deepest realm of the Universal Collective Mind is the lower astral or 'shadow layer' sometimes called the 'abyss'. You may well ask how it is possible for a perfectly balanced system to house imperfect levels of consciousness. Once again, I will need to use an analogy to try to explain this:

THE ANALOGY OF THE FLOWER

The unfoldment of the Universal Collective Mind is like a flower slowly opening. However, even as the petals open, the centre of the flower is still largely bathed in shadows. If we keep in mind that the Collective Mind is the consciousness of the expanding universe, the idea of a 'shadow realm' would be symbolic of those areas which have not yet fully unfolded and still embody elements of the original primordial chaos before creation and order as we know it.

In other words, in this less-evolved area of the collective mind, primordial chaos still has a hold. As such, it is a storehouse for negative thoughts and feelings and is said to form a 'cloud' of negativity around the Earth. If we inadvertently enter this shadow realm or *astral cloud* unprepared, it can cause major mood upsets and even *existential angst*, the feeling that one is alone and abandoned in this world. This usually happens when our consciousness has been lowered due to substance abuse or mental disorders. Once we have entered, it's 'heaviness' lowers our consciousness even more and our worst fears seem to come alive and take on grotesque forms.

A BAD MISCALCULATION

I once entered this low level of mind during a visualisation by mistake and immediately had intense feelings of *dread, despair and misery*. I was very glad to realise my mistake and got out of there as quickly as possible.

Although most times this is unlikely, it can happen if you inadvertently create a visualised scenario in which your spontaneous imagery takes you *downwards into the dark depths* instead of upwards towards the light. As I said, this is often linked to being intoxicated or under the influence of drugs and it is certainly not a good idea to try to meditate while in these states.

LIVING ON THE THRESHOLD OF THIS SHADOW REALM

Our consciousness has now evolved to a point where we are born into the *threshold* of this realm. But, as I said, for a variety of reasons, including psychosis and excessive alcohol or drug usage, we can sometimes regress to this level and it can be quite frightening.

What I didn't tell you earlier, is that it is also populated by elemental personalities I call 'shadow-entities', most of whom are not hospitable. As I said, we ourselves have provided much of the 'bad stuff' for this *basement area* of the collective mind. All our negative thinking patterns, destructive thought-forms and emotions since the dawn of human consciousness have sunk like sediment to this lowest level. These negative emotions and thoughts take on unpleasant forms during dreams or visualisations if they haven't been resolved, and is probably the reason that many people avoid meditation. However, with a disciplined and quiet mind, they can be easily managed.

You may find scattered, disembodied images and personality-patterns of some deceased persons trapped in this deep recess of the collective mind, those personalities which have not developed sufficiently to take them to higher levels. This realm reminds me of the 'underworld' in mythology, as well as the notions of Hell or Purgatory as described in religious scriptures. When it comes to meditation and deep mental processing, this area is best left alone.

However, some robust individuals are suited for work there, being able to move around within the shadows and effect real change in those places where consciousness is trapped or not yet fully unfolded. Here I refer to those who work tirelessly to reduce crime, violence and mental disorders. And this can happen both on the physical and etheric levels.

THE HIGHER ASTRAL LAYERS

On the higher levels of the astral are those personalities who have not yet moved on, or have freely chosen to remain close to the Earth sphere to help others. This is the level normally engaged by clairvoyants when they give us messages from loved ones who have 'crossed over'. However, there is a lot going on in these realms and it is usually best to avoid them unless you are called to work with deceased personalities, as you may be approached by those seeking help. I discuss the activities in these higher astral layers in more detail in the section on 'What happens after death'.

THE WORLD OF NATURE SPIRITS AND ELEMENTALS

'Millions of spiritual creatures walk the earth unseen, both when we wake and when we sleep.'

John Milton, Paradise Lost

On the lower levels of the Collective Mind, we may meet up with the archetypal beings associated with Nature. I am sure that many of you have seen what appear to be faces in the foliage of trees and bushes when out walking in natural settings. In some cases, it could well be your imagination, but if you were in the right state of mind, it could very well have been what is called an elemental or nature spirit. This is usually the stuff of fairy tales, but due to my research, I believe I can say with confidence that these elementals do exist, although probably not as we have pictured them.

Let's look at the reasons why I say this:

ELEMENTALS

In a universe of consciousness, the presence of life indicates consciousness, and plants and trees have large concentrations of natural, living energy. Elemental archetypes, or 'nature spirits', are found within this realm which is just above our own, part of the etheric envelope of the planet. As they exist in a realm which is on a slightly higher level of the light-spectrum (the astral), we don't normally see them, although, as with other archetypes of the Universal Mind, they can present themselves in our visual screens during *superimposed spontaneous imagery.*

Elementals are so-called because they are associated with the four elements, earth (fields and forests), air (the wind), fire (fire-storms and lightning) and water (the sea, rivers and lakes). It seems that these concentrations of natural energy create portals for them to come through and interact with us. In the same way as celestials, they can also be identified by their energy-signatures, which in their case, is heavier than that of the celestials.

There are so many classes of elementals that they seem to form a hierarchy, extending from light energy beings (faeries) who prefer the bright light and colour of beautiful flowers to the weighty energy of elementals such as 'gnomes' who prefer rotting undergrowth, fungi, toadstools and can be quite temperamental, mischievous and deceptive. Some of the lower-level elementals can also appear as reptile-like creatures coming out of the earth at night.

If you are camping or sleeping out in nature, elemental spirits may come to you in lucid dreams and challenge you and I believe this is where the legend of the '*tokoloshe*' in South-African folklore came about. They may also offer you gifts but always refuse kindly with manners and respect, as disrespect can have them banging on your etheric body (or envelope) and you could feel ill for a while. However, there is no need for the average person to worry about them, as they generally ignore those who cannot see them and they do know if you can. This is one of the responsibilities of having *inner sight*, as you have to contend with elementals as well as deceased personalities who want your attention.

The role of elementals seems to be that of looking after plants, trees and forests, helping with their growth and development, similar to the celestials (angels), who help us with our needs on a higher level. I have personally encountered many of them under slightly altered states of consciousness such as contemplation when walking in nature and you may find the next real-life experiences amusing:

NATURE SPIRITS CAN BE MISCHIEVOUS

Most elementals will ignore us as we are normally not aware of them. But there is a certain group who love to play tricks on people. These are called 'gnomes' by those who work with elementals. I am sure that some of you have had the experience when weeding in the garden, have just finished clearing a patch, only to look and see another weed in plain sight exactly in the area you have just been working. Others may also recall putting an item down in the kitchen and later looking for it, and later finding it in plain sight. This often happens to me. Elementals, (especially gnomes), can block, or alter our perception so that we do not see objects right in front of us. They find this very amusing. What is important about these lessons is that they show how easily our perception can be manipulated. In fact, we are also guilty of this when we superimpose our own imagery on reality.

COMMENT FROM THE PERSPECTIVE OF SCIENCE

As in the case of celestials, the energy-characteristics of elementals become cues for perception and we will see what we believe to be physical and personality traits, such as size, form, dress, features and even different personalities. Once again, this is due to our mind's ability to translate impressions into images (Synesthesia) and form images from subtle cues (Pareidolia). In a similar manner to engaging the higher archetypes in the collective mind, seeing and interacting with elementals needs a slightly enhanced (introspective) state of mind to allow for superimposed spontaneous imagery. During nature walks, they will appear as faces or semi-transparent outlines in your left peripheral vision, but I have also noticed that they can change their appearance within your mind (see the case study below).

SHAPE-SHIFTING ELEMENTALS

THE ALLURING WOMAN

I have found that elementals can change *form in your mind* to mask what they really are. They can even appear in lucid dreams as attractive members of the opposite sex, and if you encroach on their areas, such as when camping, they could approach you with the view of forming some sort of relationship.

I recall one of the first encounters of this type I had many years ago when visiting a rural area. An attractive woman appeared to me in a lucid dream. She was doing a sort of ritualistic dance and wanting me to accept her as a partner. At the time I was not knowledgeable about elementals and was about to fall into the trap when a voice in my head called out to me - 'No'. This brought me to my senses and I then refused her advances. I believe that this was either my higher self or a celestial guide warning me of the danger and I certainly was grateful for that lesson. Always respond with a respectful *'No thank you'*, as any kind of commitment or relationship with an elemental will bind you to the Earth plane and this is not a good idea.

COMMENT

As I said, forming relationships with elementals can be a problem, although I believe that some earth-followers may do this. The problem is that binding yourself to one might give you access to them and a sense of power, but it will create an opportunity for them to enter the earth sphere through you and this will ultimately bind you to this plane, even after you pass on. Once you have mastered spontaneous imagery or inner sight you will have to be more careful and follow the *rules of engagement* (basically, respect and good manners), as they know when you can see them and may see your intrusion as a challenge.

Let me give you an amusing example of this:

A RUN-IN WITH AN ELEMENTAL

I thought I would include this little story as it is quite interesting and demonstrates some of the problems involved when working with elementals. A few years ago I was at a shopping mall and had just emerged when I noticed a gust of wind. As I glanced into the parking area, I saw a circular movement of dust a few meters in front of me. Looking into the swirling wind, I saw a face and immediately recognised it as an (air) elemental. The next second I felt a blow to my solar plexus, like a punch. He had obviously taken a shot at my etheric body. I was quite shocked as I had done nothing to provoke this response.

COMMENT

After further reading and study, I eventually found out that the moment one sees an elemental, it can sometimes be interpreted as a challenge and wind elementals are especially temperamental. However, other 'lighter' elementals such as the faerie folk, are generally very shy and wary but will interact with us in a friendly way if we have a genuine love and respect for nature and our minds are completely open to their existence. You might see patches of flowers and mushrooms growing in strange circles as you wander around in remote areas of a forest. These circles provide the earth-energy for their activities. Although the faerie folk themselves are usually friendly, as you have seen from the examples, there are some classes of elementals who are not. So always approach these areas with love and respect. And if you feel uncomfortable, take this as a warning and rather do not go any closer.

BE WARY OF OPENING YOURSELF TO ELEMENTALS

From my experiences, I have noted that alcohol, and I would assume drugs as well, will open you to the influence of elementals. Alcohol lowers your consciousness to the point where they can bypass the conscious blocks you may have in place and prevent your ability to deal effectively with them. I realised this from a recent experience in which I had a lucid dream in which I was confronted by a group of elementals in different forms. Some assumed the image of aggressive Vikings with swords and others simply remained as grotesque little figures. Having had a few drinks earlier that night, I found I was not able to easily overcome them and had to actually wake up and consciously engage with them during spontaneous imagery to teach them a lesson.

THE POWER OF LOVE

The funny thing is that I learnt a few good lessons that night. The first being that it is quite possible that it is the task of elementals to challenge those who can 'see' with the purpose of making you stronger, as you have to use a lot of intention and will-power to face and overcome them. The second lesson was that they seek *emotional energy* and feed off the fear that they can arouse within you. This is why it is important to face them without fear or doubt.

The third, and most important lesson, was that *love itself* is the 'gold standard' when it comes to emotional energy, and I found that these elementals responded very well when I stopped fighting and began to radiate love towards them. Their attitudes changed completely during the lucid dream and they immediately became respectful and docile. They were absorbing the love I was sending them and seemed very satisfied. So it is true that *love conquers all* and I can now say that I have now seen this in the shadow realms as well.

COMMENT

I found it easy to love them after I came to the realisation that we are all just like 'lost children' of the one Father (the Universal Mind) and we are all just trying to find our way home.

WHAT ARE THE DEVA?

The deva are more powerful archetypal elemental forms concerned with broader issues in Nature on the Earth plane, even structuring what we see as physical reality, pretty much the same as the role of the higher celestials (archangels) on the 'spiritual' planes. Some deva are attached to high concentrations of energy such as mountains, lakes and even the sea. It is quite possible that many of the old deities linked to the four elements and to Nature itself who were worshipped in ancient times are actually deva, as they are powerful and best left alone to do their work. I think the Jinn referred to in Eastern metaphysical teachings would probably also fit into this category.

THE LADY OF THE LAKE

Deva and elementals have the power to change their appearance by manipulating our perception to appear in more familiar and less threatening forms. I once remember an experience in which I made contact with a very large water deva in a lake in the mountains which, when seen in her natural state, could best be described as a small whale with a face. However, when she saw me, she assumed the shape and form of a beautiful young woman and came to the shore. Once I told her that this was not necessary, she returned once more to her more elemental form. I believe this that ability of water-deva to assume such a form could have led to the myths and legends of the 'Lady of the Lake' as mentioned in early literature.

ATHENA

Many years ago I often used to meditate when I was out on nature rambles or walks. In fact, I had a favourite spot where I used to sit at the base of a large tree. After a few such meditations, in my visual screen, I noted the presence of a powerful (giant) figure of a woman wearing clothing that one would usually wear in ancient times for battle or hunting, skins complete with bow and arrow. After a few such engagements, I learnt that she was Athena, the ancient Greek deity (archetype). She often had an eagle on her shoulder and I got the distinct impression that she was a deva responsible for overseeing and protecting Nature.

I frequently engaged with her during my meditations using *superimposed spontaneous imagery*, paying my respects (but never worship), until we had an amicable relationship. She often used to lay her hands on my shoulders as a sort of blessing from Nature. I have always had a great fondness for Nature, especially wild animals, and even more so after these experiences.

On one occasion I was ill with stomach cramps and she gestured to me to eat a leaf from a bush that was nearby. I did so and within a few moments, my cramps had stopped. I do not believe that it was actually the leaf that made a difference, but rather my faith that she was able to help me which brought about the actual healing.

After a number of years, I stopped meditating at the tree, which had, in fact, now been cut down, and never saw Athena there again, although I was sure she would come if I asked her. In fact, immediately after writing this section, she appeared to me again at home just to let me know that she is still around. I think it was because I was thinking of her and used her name as I wrote down this experience. If you know the name of an elemental or deva you can call them to you. That is why they are reluctant to give up their names, as we saw in the old fairy tale of Rumpelstiltskin. It seems the old tales and legends may have an element of truth to them after all.

These experiences have led to my belief that many of the deities of Ancient Greek, Roman and Norse mythology were deva, responsible for the different natural phenomena. I am fortunate to have good relationships with deva, as they are powerful nature-archetypes within the collective mind and are not to be trifled with.

COMMENT

WORKING WITH ELEMENTALS AND DEVA

When it comes to the archetypes formed in the Earth realm of the collective mind (Nature), I believe that it is not a good idea to enlist their help. Elementals can be devious and we should also not interfere with devas in their work. I certainly don't normally ask them for help, as it is, strictly speaking, not in their job description. But as is the case in the everyday world, sometimes people will help you even when they have not been asked, and you may find that, if you have been a world-server for a while, especially when working to improve the quality of the global etheric, your actions could suddenly improve and you realise that you have had help, and may see the face of a deva involved in the process. In terms of metaphysical law, if devas decide to help you of their own volition, that is fine.

Always remember to show gratitude for any help you receive, whether it is from celestial, cosmic, or other archetypes within, or connected to the collective mind. Just ensure that the help is from a benevolent source and not a shadow-being. Let me now tell you about this class of archetype.

THE DENIZENS OF THE SHADOW REALM

I mentioned earlier that we should avoid lower realms of the collective mind during meditations, as they house many un-evolved personalities, as well as the 'shadow entities', of which I spoke about earlier. Inadvertently, or even consciously, entering this realm during meditation and spontaneous imagery could be like making a wrong turn on a road trip and ending up in a rough neighbourhood in a 'dodgy' part of town.

First, the energy at this level is uncomfortable and disturbing for those who are not familiar with it. Second, 'shadow-beings', also archetypal personalities, live in this '*shadow*' of the collective mind. They have many names and are portrayed in medieval art as demons and monster-like entities. But once again, we must blame the translation of their attributes into these forms on our imagery. I personally do not see them as hideous entities, but rather hooded, humanlike figures with *heavy energy* drawn to our egoistic and selfish instinctual drives, and who tempt us to abuse power with destructive thoughts and actions. Unfortunately, they seem to have the ability to enter our sphere and minds at will and thus create problems for us, especially when we are in a negative state of mind and consciousness.

DOES THIS MAKE SENSE FROM A SCIENTIFIC PERSPECTIVE?

If we take the time to understand the principles involving the transmutation of energy, from a scientific viewpoint, the 'shadow-beings' would exist in those regions of the universe in which the forces of creation are still in flux, and in which the two principles of chaos and order are busy with a tenuous and unsteady 'dance'. This idea of *order and chaos being able to co-exist* may seem to be a contradiction. However, the problem is that we do not as yet fully understand their true nature and we are also acting on the assumption that the creation of the universe is complete. The fact of the matter is that our universe is still expanding, and life in its many forms, (including ourselves), is still busy with a process of evolution and unfoldment. This means that things are not as complete as we believe them to be, and in terms of the systems theory analogy, there is still a process of 'balancing' taking place within the universal mega-system.

THE BATTLE BETWEEN CHAOS AND ORDER

Although I personally don't view life in this way, if we try to see this engagement with the shadow-beings as a battle between 'good' and 'evil', this world could be seen as the *testing-ground* for the unfoldment of our personalities and souls. It is said by some metaphysicians that these tribulations are not possible in the higher realms of the Universal Mind, and it is only by moving around in a lower *world of shadows* that the full range of experiences are possible. And to evolve, we need to move through a struggle process, as butterflies do to free themselves from the chrysalis. In this way, by living in a world alongside shadow-beings, our purpose could be seen as that of warriors in the front-line of the battle for balance, order, common-sense, reason and enlightenment.

DO THEY HAVE A ROLE?

If we examine their actions more carefully, we may see that even these shadow-beings have a role to play in the natural unfoldment of the collective mind. Perhaps they do help us to build our will-power and resilience by resisting temptation, and when we fail, to learn from our mistakes. For instance, if we correctly process the lessons that painful experiences bring, we will eventually find our way back to the path of conscious growth. Learning to '*move through the pain*' and make better choices is a necessary part of human growth and development. In other words, the shadow-beings could be part and parcel of the process of moral and spiritual growth and by confronting and overcoming them, we become masters of our own lives.

However, deliberate contacts with these entities are not helpful and they are best avoided or left alone unless you intend working with them as part of your global service. In this case, you should learn the rules of safe engagement as explained in my book *Multi-Dimensional Perception*.

ENDNOTE REFERENCES

1. The Abyss –The lower part of the etheric 'cloud' said to surround the earth sphere which contains within itself the negativity of the world. https://www.heartofshambhala.com/?p=436

2. The Seven races of Mankind- A belief in the Hindu tradition which suggests that there are seven races of mankind in the cycle of human development, incarnating from the spiritual, through the physical, eventually returning to the spiritual again. http://www.awarenessofnothing.com/the-seven-root-races-of-mankind.html

3. The seeding of souls – The entry of the soul into a human body, bringing with it consciousness and self-awareness.

4. The Christ Consciousness – The highest level of consciousness (spiritual expression) available to us as human beings. https://spirituallifemedia.com/what-is-christ-consciousness/

CHAPTER EIGHT

ENERGY

THE METAPHYSICS OF ENERGY

If you have ever doubted the power of metaphysical processes, this is the section of the book that will change your mind. In this chapter, I show you what energy actually is and how to create and transmute it with your mind and consciousness to bring about amazing inner experiences. This is an advanced section and you *must* have mastered meditation and spontaneous imagery to even attempt it.

In this chapter, I first provide some scientific research that shows how our minds can affect matter and energy. Second, I then discuss the different sources of energy in the universe and how to make use of them. A number of interesting examples are included to show how this is done. Finally, I explain how to sense, connect and work with your own etheric body-energy using the power of your mind and consciousness.

The final section of this chapter deals with using your knowledge of energy to assist others, and also includes some examples. However, I point out some of the rules that apply when working with healing energies.

TAPPING INTO THE ENERGIES OF THE UNIVERSE

'Energy cannot be created or destroyed,
it can only be changed from one form to another.'

Albert Einstein

THE METAPHYSICAL VIEW OF ENERGY

In metaphysics, energy is seen as having a *dual nature*, which, in terms of this present framework, would arise from the consciousness (conscious energy) of the Universal Mind. Earlier on in the book, I mentioned two main modes of energy in the universe, namely the 'divine masculine' energy (representing activity, will-power and intent) and the 'divine feminine', energy of a more passive, gentle, flowing nature. Many powerful archetypes embody the 'masculine' energy, which makes them appear 'male' in our imagery, while those who express the passive energy appear in our minds in 'female' forms. In ancient times, the female Egyptian, Greek, Roman, Aryan and Norse deities would have represented this passive, but still, powerful energy, while in Christian mysticism, it would be the Mother Mary. In actual fact, these two modes of energy are complementary, as the duality that underlies all of creation. Let us examine these two energies in more detail.

POSITIVE, ACTIVE (MASCULINE) ENERGY

This would be the 'Yang' energy as mentioned in Eastern philosophy and the martial arts. We tap into this active and forceful energy when we actively use willpower and intent to move it around or to bring about transmutation and change. If translated into words, the mental action involved would be something along the lines of 'It is done', which is similar to a command. However, I have found that continually keeping up the sustained intention needed to work with this energy is demanding.

The amount of focus, attention and concentration needed for advanced imagery such as creating and sustaining mental *'membranes'* or *'portals'* for passage into higher dimensions of the collective mind, places huge demands on our energy resources. In fact, the deeper we explore, the more active energy we need for our minds to be able to construct for us a workable sense of reality and to translate the archetypal energies we interact with, into recognisable forms.

PASSIVE (FEMININE) ENERGY

During my meditations, I have recently been introduced to the loving, passive flowing energy of the 'divine feminine' principle. This is the other side of the 'energy coin', the 'Yin; energy as mentioned in the martial arts. One that is less demanding, more grounding, and certainly much 'kinder' to our neural circuitry. Instead of using only willpower and intent, when we use passive feminine energy, the process is more of simply 'allowing' the changes to take place, in other words, opening up to a gentle flow which will bring about healing, balancing or transformation within its own time and not simply at our command. In this case, the mental effort would be more one of faith, and the words chosen to represent this action would be 'let it be'.

THE SCIENTIFIC VIEW OF ENERGY

Let us now compare the metaphysical view of energy with that of science. Physics recognises a number of different modes of energy, including mechanical energy, radiated energy from the Sun, electrochemical energy, electricity from power generation, and more recently, nuclear energy. In metaphysics, this list is extended to include *mental energy* created by our will-power and intent, etheric energy radiated by the electrochemical action of our bodies and conscious energy, which is believed to be given off by all living beings as emanations and impressions.

MENTAL ENERGY

There is some scientific evidence to support the existence and power of *mental energy*, such as the *wave-particle theory*[1] in quantum physics which shows how sub-atomic particles change their behaviour as *we observe them*, (pointing to the influence of our minds on these particles), as well as *Dr Masaru Emoto's*[2] experiments which demonstrated the power of thought and emotions to cause different patterns in the forming of ice crystals. If you wish you can read further about these experiments using the hyperlink references I have included.

THE TRUTH OF THE MATTER

When it comes to our minds actually influencing material things, it is quite clear that the level of energy in this physical world is much denser and slower-moving than the energy of our minds and it seems to most people that mind-control of the physical universe is not possible. However, the experiments conducted by quantum physicists and those of Dr Emoto's, have shown that our minds do have an effect on matter, although it is not pronounced. However, imagine then the power of a vastly superior universal consciousness (the Universal Mind) able to transmute energy to form energy-matrices and provide the underlying templates for what we experience as the physical universe.

At our present level of reality, most of our creative actions are done mechanically using our hands, tools and machines. From an evolutionary viewpoint, it is interesting to see how our hands have specifically evolved to shape and manipulate matter on this plane, but it is a slow process. This is probably a good thing. Imagine the havoc that could take place in the world if everyone, (including selfish and undisciplined persons), had the power to control or create matter and energy with their minds, or to bring about immediate changes in circumstances or events. This kind of mental power is reserved for advanced beings who have reached the necessary level of wisdom, consciousness and understanding to use it wisely, such as world-servers and masters who, through the ages, have demonstrated this ability with (so-called) miracles.

ENERGY FROM A PSYCHOLOGICAL POINT OF VIEW

We also know from psychology that thoughts have power, in that thought alone can unlock huge amounts of physical energy and activity, such as the knowledge that one has the support of fans at a sports match, or the excitement in a person who has just learnt that he or she has won a large amount of money. In this same way, during meditation, the energy of the mind can be increased dramatically by positive thoughts which generate powerful emotions such as joy or excitement which can be transformed into energy and harnessed for inner work. In other words, body energy appears to be linked to our emotions.

Let us go a bit deeper into this matter with a look at the different energies within the body that are available for transmutation, and how this is done in metaphysics.

WORKING WITH OUR BODY-ENERGY

'Every cell has life. Matter, too, has life; it is energy solidified...'

Albert Einstein

The simple mental manipulation of the different energies *within our own bodies* is not that difficult. For example, we already transform our physical energy spontaneously into mental energy when we read or study. Students can study for hours if their bodies are able to supply the energy to their brains to keep them focussed and alert. Likewise, mental energy, (sustained intention), can direct the energy envelope infusing and surrounding our bodies, called the *etheric body* in metaphysics.

This control of *etheric energy* (Qi) is the basis of Yoga, Tai chi, Qigong, as well as other martial arts. Qi means 'breath' or 'air' and is considered the 'vital-life-force' or 'life-force energy' of the body. Qigong practitioners believe that this energy is available from the universe and penetrates and permeates everything. This would be the *active energy component* of the Universal Mind, corresponding to the Greek *'pneuma'* and the Sanskrit *'prana'*. When applied to the body, it would be the Western medical equivalent of 'bioelectricity'.

As our bodies have an electrochemical basis, it is not unreasonable to believe that they can take in this universal energy, producing a flow of radiated body-energy able to assume the form of the body, surrounding it in an etheric envelope. This energy can be moved, extended and shaped into different forms by skilled metaphysical practitioners. However, being able to work with this energy and transmute it into other forms is a great responsibility and I would advise you to get guidance before attempting it on your own. In my case, it took me quite a few years before I fully understood the responsibilities involved and was allowed to work with these universal energies.

In being able to transmute our physical energy into mental energy and control our etheric energy, we can develop a number of skills, such as projecting consciousness, (as seen in the case study of the rose), creating mental fields for sensing or protection, creating portals for entry into higher levels of the collective mind or powerful etheric thought-forms able to house our consciousness for more advanced work. I will deal with these skills in the section on mental creation.

INCREASING OUR BODY AND ETHERIC ENERGIES

When in an enhanced state of mind we can directly access the global energy-matrix and even the source of universal energy caused by the activity of the Universal Mind. This radically increases our own flow of body-energy or etheric energy (Qi), as well as our ability to sense other energies. Being able to move and direct Qi around our bodies is good for our health and inner strength. It also forms the basis for more advanced forms of etheric projection.

The way this is done is through what I call 'sustained or programmed intention', which demands a lot of practice. During visualisation and imagery, we use intentions, (intent), to continuously change the scene. Moving body-energy (Qi) around the body is similar but more complicated, as it means combining spontaneous imagery with a sustained focus and intention to actually 'see' the body-energy (Qi) moving up and down through your arms, legs and even your hands. This is based on the metaphysical principle of *energy follows thought* (intent). Once you have perfected this skill you will actually feel the energy moving and later on, you can program your subconscious mind to take over and do most of the work for you.

HOW TO FEEL YOUR BODY-ENERGY OR QI

- A simple exercise to help you become aware of and increase your sensitivity to body-energy (Qi) is to stand with your palms facing each other and try to feel the pressure of body-energy between your hands.

- At the same time take a deep breath and hold it in.

- Once you have the feeling of a subtle resistance between your hands, separate them and raise your right-hand palms up and try to still feel the body-energy in your right palm.

- Now, using your willpower and sustained intention, try to move the energy up your arm and down and out of your palm again.

THE POWER OF GESTURES

In metaphysics, we learn to shape etheric energy for healing or other advanced forms of mental creation. To move this body-energy or Qi, the correct positioning of body parts such as legs, arms and hands is important, as there are natural pathways in the nervous system which have to be opened. The idea is to move the Qi to a single part of your body such as your hands for healing, or more advanced forms of mental work such as creating portals or protective shields. Both energy-workers and martial arts practitioners claim that the right body movements and gestures cause a flow of energy through the various meridians in the body to where it is directed.

The position and movement of the hands is a very useful way of working with the body's energy. Apart from having powerful energy-centres in the palms of our hands which allow us to sense and direct this energy, programmed symbolic gestures can be used to reinforce intention and guide the flow of this etheric energy, even outside the body.

PROGRAMMING GESTURES

Gestures can also be programmed to bring about changes to our consciousness or states of mind. This is especially helpful if we wish to enter into meditation quickly. The connection between a gesture and a shift in body-energy (Qi), or state of mind of consciousness, is set over time by using repetitive association (programming). For a period of time, (usually a few weeks), you will have to learn to couple a specific body movement or gesture to a shift in your body-energy or state of mind. This is done in combination with affirmations and intentions. For example, continually saying to yourself; 'When I raise my right-hand (and face it forward), I immediately stop my thinking', or 'When I move the open palm of my right-hand across the front of my face I clear of my mind of all thought' or 'When I raise my right index finger I reinforce my decision, intent and will-power.'

Initially, you have to bring about the change or shift yourself, in other words, make a conscious effort to move the energy along your arm to your right-hand when you open it facing upwards, or to stop thinking when the palm of your right-hand passes in front of your face. However, once you have formed the subliminal link (association) between the two, the body movement or gesture by itself, will act as a cue to your subconscious mind to bring about the shift or change in body-energy or consciousness, which is now a conditioned response.

WORKING WITH QI OR ETHERIC ENERGY

Earlier I mentioned how we can transmute mental energy into etheric energy and move it along the body using only the mind. In this section, we will combine spontaneous imagery with the effect of programmed gestures for the projection of etheric energy. This is performed best in a relaxed and slightly altered state of consciousness.

- Sit comfortably and set your intention that your left hand is the grounding hand and will contain the '*yin*' etheric energy and the right-hand, the more active '*yang*' etheric energy.

- Start by holding both hands relaxed in your lap and focus and concentrate (but not too intensely), until you feel the energy in each hand. Use spontaneous imagery and sustained intention to see the energy passing from your right-hand to your left. It will help if you change the position of your hands, bring them closer together and almost 'pour' the yang energy into your left hand to combine with the yin energy. 'Pour' it back again from your left hand to your right, and continue exchanging the energy from right to left and left to right in this way.

- A good method of knowing if you have been successful in making the yin/yang connection is by moving your little fingers on each hand slightly in turn, and you should feel the change, (or a subtle shift in energy), in your other hand. Being able to feel and project your etheric energy is important for later energy work such as healing or directing energy during your world-service.

USING YOUR BREATH TO SUPPORT FOCUS AND INTENTION

The power of breath is also well known in metaphysics. There are many books written on special breathing techniques to reduce anxiety and induce different states of consciousness. However, this is outside the scope of this book and here I will merely show how your breath can be used to improve your focus and sustained intention.

To move Qi or etheric energy around our bodies we normally use focussed thought and intent. However, I have also found that using my breath helps to reinforce my sustained focus and intent. For example, blowing slowly when using the right posture and gesture seems to help to move the Qi energy where it is needed. It is almost as if you are, (metaphorically), blowing the energy along your limbs to your extremities. In later examples, you will see how it is possible to use this skill in working with etheric energy and projecting consciousness.

THE AURA

I have already mentioned how our radiated body-energies can collect around our bodies to form an electromagnetic envelope, much like the Earth's magnetic field. In metaphysics, when this envelope is populated with images, thoughts or emotions it is called the *aura*, which is also under the control of the subconscious mind. The state of health of our bodies, as well as our dominant emotions, can be seen as colours in this etheric envelope by persons who are sensitive to energy. This is how most energy readings are done.

SOURCES OF ENERGY

'It followed from the special theory of relativity that mass and energy are both but different manifestations of the same thing...'

Albert Einstein

My meditations have led me to believe that the highest 'conscious' energy of the Universal Mind is transmuted into three types. The first is *celestial energy*, which has a pleasant feel, is given off by celestial archetypes (angels and archangels), and is seen by us in the form of light, especially rainbow colours.

The second (conscious) energy is *cosmic energy*, which exists throughout the universe and flows through the galaxies in 'meridians' very much like our own bodies. This energy surrounds, sustains and balances the planets, solar systems and galaxies and is embodied in cosmic personalities, those super-intelligent beings who have ascended beyond the physical realm of the Universal Mind. This energy feels more clinical and is usually seen as a whitish colour.

Finally, we have the heavier, 'natural' energies which also permeate the universe and all of Nature and manifest in its many life forms, including our human etheric or electromagnetic body energy (Qi). This energy seems to be related to the principle of life itself.

MORE INFORMATION ON COSMIC AND CELESTIAL ENERGIES

Remember that in a universe of consciousness, all energy would have a conscious component. You may not realise this immediately, especially when it comes to the natural energies known to science, but when working with archetypal energies you will quickly realise that what I say is true.

ANCIENT, ARCHETYPAL COSMIC ENERGIES

When it comes to sources of cosmic energy in the universe, my own personal experiences, as well as those of other metaphysical practitioners, point to scattered, primordial or ancient patterns of archetypal energy still existing in the universe, possibly left over from the earliest times of creation. When engaged, these accumulations of *conscious cosmic energy* will take form in our minds as dragon-like beings, or other mythological creatures. I find it best to not engage with these ancient archetypes and their heavier energies unless you are called to work with them.

Celestial energy of a more refined nature is available from celestial personalities such as angels, archangels, thrones, powers and principalities all existing within the Universal Collective Mind. Relationships with these archetypal personalities are to be encouraged.

REPLENISHING YOUR ENERGY

It is possible to replenish your mental and etheric energies by using meditation, prayers or petitions to the higher celestial personalities. In religious terms, this would be asking or praying to God, the angels, or even saints for the strength to cope with a difficult situation.

There are some provisos when praying or petitioning for energy:

- What we ask for must be in line with our real developmental needs. As our guardians and protectors, our subconscious minds will block any requests which are selfish or could be damaging to us or others.

- No prayer or petition will go unnoticed or unacknowledged if it is unselfish and in line with our best interests, our continued inner development and the plan of the Universal Collective Mind, although it may not work out exactly as we imagined it.

- Help comes from that level which is closest and most suitable for our needs. In other words, it's no use expecting a celestial to come down and help us move the furniture. Practical help usually comes from other people who have been inspired, moved, or directed, to assist us, as we are all connected within the collective mind.

Celestial energy is also available from our own souls, which, as I ventured to say earlier, are also archetypes of the Collective Mind and components of the Universal Soul. For instance, when you connect with your higher selves, or soul-consciousness, (the 'I' meditation), you may recall that this brings on a sudden, unexpected deep breath and a rush of energy which makes you gasp.

HOW TO DRAW IN CELESTIAL ENERGY

- When you wish to draw celestial energy from the collective mind, enter into meditation and engage spontaneous imagery.

- Then begin to imagine the light of different colours flowing in and out of your body. Each colour is linked to a specific aspect of the collective mind. For instance, a golden ray represents spiritual wisdom, orange light describes vitalizing energy, yellow light is linked to intellect and inspiration, silver and blue for protection, and white and gold light for a celestial presence.

- Once your subconscious mind accepts your programmed intentions and responds, you will spontaneously see colours surrounding your body. Seeing this in your mind's eye will confirm your belief that you are actually receiving energy and you should soon feel the difference.

COSMIC ENERGY

As I said earlier, massive pockets of cosmic energy are to be found in the Universe surrounding celestial bodies such as stars (suns), galaxies and nebulae. The good news is that we do not have to travel to access this energy. With the right knowledge and advanced visualisations, it is possible to tap into these energies at a distance.

I confirmed this for myself during a projection of my consciousness through a visualised scene of outer space. By creating images of the planets, the Sun and star systems during meditation and spontaneous imagery, I used the experience of moving out into space through portals and past star systems to distant points within the galaxy which contained masses of cosmic energy. As I said before, this is only happening in your mind, but due to the principle of affinity, (sympathetic connection), between mental images and their real counterparts, it is enough to access the actual energy available within the universe.

However, this is not all that easy, and you will find that you need to use plenty of will-power and sustained intention to keep moving forward in your imagined universe. But you will find that when you complete your meditation, you will feel recharged with etheric energy and this will assist you further with your inner work. I can show you how this is done using a few real-life examples:

JANE GATHERS ENERGY DIRECTLY FROM THE COSMOS

After preparation and setting the correct intention, Jane connected with the consciousness of the Universal Mind. Using spontaneous imagery she passed through portals and entered ever deeper, until suddenly, everything went quiet, like the eye of a storm, a centre of calm and 'nothingness' (apart from pure awareness). She then saw that this centre gave rise to a cloudlike formation, the original energy of the universe itself and what she interpreted as a 'cosmic flow' of energy, almost like a milky river flowing through the universe. Jane found that using intention, she was able to connect with this flow and when she returned to normal consciousness, she reported seeing strange symbols enter her mind and found that her day-to-day energy and awareness had increased, although only for a short while.

COMMENT

According to the Law of Affinity, I believe there is a direct link between the physical universe and its etheric (energy) counterpart (template) in the Universal Mind. This makes sense in terms of metaphysics, like the Earth, other planets and whole star systems may, indeed, be physical manifestations of different spheres of consciousness and existence. Something to think about!

MOVING THROUGH INTER-DIMENSIONAL 'PORTALS' TO ACCESS COSMIC AND CELESTIAL ENERGIES

One evening, I again entered into deep meditation and set an intention to pass into even higher realms of the collective mind. I have always been a bit daring in this way and have been *'spiritually rapped over the knuckles'* a few times for going too fast or too deep during a meditation. As I said earlier, one has to be ready for the experience otherwise it can be unnerving.

I engaged spontaneous imagery, set the intention and immediately found myself in the presence of celestial helpers. At the same time, I saw an energy-portal appearing in my inner visual field. My eyes were half-closed at the time, but this portal looked like a semi-transparent membrane, which, of its own accord, moved slowly towards me. To me, this meant that I would be allowed to enter, but I know how important it is to ask permission when entering the higher realms of the collective mind, otherwise one can inadvertently *'tramp on spiritual toes'*, so to speak. So I asked the celestial personalities present if I could continue and intuitively received a 'go-ahead', at which time I set a second intention to pass through the membrane.

Keeping my focus and intention going, I moved through the membrane and noticed an immediate change in my surroundings. It felt like I was poking my face through the atmosphere of the Earth and peering out into the great mystery beyond. This new vista appeared to me like outer space, dark and unstructured.

I continued applying willpower to project myself forward and felt a rapid acceleration through this space. The changing scene was unfolding of its own accord and I recall passing many planets at great speed. This continued until I could see entire solar systems and galaxies receding into the background until suddenly, everything became bathed in bright white light. In this light, I noticed that there were other figures or intelligences, but could not make out their forms or interpret their messages as the light was too intense.

I then accelerated even further until I entered a sort of limbo. Everything seemed so totally quiet and was moving slower. My consciousness seemed to 'hang' effortlessly and 'drifted' very slowly in this empty space. This new state was very fluid and totally different from the lightness I normally experience during meditation. It was more of a 'physical' experience than mental imagery.

I found out that in this dimension I was able to briefly (mentally) create images of objects which appeared quite real, but I could not sustain them for very long. After a few seconds, I gained the impression that it would be best for me to return and practise later again, as the experience was becoming too much for my symbolic processes to handle. I set the intention to return and found myself passing quickly back through the membrane and re-entering my earlier 'representation' of the Earth sphere.

After this meditation, I felt very alert (my consciousness had radically increased) and I saw strange multi-dimensional geometric figures appearing in my inner visual screen and I intuitively felt that this meant a gift of cosmic energy.

COMMENT

I am fortunate to have built up a powerful co-operative relationship with my subconscious mind over many years. As a result, my set intentions and the subliminal state induced by my meditation was enough to create spontaneous images of membranes, planets, star systems and even figures in my inner visual field. In this case, the image of a 'membrane' could be explained as a symbolic representation of a passage to higher consciousness constructed from my knowledge of science, (semi-permeable membranes), or it may, in fact, have been an actual wormhole in the energy matrix of the universe, able to transport my consciousness to other parts of the universe.

I experienced the movement through the portal as an entry into a plane way beyond the Earth sphere. The rapid spontaneous shifting of my consciousness was represented by the feeling of a speedy movement through space and the images of rapidly passing planets and star systems. At this point, it must be clearly understood that no actual movement or out-of-body experience had taken place. The changing vistas I experienced were being constructed with the assistance of my subconscious mind and were only symbolic of shifts taking place in my consciousness and inner perception which were being translated into meaningful images.

The white light would suggest a level, (of the Universal Collective Mind), where differentiation, (into colours), has not yet taken place and symbolised union with the conscious origins of our universe. My inability to form definite images of the intelligences within the white light suggested that at this very high level my perceptual processes were starting to break down and I was unable to process any more detailed information. I had ended the mediation safely by following the same route back to normal consciousness.

The 'gift' of cosmic energy was represented by complex geometric figures appearing in my mind. It seems that projecting our consciousness deep into the collective mind allows us to gather energy as well, or perhaps it was the cosmic intelligences that had rewarded me? I can't say for sure.

OBTAINING ENERGY FROM NATURE

Other modes of energy can be found on Earth as well, as concentrated in clusters in our etheric bodies themselves. We can actually draw energy directly from Nature. For example, 'soaking up the sun' is often a good way of improving our mood. In other words, the Sun gives us positive (yang) energy. I have also found that spending time at mountain resorts revitalises me, especially if I use the opportunity to go for nature hikes. It seems to be the mountains themselves. I notice it especially when I return and find that I can use this positive energy to bring about major shifts during meditations or lucid dreams. Just walking around in natural surroundings can energise us. Trees and bushes have natural energy which we can tap into if we open ourselves to it.

On the other hand, the sea has a more passive (yin) energy that is great for relaxing. I always come back from a coastal resort feeling calmer and more relaxed than when I left.

ANCIENT EARTH-BOUND ENERGIES

Throughout history, ancient archetypal sources of earth-bound energy have been around and have been given many names such as jinn, serpents and dragons. And although it is possible to access and engage with these archetypes, I certainly can't recommend this without the proper training. Energy-practitioners believe that most persons are simply not 'wired' to work with these powerful serpentine earth-energies which can disrupt our minds and even badly affect our health. There are, however, shamans who can seek out and use these energies wisely. As is the case with the ancient archetypal 'cosmic' energies, unless you are called to work with these primordial earth-energies, I would recommend avoiding them altogether.

WORKING WITH HEALING ENERGIES

'You have the power to heal your life, and you need to know that. We think so often that we are helpless, but we're not. We always have the power of our minds⬚Claim and consciously use your power.'

Louise L. Hay: American motivational author

Before I go into the different methods of healing, I need to give a few words of warning. We often level criticism at energy and 'spiritual' healers who refuse, or are not able, to heal a certain person. For this reason, I think it is important that I give you the metaphysical explanation as to why healing may, in line with universal principles, sometimes not happen.

Energy, or spiritual healing, occurs within a framework of metaphysical laws and principles and one needs to know these requirements and criteria to be truly effective. A true healer will be guided, or at least have highly-developed metaphysical insight. This is necessary to identify the true causes and underlying issues associated with a person's illness, as simply removing the symptoms will not help in the long run. This section discusses these important rules and principles.

KNOWING THE RULES

Healers must always approach the case holistically, and this should ideally include a consultation with the person involved if at all possible, or at least with a close family member or friend. In my opinion, any healer who offers unconditional healing to all and sundry, without insight into their background, or circumstances, can at best, offer only temporary relief or partial healing on an emotional level. They may also be going against some important metaphysical principles. These problems will become clear if I explain the five instances in which energy or spiritual healing may not work:

- Firstly, within a religious framework, it may be *'God's will'* that a particular soul should return after having completed the tasks which were assigned to them. In other words, it could be their 'time to go'.

- Secondly, on a general metaphysical level, this person could have made a soul-choice (of which they are usually not aware), that their mission is complete and they wish to return to their source. As this decision is lined up with 'God's will' or universal laws, depending on your beliefs, any effort to save such a dying person will be ultimately unsuccessful.

249

- Thirdly, illness can sometimes also be important for the individual's growth or development in the form of a 'soul-lesson'. In other words, someone may actually draw an illness to themselves to develop attributes such as love, empathy, patience and tolerance, or to learn a necessary lesson in human experience. A healer who thus prematurely removes the 'thorn from their side' in fact, performs a disservice. This person may, or may not, have reached the point where they are ready to be healed.

In counselling, it is quite a well-known fact that a person must have reached a certain point of despair where they are willing to ask for help and actually be prepared to change before therapy will be effective. This is the reason why it is of utmost importance that the person ask, or at least be willing, to receive healing and not be forced into the situation. The metaphysical principles of free-will and personal choice are very important in this case. In other words, the person may not yet have reached the point where they are ready to ask for help, and healing has been asked for by another person. In this case, the patient themselves may not be willing, or ready, to let go of the underlying causes due to a lack of faith, or just plain stubbornness. This attempt at healing in such cases will also not be successful.

- Fourthly, an illness could also be the result of certain bad habits in their thinking, emotional life or their behaviour (lifestyle). Research has shown that stress from home or work and intense pent-up emotions such as rage, resentment or others linked to depression, can lead to illness. The illness may therefore only be a symptom of an unbalanced psychological or emotional state. Healing in this case has to address the 'whole' person and their living circumstances and not just by pronouncing the person 'healed.' It is important that the underlying or lifestyle issues be dealt with before they can be healed. At the very least, they must commit to these changes.

- Finally, in rare cases, an illness may also be caused by other metaphysical factors such as the belief in black magic, (believing oneself to be cursed), or the attentions of unpleasant, astral entities which may have intentionally, or unintentionally, been invited in by the victim. Treatment in such cases will need to be more than the laying on of hands, as the real cause needs to be dealt with first.

Some healers mask or remove symptoms temporarily by moving the patient's focus and attention from negative thinking, emotional trauma, or self-destructive behaviour, to more positive thoughts and actions. If the person, by virtue of his or her healing experience, can let go, immediately change these patterns, or come to terms with these issues, then more permanent healing could occur. However, if there are deeper causes and they are not dealt with during the process, the person could very well return later to the earlier patterns of thinking, emotion, or behaviour, and the illnesses will re-surface.

It is advisable for healers to make themselves aware of the underlying causes of the illness during a brief diagnosis and remedy them before attempting healing. This can also be done intuitively. If the patient is not ready or willing to release negative and destructive patterns, permanent healing will not be possible and the healer will be wasting his or her time.

On a metaphysical level, it is also possible to 'tune into' celestials who are dealing with this person using a light meditation and spontaneous imagery and to act on their guidance in all cases. This principle also explains why a true healer may sometimes not wish to attend to a person and why some healings are not permanent. Merely masking the illness with an emotional 'high', will at best, only provide temporary relief. We need to look holistically at the problem and follow the 'rules'.

THE USE OF ETHERIC ENERGY FOR HEALING AND OTHER MODALITIES

Having said this, I will now deal with the correct metaphysical tools for the use of etheric energy for healing as well as for channelling other aspects of the collective mind such as strength, comfort, protection, wisdom, understanding, compassion and love. When working with your own mind and etheric energy you will be most likely be using the positive aspect of the dual nature of energy which is powerful and you have to be careful that it doesn't disrupt your own energy and body.

The interconnected webs of energy in the Universal Mind are the lines of communication for the transfer of mental and etheric energies. In the case of healing, an etheric link to a person needing healing is created by setting intent for a *loving, healing* thought, or even using direct healing such as 'touch'. In cases where the person is actually present, you can lay your hands directly on them, but if they are not present, you will have to do absent healing. This means that an etheric connection has to be set up between you and that person. It is the same for channelling the other energies such as love, strength, comfort, protection and wisdom (understanding).

- Simply enter a meditative state and dial-up their 'energy addresses' by using photographs, their names, or the names of people you know who are close to them. As with our DNA, each person has a unique 'energy-signature' which we can tune into by directing our thoughts and intent towards them. This is the metaphysical principle I mentioned earlier of a *sympathetic connection* which states that there is an energy (quantum) connection between a person and their photo or name. Thoughts, feelings and different healing, or uplifting energies, in the form of colours, can be sent, which, if they are open to it, they will sense and pick up.

- During your meditation first seek balance and then visualise the person, express your intent and a feeling of *love* towards them, (this establishes a relationship), and then channel either your own energy, (holding an experience of health, love, strength, protection and wisdom in your mind), or drawing the specific type of energy from the universe (collective mind) itself.

- Become aware of this life-energy of the universe surrounding you. Using spontaneous imagery, try to see and feel this energy as it impacts on your own etheric envelope. Once you have the experience, direct it to the person needing it.

- You can also use your hands and sustained intent to assist in the movement and direction of this energy. As I said earlier, you can also use colours, as metaphysically, each colour is associated with unique energy present in the collective mind. For example, green and light blue are normally colours used for absent healing. In this way, you become the channel for the flow of *universal energy* (this is the basis of Reiki).

ABSENT HEALING

The following is a real-life example of absent healing which shows you the different skills needed:

Joan often sees messages on social media asking for the healing of friends or a family member. In this case, she decides to help and starts to meditate, visualising the image of the person as given in the posting (you can also use their names). To *sense and feel* the connection on a body-energy level, Joan raises her right-hand facing forward and uses sustained intention, allowing energy to accumulate in her palm. The open palm of the right-hand is particularly sensitive to changes in energy and she keeps this hand up during the entire process.

Joan knows that she has been successful in connecting with the person, (as visualised), on an energetic level when she feels pressure, like a 'bump' on the energy pocket in the palm of her right-hand (sometimes the connection can also be intuitively sensed). Joan *engages spontaneous imagery* and connects with the celestial helpers of this person to find out if she can go ahead, or if there is not some metaphysical obstacle to the healing.

Once she receives the go-ahead by seeing the celestials in her inner visual screen nodding their approval, Joan finds it easy to use the energy-connection to send focussed thoughts of peace, harmony and healing to the person. She colours her etheric energy with one of the healing colours. What is interesting is that, as she is using spontaneous imagery, an image of the person actually starts to form in her mind, as well as the colour she uses and the acknowledgement from the guides. Joan then gives thanks and exits slowly from her mediation in the usual way.

COMMENT

Joan demonstrates most of the requirements for absent healing. However, she could have used her breath to reinforce the movement of the healing etheric energy. In other words, while you are releasing the energy, blow lightly as if you were blowing a cooling breeze towards the person. This use of breath reinforces your gestures and sustained intention.

INTERCESSION AS A FORM OF HEALING

We can say that intercession takes place when we 'step into the breach', or intercede on behalf of someone else, or even on behalf of something that cannot act or speak of its own accord, such as a vulnerable adult, small child, or even an animal. Once again, intercession is based on ethical principles similar to healing. In other words, we must ensure that the intercession is asked for, actually needed, and does not involve removing some situation or obstacle which is actually part of the person's growth and development. The best way to make sure of this is to first consult with the person's celestial helpers during meditation, connection and spontaneous imagery. When visualising the person involved you will generally 'see' the helpers in the background and you can pose the question to them whether it is fine to go ahead with healing or intercession. If there is a problem, they will tell you intuitively, or use gestures such as shaking their heads.

THE HEALING OF THE PUPPY

In one case I was moved to intercede on behalf of a sick puppy that had been given to us. When I visualised the puppy during meditation and projection, I received an intuitive positive response that the intercession was necessary and indeed possible. Being experienced in working with helpful celestial personalities within the collective mind, I immediately petitioned for the healing of the little animal. In my spontaneous reconstruction of the scene, I saw a short, stocky, friendly Indian lady in traditional attire with markings on her arms. She informed me that her name was Rajmee and she was a deceased Reiki master who specialised in healing animals.

In my mind's eye, I saw her picking up and caressing the puppy (or at least an image of the animal). After a few words and moments, she announced that the puppy would be fine and put her down. When approached as to why these vulnerable animals are not automatically healed, she replied that 'one has to ask'.

Soon after I thanked Rajmee, the puppy recovered in spite of her sibling having died of the same illness a few days earlier. The puppy is still with us and is now an adult dog. I have successfully called on Rajmee a few times since this particular incident and have even given her name to other metaphysical practitioners.

COMMENT

This case serves to reinforce my belief in the power and validity of intercession (and prayer). In this particular case, using spontaneous imagery I was actually able to see her and how she acted to heal the puppy. I am also able to confirm that the healing actually took place. You can now understand how difficult it must be to rely on blind faith *without the ability to actually see the events taking place* using spontaneous imagery or inner sight.

SUPERIMPOSING HEALING ENERGY

A final, and even more powerful method of healing with the mind, is to use spontaneous imagery to create a new reality in your mind and impose this new reality on the old. For example, the most powerful form of healing a person is to imagine and bring forward the perfection of the pure human template from the Universal Mind and allow it to superimpose itself on the sick person to correct their imbalance. Try to hold them in the light of a new state of health for as long as you can. Using spontaneous imagery you will see colours and real energy surrounding them, and if they respond well to it, it can bring about great results.

ENDNOTE REFERENCES

1. Wave-particle theory- a scientific theory which shows that sub-atomic particles can assume the form of either a wave or a particle http://theconversation.com/explainer-what-is-wave-particle-duality-7414

2. Dr Masaru Emoto - a scientist who showed that thought and emotion can affect the formation of ice-crystals https://thewellnessenterprise.com/emoto/

CHAPTER NINE

NEW MENTAL SKILLS

*'Only those who risk going too far can possibly
find out how far one can go.'*

T.S. Eliot

DEVELOPING NEW MENTAL SKILLS

In this chapter, I show how metaphysical practices bring about increased cooperation from our subconscious minds. This, in turn, boosts our mental capacity, resulting in a raised consciousness, a realisation of the soul and the mastery of will-power, intent and advanced spontaneous imagery. Practical guidelines to further develop these skills are given.

We also look at ways of unfolding even more latent mental abilities, such as opening ourselves to visions, learning to control lucid dreams, developing telepathic abilities, enhancing our intuition and having out-of-body experiences.

In this chapter, this process of unfoldment is linked to a series of exercises as well as tips from several real-life examples.

A GREATER REALISATION OF SOUL

'The soul given to each of us is moved by the same living spirit that moves the Universe.'

Albert Einstein

Once we can reconnect with our souls due to regular meditation, we will experience higher levels of perception and understanding. This new realisation of soul begins when we start to feel a sense of *connectedness*, together with an inner joy, which tells us that this is indeed who we truly are, a spiritual being of light, or a 'soul'.

DISCOVERING OUR SOUL-CONNECTION

Although it has been covered up by piles of emotional and psychological rubble spanning many years of conditioning, our soul-consciousness can be slowly awakened from its slumber and its 'dreaming' in the body by practising regular meditation and other metaphysical practices. These practices must all be aimed at stripping away all pretence, masks and conditioned thoughts and actions to clear the path for the light of the soul and for us to become *'real'* and *authentic* again. As you have seen, the important elements for this are a quiet mind, the resolution of inner conflicts, and finally, the important realisation that the egos no longer have any legitimacy in their present form. They served their purpose during our early development and we now need to be 'reborn' into a soul-consciousness.

To me, this is the true meaning of the religious idea of *salvation*, not tied to any dogma or religion, but to a natural process of releasing the outdated evolutionary instincts and drives and moving through shadows of chaos and delusion to an understanding and acceptance of our true nature.

The following real-life examples show how our original soul-connection can be regained through regular meditation and engagement with the Universal Collective Mind. It has always been there but has gone unnoticed in the distractions and delusions of this life, but the time has now come for us to unfold this *flower of life* (the soul) fully.

THE PROCESS

Once again the soul-connection can be brought on by using meditation and spontaneous imagery. In this case, we have to choreograph a suitable scenario to suggest to our 'lover' (subconscious mind) that we want to uncover or release the inner part of ourselves (our soul). I have personally had some measure of success with imagery of myself emerging from an Egyptian sarcophagus (the soul emerging from the 'body'), or a cocoon (a butterfly emerging from a chrysalis).

A soul-connection can happen spontaneously. as soon as we clear away the debris from years of conditioning. However, it can also be speeded up by sincerely asking for it in meditation or prayer.

THE GIFT OF A SOUL-CONNECTION

This happened to John as a spiritual gift for his 50th birthday after many weeks of petitioning. During meditation and spontaneous imagery on the eve of his birthday, he was visited by several celestial guides who informed him that a new connection to his soul had been granted to him. This would allow him to access its wisdom more easily, bringing extra inspiration and insight which would assist him in his spiritual work. The importance of mastery of the practice of spontaneous imagery is evident. Without inner sight, John would not have been aware of this gift.

A SPONTANEOUS CONNECTION TO SOUL

During a meditation, Sue was suddenly completely overcome by a spontaneous connection to her soul, which she found herself channelling. The words just flowed as she spoke out loud:

> 'This is the gift I give to you to know me when you put aside your human personality to express me and my power when you need it.'

The experience was so powerful that after this Sue could no longer continue. She exited the meditation and spent the next few minutes expressing her gratitude for this privilege.

COMMENT

What is very interesting is that her soul appeared to have a separate personality of its own. This was certainly a powerful experience for Sue, to channel her soul to the point where her personality ceased to exist and only her 'nameless' soul remained.

WHAT'S IN A NAME?

This example points to the fact that our souls are not the same as our human personalities, but so much more. According to metaphysical philosophy, our personalities start forming when our souls enter our bodies at birth, bodies which contain early evolutionary drives and instincts, as well as inherited personality traits from our parents. These form the basis for our personalities which are later further shaped by our early experiences as children.

This experience also showed that our souls are the source of our lives and consciousness and are ultimately our true identities. In other words, our souls are eternal and actually nameless, and we only take on names at birth. I have noted that many of my friends who also study metaphysics have accepted new 'spirit' names. Perhaps this is due to their experiencing a soul-connection and giving it a name different from their birth name.

A MASTERY OF WILL-POWER AND INTENT

'You need to draw upon your willpower to accomplish the self-assigned task of mastering self-control.'

Dr Prem Jagyasi: Speaker and bestseller author.

Another important skill you can develop with regular meditation and engagement with the Universal Collective Mind is the understanding and correct use of *will-power or intent*. This is the use of the metaphorical *'divine masculine'* or active, positive energy I discussed earlier.

It is important to develop our will-power to create and be able to sustain our imaginary scenarios for long periods during visualisation and this development can sometimes take quite a while. I call this ability to maintain our will-power for any length of time, *sustained intent*, as, if our intent is to visualise ourselves walking down a path or a winding road, we will have to keep this intent, focus and concentration active for the entire walk in the scene, which could take a few minutes.

We can develop our will-power naturally as we master the skills of meditation and visualisation, but there are other specific exercises that can help us speed up the process.

A USEFUL EXERCISE FOR DEVELOPING WILL-POWER

The idea behind this process is to create an imaginary (visualised) situation in your mind in which you would need to use will-power. If you have mastered spontaneous imagery, you will also be able to see the results of your effort.

RAISING ROCKS AND BOULDERS IN YOUR SCENE

- Go into meditation and engage *spontaneous imagery.* Now imagine a grassy field full of large rocks or boulders. Take your time and try to make the boulders and the entire scene look as three-dimensional and as realistic as possible.

- Your next step will be to set an intention to use the power of your mind to raise one of these large rocks off the ground in your visualised scene with a view to practising your willpower and *sustained intent.*

- A positive spin-off will be that such an unusual and bizarre situation, beyond our normal belief systems and the laws of science, should also be a strong challenge to your outdated schemas and scripts about reality.

- Pick one of the rocks and imagine it lifting slowly until it is about a meter off the ground. You can use hand gestures to support your sustained intention. In other words, move your hand as if you were lifting the rock with your hand. You may be surprised by the mental effort needed to do this. It will not be easy.

- Although this is only an imaginary situation, you will find that your body and mind will act as if it is real and you should feel quite a strain. You may find it difficult to keep your focus and attention for long and may tire quickly. In fact, it could take weeks before you are actually able to raise and steady any rocks in the visualised scene.

COMMENT

When I first did this exercise it took a number of attempts before I was successful. I cannot explain the thrill and exhilaration I experienced when this happened for the first time, as this type of help from our subconscious minds is so useful and important for more advanced work. This convinced me of the huge amount of mental energy needed for sustained visualisation or imagery.

I ALSO NOTICED SOME INTERESTING POINTS:

Once you have mastered spontaneous imagery all sorts of exciting things begin to happen in your scene and it will seem to take on a life of its own. For instance, after you engage *spontaneous imagery* and do this exercise of lifting the boulder in your mind, you may see it 'wobble' or notice sand or grass falling from it.

It may behave in other strange ways without conscious involvement. For instance, the background scene may even change. This means that your imagery is now being taken over and controlled by your 'lover' (subconscious mind). However, I noted that, over time, my own focus and willpower had improved, as it became easier to work with the rocks and boulders.

NOTE

If you have any religious qualms about going against the laws of nature, remember that you are actually not doing so. This is an imaginary scenario in your mind, so there can be no judgment.

THE DISAPPEARING ROCK

One day I was busy with this exercise for improving willpower using spontaneous imagery and had just succeeded in raising a huge boulder in my mind when I heard the words, '*Know the rock*'. In response to this message from my subconscious mind, I focussed more on the boulder itself, surrounding it with light using gestures from my hands. To my amazement, the rock suddenly disappeared completely from the scene.

At this point, I stopped the meditation and took the time to consider what had actually just happened.

COMMENT

I started thinking deeply about the disappearing rock and received the following insight. As a result of my frequent practice with raising the rocks a new level of intent and perception had been given to me. This new level was of such a nature that it was able to alter the assembling of the rock in my mind. In other words, I was now able to see it as energy, which is not visible to the naked eye. This took me back to the quantum scientific explanation of matter as pure energy, which, to me, had now been confirmed by this strange experience.

I must stress that this was not a real boulder but one formed in my imagination. However, I believe that the principle is the same and is important for our present view of reality. If we can focus on the essence of reality during enhanced states of consciousness such as meditation, we may be able to see through to the energy matrix in the collective mind which gives rise to reality itself. This has been confirmed in later examples.

A PHILOSOPHICAL VIEW

There was an even deeper philosophical side to this. This lesson carries the realisation that we do not always have to tackle obstacles in our lives immediately with actions. Each challenge in life has a lesson or a message, and by getting through to the real essence of the problem or challenge (understanding the lesson), the problem will simply disappear, as the rock did.

This approach has worked quite well for me since this insight. Instead of panicking at the first sight of a challenge, I meditate and contemplate on it, asking for inner guidance as to its true essence, (what is the lesson here), and what has to be done. This results in really creative ways of solving problems and challenges.

A RADICAL IMPROVEMENT IN THE POWER OF SPONTANEOUS IMAGERY

'[Visualisation] works most powerfully when you realize that it is already a reality on the unseen level. It's already there.'

Eckhart Tolle

SPONTANEOUS CHANGES IN COMPLEX VISUAL-ISED SCENARIOS

Regular meditation and engagement with the collective mind will soon bring a radical increase in the power and involvement of our subconscious 'lovers' (minds) during spontaneous imagery. The following example is an advanced case in which the subconscious mind completely took over the scene. The power of spontaneous imagery, combined with will-power and intent, can also clearly be seen in this classic example.

'JOAN' THE WARRIOR PRINCESS

Our subconscious minds also regulate our autonomic bodily responses, so a realistic visualisation can bring about genuine emotions and even a *degree of stress*. This is quite evident in this real-life example. Joan's name has been changed for reasons of confidentiality.

One evening, Joan entered into an advanced three-dimensional visualisation in which she saw herself as a sort of 'warrior princess' in an ancient battle. Joan has always been successful with spontaneous imagery and this time found the scene once again shifting, changing and unfolding of its own accord as her subconscious mind played out its own programme. As soon as she released the scene, her subconscious took over and she found herself in the first-person in the midst of this great battle in which the enemy was firing arrows and slinging giant rocks at her using a catapult. In her mind's eye, she could actually see the arrows and boulders travelling through the air directly towards her.

Being practised in the use of willpower, sustained intent and symbolic gestures, Joan saw herself raising her right-hand in a 'stop' motion and was able to freeze the boulders and arrows in mid-air during their flight and cause them to fall to the ground in front of her. She had created a protective 'shield' in her mind and by moving her right-hand to the left or right, she was also able to deflect the boulders and arrows.

Obviously, her subconscious 'lover' (mind) was now enjoying this 'game' and without any action on her own part, she noticed that the assault on her had increased, with more spears, warriors, or even giant wooden machines, appearing out of nowhere and joining the attack. Once again, she had to use constant willpower, (sustained intent), to put up barriers and overcome all these attacks.

Soon Joan began to notice that her focus and concentration were weakening. She was obviously using up her mental energy at quite a rate. As it became even more demanding on her body, she began to have lapses in her concentration and some rocks and arrows actually began to penetrate her protection and she started to feel *real anxiety*. These penetrations she experienced as mild shocks or feelings of discomfort, suggesting that her mind and body had actually been affected by the imaginary 'wounding'. She soon realised what was happening and slowly exited from the imagery by withdrawing from the battlefield scene.

COMMENT

Several important lessons emerge from this case study:

Once again, it shows how spontaneous imagery can be used as a powerful tool for developing mental skills and willpower. It also shows that the subconscious mind is quite willing to help with these exercises by automatically increasing the *difficulty level* (almost like a computer game). As a result of overcoming the challenges set by our subconscious, over time we actually improve our intent, focus, willpower and concentration. Finally, this case study shows the demands that are made on our mental energy and concentration when using advanced mental skills and how much practice is needed.

USING SPONTANEOUS IMAGERY TO RESOLVE OUR 'SHADOW SELVES'

After a while, our spontaneous imagery becomes so powerful that we can even use it to balance and even transmute the deepest areas of our psyche, including our '*shadow-selves*'.

To explain what a shadow-self is, I need to return to the issue of archetypes.

In an earlier section, I showed you how some of our archetypes can be negative or unpleasant if we have not balanced or dealt with them effectively. In my earlier example of me facing my own archetypes, you saw how one archetype, *Greed*, introduced others and how another, *Deception*, claimed to be the son of *Ignorance*. This points to another characteristic of archetypes, that unresolved archetypes can form associations or 'band together' with our basic selfish drives and instincts left over from earlier evolutionary stages to form what is called in metaphysics, a *shadow-self*, a sub-personality which contains all our repressed anger, negativity and pain, as well as all the un-evolved aspects of our personalities which have sunk like heavy sediment into the depths of our subconscious minds.

These shadow-selves can come out and take over our personalities if we lose conscious control of our faculties during uncontrolled rage or drug or alcohol abuse and this experience will not be pleasant, especially for family members and friends. The many instances of domestic violence in this country due to substance abuse shows this to be true.

However, we need not be ashamed of this side of ourselves, as it is an integral part of our psyche and a challenge along the path of inner development. In psychology, we are actually encouraged to embrace and accept our shadow selves, but in metaphysics, we find ways of actually engaging with it and transmuting its energy with a view to further growth. This is another instance in which metaphysics takes us beyond the normal methods of personal growth.

By balancing, or transmuting our archetypes, we eventually dismantle our shadow-self piece by piece. However, sometimes it can take form in our mind during lucid dreams and this then gives us the opportunity to challenge and possible change, or at least redirect its energy as a whole. In the following example, David's shadow-self emerged in a lucid dream and the way he dealt with it should give you a number of useful guidelines, if you feel ready to take on this challenge.

DAVID ENGAGES HIS SHADOW-SELF

One night, David decided that he was going to engage with his shadow-self during meditation and used spontaneous imagery. He did not find this particularly harrowing, as he had worked with many of his archetypes on previous occasions. During the meditation, David's shadow-self did not present itself or take on any form, but he sensed its presence as a 'heavy' feeling surrounding him. So not much came out of this meditation and David went to bed a bit disappointed.

However, that night he had a lucid dream in which he was confronted by a group of sinister-looking 'reptiles' and it was quite a battle for David to subjugate and control them. For some reason, these archetypes of the shadow-self had not been there to present themselves during his meditation, possibly as a result of the power of his subconscious mind to offer him a measure of protection, as sometimes a subconscious experience can be a bit disturbing. But that night when he was asleep and his subconscious mind became active, it allowed the shadow-self to present itself to him in symbolic forms as large reptiles, and during the lucid dream, he was able to make a decision and muster the intention and willpower to subdue them.

COMMENT

One has to look at these reptiles metaphorically. A reptile is a relatively un-evolved form of animal, which suggests that David engaged his own shadow-self and the reptiles merely represented those un-evolved aspects of his own personality, or else some earlier evolutionary survival drives and instincts which may have existed in his DNA. This probably applies to us all at some stage.

Second, the fact that they seemed quite fierce, pointed to them being certainly no longer helpful to his development, in fact, now a probable threat. I personally believe that many of our unthinking behaviours are due to these earlier selfish survival programs in our genetic make-up, as this would account for the senseless violence we often see in our societies.

Finally, the fact that he was able to subdue them in a battle of wills showed that is possible for us to control our irrational urges and then to move forward with our inner development.

DAVID TRANSMUTES HIS SHADOW-SELF

During meditation one evening, David again engaged spontaneous imagery and set the intention to connect with his higher self. To his surprise, his subconscious mind took over and he saw himself in a darker place and experienced his shadow-self again. This time, David used this opportunity to address it in the same way as he would an archetype, telling it that it had fulfilled its role and thanking it for its contribution to his growth. He then asked it to transform its energy and add it to the light of his higher self. David reported that at that moment he saw himself separating from his shadow-self and said it felt like a load had been lifted from his shoulders and he was like a being of light emerging from a chrysalis.

COMMENT

The shadow-self accompanies us on our life-journey until we are prepared to let go of the past, embrace forgiveness and accept full responsibility for our own actions and our situation in life. As long as we continue to blame others for our misfortunes, we can never release the shadow-self. It is only by acknowledging and releasing or transmuting it that we can leave it behind. Remember Einstein's words that energy cannot be created or destroyed, only changed from one form to another.

Also notice the cardinal rule that David applied that when engaging with archetypes, confidence, good manners and gratitude are part of good metaphysical etiquette. Speak decently without fear, even kindly and with love and understanding if at all possible, and show appreciation for the lessons that they have brought into your life. Remember that these entities are metaphorically your 'children'. You spawned them and they are part of you.

INCREASED COOPERATION FROM YOUR 'LOVER' (SUBCONSCIOUS MIND)

'The subconscious mind is more susceptible to influence by impulses of thought mixed with 'feeling' or emotion, than by those originating solely in the reasoning portion of the mind.'

Napoleon Hill: American self-help author

As the power of our minds and intention improve with the practice of metaphysical processes, so will our ability to gain the cooperation of our subconscious minds. In this section, we reveal the true power of our subconscious 'lover' (mind) by showing how it is possible to challenge and even implode outdated schemas and scripts, simply by using spontaneous imagery.

A RETURN TO SCHEMAS AND SCRIPTS

We awaken each day to this present sense of reality because our neural systems are biologically hard-wired to do so and our consciousness is being controlled by our schemas and scripts relating to self and reality. Using our computer metaphor, this means that these outdated programs limit our processing of reality and our acceptance of 'what is possible'.

Earlier I showed you how you to clear out negative thinking and change unhelpful schemas and scripts by challenging your inner dialogue with new self-talk statements. However, I did mention that our subconscious minds respond better to imaginary enactments, (radically new experiences), than they do to words, and how we can use spontaneous imagery to radically challenge these outdated schemas and scripts, stretching them to the limit where they *implode*, releasing their hold on our thinking and perceptions.

For instance, I used the example of Peter and his *'dog schema'*, which was completely shattered and re-formed after his unfortunate encounter with a vicious dog. His *'nice doggy'* schema could simply not come to terms with the new experience and an alternate, negative schema was formed.

THE PROCESS

By now we know that our subconscious minds respond to imaginary situations as if they were real, and we have used this tool to clear our minds on many occasions. So, in this process, we use dramatisations to radically challenge them and dismantle the unhelpful schemas and scripts.

I have already given you some simple scenarios to use as examples. Remember the analogy of water washing out the cave? This will work for a general spring-cleaning of your subconscious schemas and scripts, while the exercises on lifting the rocks should help to stretch your schemas and scripts for reality and the 'warrior princess' example could work in changing your existing schema for self, allowing you to integrate a more powerful view of yourself and your abilities.

In this book, we follow a 'graded' path and the processes get more difficult as the reader proceeds through the book. We will now look at some very powerful dramatisations called pseudo-realities.

USING PSEUDO-REALITIES TO SHATTER YOUR OLD SCHEMAS AND SCRIPTS

Earlier I mentioned research which suggests that *fantastical* experiences way out of the 'range' of these schemas and scripts could end up stretching, or even shattering, them completely. In other words, by changing our schemas and scripts, we change the 'rules' for what we can and cannot experience of reality, opening us up to amazing shifts in consciousness and perception. I now show how this can be achieved with advanced scenarios of spontaneous imagery and the creation of *'pseudo-realities'* which act as catalysts for this schema change. But before I do this, you will need to make a few decisions.

Firstly, you need to remember that some of your schemas and scripts could have been put in place by your ethical, moral, or religious convictions. In other words, any inner conflict you have about the 'rightness' or 'wrongness' of the processes I will be sharing with you will be a stumbling block to your success. This is why it may be better for you to first take time off for self-examination before you begin with this advanced work and ensure you do not have any serious ethical or religious issues that will stop you. As I said at the beginning, I personally do not believe this path of metaphysics to be 'dark' or 'bad', as your motive will be personal growth and self-actualisation, but there may be those, even in your family, who will try to put you off this type of study.

MORAL AND ETHICAL RULES

However, as you are only working within your own mind, your work will not affect anyone else in a negative way and I do not believe that there can be any judgment. In fact, your work will ultimately be of benefit to the whole world, (see the final chapter on World-Service in this regard).

If you still have some ethical blocks to continuing, try to reaffirm your good intentions and motives. And if you do have outstanding issues concerned about the coming work, try making new commitments, or put protocols in place which will satisfy your moral and ethical needs. As you move deeper into the Collective Mind you will have to unlock more and more psychological 'gates' to get the full co-operation of your subconscious mind and to do this you need complete confidence, a positive state of mind and no doubt at all that what you are doing is correct.

IF YOU FEEL READY, LET US NOW LOOK AT HOW IT IS DONE:

THE PROCESS

As I said, this particular method expects you to experiment with new pseudo-realities, self-created 'worlds', or even 'universes' of inner experience. However, to have success at this level of mind, you must have mastered the skills of meditation, the use of sustained intention and advanced spontaneous imagery. If you have not yet reached this level, please read my earlier book *Multi-Dimensional Thinking*, in which these processes are fully explained.

The aim of creating bizarre imaginary scenarios or enactments is to challenge your present self-limiting schemas and scripts with the view to convince your subconscious mind to help you be more open to powerful new inner experiences. Your imaginary scenarios should also have good storylines which will make sense to your subconscious mind and will lead it into accepting that the alternative realities that you are creating in your mind are 'possible' and real. The following is an example of such a powerful programme.

THE 'WORLD OF FLOATING ROCKS'

You may remember the earlier exercise on raising the rocks in your mind to build your will-power.

This is a similar exercise but one that is even more bizarre and difficult to hold in your mind.

- Enter into a deep meditation with your eyes closed and use visualisation to imagine a visit to a strange planet with zero gravity in which rocks are floating, suspended in the air. See yourself entering this world from a space-ship and being able to touch and move the floating rocks, making them spin and twirl. Open your mind to your feelings, as well as sounds and scents, to increase the depth and multi-dimensional nature of the enactment. Try to make it as real as possible.

- Now engage spontaneous imagery (let go of the scene) and let it float in your imagination. Reach for one of the floating rocks twirling all around you. Touch one and see it move off as soon as you push it. Let yourself be lost in the experience for a few minutes.

- Now begin to open and close your eyes slowly and try to shift your perception between this 'world' of floating rocks and the reality of the room you are in. Do this a few times. If you are successful it will seem as if the floating rocks are 'superimposed' in the air in the actual room you are sitting in. Stay in this state for a while, try to enjoy the newness of this illusion and realise the true power of your mind.

- If you start to feel your energy waning, stop and exit the visualisation slowly. Always remember to end your storyline naturally before ending the meditation and visualisation. In other words, re-enter the rocket you came in and return to Earth. Do this a few times until you feel changes taking place in your perception of reality, but don't stay in this enhanced state for too long as you could get a little 'lost' in the experience.

THE POWER OF SUPERIMPOSED REALITIES

The effect of this powerful experience on your schemas and scripts for reality can be extreme. They can be stretched to capacity and possibly implode altogether. This will release their hold on you. You know this when you can superimpose images on your room during spontaneous imagery and begin to doubt your view of reality. You could feel a little confused from time to time, but this is natural, as you are now in the process of rebuilding your schemas and scripts and your subconscious mind is allowing you a more open and fluid sense of perception. This means you will now be able to process more complex inner experiences.

If you continue with this type of exercise, your abilities will grow and deepen in order to cope with the pseudo-realities and your subconscious mind will not be able to tell what is real and what is not during your visualisations. This will make it possible for you to shift your perception at will, allowing you to access multi-dimensional spiritual experiences which would normally go unnoticed in your everyday life. And with further practice, this exercise will enable you to access higher realms of the Collective Mind.

Regularly continue with this type of exercise. Change your imaginary scenes to include fantastical, bizarre images and colours which will further challenge your existing framework of perception. A word of warning, I did say that this way of altering perception is advanced and not suggested for novices as this is powerful stuff, and you could feel confused and disoriented for a while as it is so totally new to your mind. So pace yourself properly and do not get lost in the fantasy.

CHANGES TO THE QUANTUM REALITY

There is another even more powerful aspect of visualised superimposed scenes or thought-forms. As they are formed from the energy of our minds, they actually become an energy template for change. In other words, if you are troubled by a difficult situation in your life, you can create an improved, or 'resolved' pseudo-reality and superimpose it on your current situation. On a *quantum* (sub-atomic) level, you are then setting up the conditions for change. Obviously, you would have to do this a few times with intent and emotion before the template would produce real change. Many NLP practitioners and motivational speakers teach this as a means of self-empowerment, but I don't know if they are aware of the metaphysical aspects of what they are doing. And then again, perhaps they do and just don't tell us.

Finally, the following is a real-life example of 'Joan' using this method of an imaginary pseudo-reality to change her schemas which ultimately affected her view of reality.

A VISION OF REALITY

One evening, Joan began her meditations as usual, but this time set an intention for a deeper view of reality. Her meditation involved visualisation, (spontaneous imagery), in which she first recreated a complete view of the room in which she was sitting in her mind. After asking for a vision of reality, she let go of control of the scene and immediately felt that she had entered an enhanced state of consciousness. She was amazed to see that the walls seemed to dissolve and fall away and she could see out into the backyard of her home. What was even more amazing was that, even when she opened her eyes for a few moments, the walls still appeared transparent. However, as soon as she allowed a thought to enter her mind, they became solid again. She returned to normal consciousness and recorded this important vision.

COMMENT

This lesson points to the metaphysical principle that nothing is truly solid and to a very high consciousness, obstacles such as walls and structures do not exist. Another important insight from this experience was how quickly this state of consciousness can be lost. A mere thought was enough to stop the vision.

THE LATENT POWERS OF YOUR MIND

'Believe in yourself! Have faith in your abilities!
Without a humble but reasonable confidence in your own
powers you cannot be successful or happy.'

Norman Vincent Peale:
Author (Power of Positive Thinking)

In building a good relationship with our subconscious 'lovers' (minds) and engaging the collective mind regularly, we can enhance many of our natural skills. It is almost as if we bring back some of this higher consciousness into our lives after our meditations. In this section, I discuss a number of more familiar areas in which your growth will be improved. To me it seems that these abilities were always there, just waiting for the opportunity to express.

THE ABILITY TO HAVE VISIONS

Mastering superimposed spontaneous imagery will give you a greater opportunity to have visions. Visions are similar to dreams in that they are messages from our subconscious minds about deep-seated emotional issues that need to be resolved, but they can also be in the form of guidance. It is possible that some intuitive imagery, (visions), may come from guiding personalities within the Universal Collective Mind.

In the case of visions, the images and interactions are actually taking place in our minds, but often become superimposed on our view of reality. If we accept that everything is processed through the mind anyway, then they can be accepted as quite real. Visions will often occur during meditations, bypassing our normal thinking processes and if our minds are properly prepared, be quite clear. However, sometimes visions can even occur when we are simply relaxed and contemplative. Carl Jung believed that images from the *collective unconscious* (Universal Mind) can impose on our normal awareness during such moments of introspection.

The following examples serve to highlight this valuable skill:

A VISION OF THE EARTH PLANE

The idea of our Source and Creator being a vastly superior collective mind, or consciousness, has important implications for the status of Earth, our home planet. For example, if our view of reality is actually constructed in our minds, then it stands to reason that the planet itself may not be exactly as we see it. This was confirmed by an interesting example I came across a few years ago.

Samuel remembers a vision he had during an advanced meditation years ago. Using spontaneous imagery he was able to bypass the limits on his perception imposed by his mind, and as a result, in his mind's eye, everything, including the very ground beneath his feet, appeared to dissolve in consciousness. At the same time, the Earth appeared not as a planet, but rather a 'sphere of existence', housing various other spheres and categories of archetypal beings formed within the collective mind. This vision included the view of a field, energy-membrane, or etheric web, forming the furthermost border of the sphere, (the Earth's electromagnetic atmosphere), and Samuel noticed how remarkably similar this was to a single human cell embodying a mass of embryonic substance, (in this case, consciousness), in the process of evolving.

COMMENT

This type of vision uses powerful imagery and in this case, shows how easily our view of reality is assembled in our minds. The powerful effect of symbols and metaphors on our minds was also shown in this particular example. For instance, the vision of different spheres in the single Earth sphere, could, by analogy, be seen as symbolic of the various levels of human consciousness, emotions and thoughts. For instance, subconscious human drives could be represented by the heavier elements on, or below the Earth's surface, the fluidity of human emotion can be compared to water, (the oceans), with more enlightened thoughts corresponding to the more subtle regions, (the air), which surround the Earth sphere.

This case study also has implications for the possible true purpose of mankind. For instance, if our Earth sphere actually represents only a single plane out of many that exist within a universal 'mental' reality, (the Collective Mind), it follows that our purpose would first be to achieve mastery over this sphere. This would include cultivating sufficient knowledge, consciousness and intent with which to move forward into the next level of the collective mind after the passing of our physical bodies. And this is the reason why, in metaphysics, death is often seen not as the end, but only as a transition from one form of existence to the next.

HOW DO VISIONS OCCUR?

Carl Jung believed that anyone can inadvertently open doorways to their subconscious minds and receive sensations, impressions and even symbolic images while conscious, as well as in dreams. Many people have reported receiving intuitive warnings of danger as images of an accident which flash briefly through their minds. This is once again, the work of our subconscious minds, which is able to introduce these images into our normal consciousness under certain conditions.

The biggest issue to discount the reality and value of 'visions' is that it is relatively easy for our thoughts and images to enter our minds and we need to *watch out for an overactive imagination*. It is always important to keep a totally clear, open mind if you wish to use your intuition or open your mind to visions. Any strongly-held belief that is lurking just below your consciousness will 'jump in' and influence what you see or experience.

You have seen in the previous sections how, during meditation and spontaneous imagery, entire 3-D (moving) scenarios can unfold in your mind. In a manner of speaking, these are also visions, as they are likewise choreographed by your subconscious minds. Although they may at first appear to be part of a daydream, the images can be quite vivid and even superimpose themselves on your normal sense of sight for brief moments. I am sure that many of you have had such experiences, so they can't all simply be discounted as fantasy.

COMMENT

As before, exactly what you see will depend on your schemas, thinking paradigms and belief systems. As with all intuitive messages or images, the key to understanding their true meaning is to interpret them correctly. In some cases, such as the accident warnings I spoke of earlier, images may be clear and understandable. However, as with dreams, intuitive visions are often shaped by our symbolic processes. As a result, we may only get clues to their meaning within the context, structure, form and composition of the imagery.

Unfortunately, this means that intuitive imagery or visions cannot always be taken literally, and you may also need to interpret what you see in terms of your personal symbols, the same as symbolic dreams. For example, a vision of an altercation between two figures could actually be mirroring your own inner conflict of which you are not aware, and if you have some insight into your present feelings and problems, this will certainly help.

IMPROVED LUCID DREAMING

Regularly connecting with the collective mind raises our consciousness and greatly increases our opportunities for lucid dreams and our ability to control them. Apart from giving us the opportunity for self-knowledge and initiations, if we act during lucid dreaming we can help to dismantle the subliminal schemas and scripts influencing our thinking and perception. Controlling a dream also means that we exercise willpower and this will improve our other metaphysical practices, as well as help us cope in everyday life. The effort and practice needed for lucid dreaming certainly builds our mental 'muscles' for the deeper work to come. The following is an example which shows the power of lucid dreams.

THE POWER TO CHANGE ONE'S VIEW OF REALITY

To show just how powerful controlling lucid dreams can be, I will tell you about a great experience I had a few years ago. One morning I was close to waking and suddenly realised for a moment that I was dreaming. In this fleeting moment, I formulated a single conscious thought; 'I am aware'.

This thought alone stopped my dream in its tracks and gave me time to make a partially conscious decision to take control. I immediately felt my self-awareness increasing and was able to set an intention to look behind the dream and see reality as it is. You must remember that a dream is constructed by our subconscious mind, which, during a lucid dream, is fully open. And even if we are only partially aware, we can metaphorically 'reach in and grab hold of the dream' and change it, leading to amazing inner experiences.

This was not easy, as keeping myself somewhat conscious during the dream was a huge strain on my energy. It was very difficult to keep my resolve, as I kept drifting back into the storyline of the dream. Eventually, with persistence, I began to have more control and was able to consciously set an intention to dissolve the dream but keep my inner visual screen open.

The results of this shift were amazing. The whole dream-scene *actually froze* and slowly, cracks started to form, spreading outwards like a stone hitting a plate glass window. Almost immediately, pieces of the backdrop to the dream, like the parts of a jigsaw puzzle, began to drop and fall away to reveal behind it, in the distance, a kaleidoscope of pure light and colour. This new vista had no definite form but was very similar to the interplay of light and colour during a sunrise.

It was becoming even more difficult to hang onto this new vision, as the pull of the original dream was strong and it would have been so easy to get lost in it again. However, once again, with persistence, I eventually managed to move aside the shattered pieces of the scene and step through into a kind of plateau which led to the mixture of light and colour in the distance. By this time, my energy reserves were depleted, but I had achieved what I had set out to do and allowed myself to awaken.

This was one of the most empowering and fulfilling experiences I have ever had, one which showed me in a very practical way that the energy-basis of what we call reality is actually light and colour, (representing different modes of energy), and how, if we apply ourselves, we can actually see it as it really is.

THE GIFT OF TELEPATHY

As a result of your new inner development from working closely with your subconscious mind, you may find that you are more sensitive to the thoughts and feelings of others and you may begin to pick up words and messages as thoughts in your mind when other people are around. This is telepathy, which happens when we connect at a subconscious level with another person and send and receive thoughts or feelings. This can be explained by the *interconnectedness of all minds* within the collective mind. The barriers separating us as individual personalities do not exist at deeper subconscious levels.

There is growing evidence that this phenomenon is very real. A simple online internet search on 'telepathy' will show you how many scientists and metaphysical practitioners attest to its validity. As mentioned, this communication with others takes place at a subliminal level and the key is, once again, to get through and communicate through the medium of the Universal Collective Mind.

It is possible to connect with another person simply by entering into a slightly enhanced, or at least a relaxed and clear state of mind, setting an intention to connect and putting together an image of that person in your mind by using a photograph, their name, or that of a family member or friend who has a relationship with this person. It is this relationship that allows thoughts to pass from one person to another, as a relationship means that there already is a link between them.

However, this does not happen easily, as you may remember, there are barriers and boundaries created by each person's subconscious mind as a protection mechanism to prevent a sensory-overload and you may not be able to get through. However, if you have a good relationship with your subconscious mind, you may at least bypass some of your own mechanisms and possibly be able to send and receive messages or feelings using the 'mental airwaves'.

Incoming messages can also occur spontaneously, as shown in the following example:

SPONTANEOUS TELEPATHY

I must mention an amusing incident that took place a few years ago when I had given a short talk on my recently published book at a local bookshop. I had just finished my talk, when clear as a bell, I heard a female voice in my mind saying the words; 'Sounds like a lot of work!!' I recall glancing to my left and seeing a young woman looking down. At that time I got a distinct impression that it was her thought which I had picked up, but I was concerned that telling her this may upset her and so I did not mention it to her.

COMMENT

What I found interesting about this case was that the telepathic contact took place spontaneously, without any intention on my part. It is true, however, that my mind was quiet and I could well have been in a receptive state of mind. The fact that I was close to her could also have played a role, as she obviously had my book (and me) in mind when she entertained that thought.

The truth is that for me, telepathic contact between people is a curiosity. I am more concerned with telepathic contact between us and celestial and cosmic intelligences during meditation, as this is important. Sometimes the messages come via our intuition, but when actually engaging face-to-face with archetypes you will find that communication is telepathic and the speech is quite clear, sometimes in your own voice, but interestingly, also sometimes in a voice that fits the profile of the archetype. Before you have mastered this skill however, you may only see gestures and will have to infer the message that is being given. However, with practice, this skill can be improved.

THE DEVELOPMENT OF INTUITION

An important by-product of a growing relationship with your subconscious mind is the development of intuition. Many names have been given to *intuition*, which include 'sixth sense', 'inner voice' or 'gut' feelings. There is no doubt that this faculty exists, as it is even acknowledged in psychology in a slightly different form as 'immediate insight' or 'immediate understanding'. However, in this case, it is linked mostly to finding spontaneous solutions to visual puzzles and it is believed that our subconscious minds simply re-arrange the elements of the problem to find a solution without any conscious thought.

However, I believe that intuition is simply guidance from our subconscious minds. As mentioned earlier, there is ongoing communication between our conscious and subconscious processes, but once again, we don't recognise it as such, for instance, those moments of intuition or inspiration when we are engrossed in art, writing or other creative work.

Messages from our subconscious minds usually come to us in our dreams but can also happen spontaneously. These messages take the form of 'intuitions', words and ideas which simply 'pop' into our minds when we are relaxed and more receptive to them. In other words, intuition is us simply becoming aware of the promptings from our subconscious minds.

However, our conscious minds have to be open to the idea of inner guidance and be reasonably clear and quiet for these messages to be heard. As a result, our intuition works best when we are in a slightly altered state of consciousness such as during introspection, self-reflection, contemplation, a light slumber, or meditation, as these promptings are subtle and can be lost in the clutter of our everyday thoughts.

As mentioned earlier, some people have also reported receiving intuitive warnings of impending danger in the form of images of an accident flashing briefly through their minds. This suggests that our intuition can be developed and primed to identify possible emotional and psychological threats to us as well. For instance, clues as to peoples' true feelings and intentions are often hidden in their actions, body language, and choice of words, and this can be picked up by our subconscious minds. In fact, most of us will admit to having had feelings of discomfort in some situations but did not give them a second thought. In most cases, we simply overlook or choose to ignore these feelings which could be intuitive warnings from our subconscious minds.

However, we do need to learn to tell the difference between real intuition and what is simply a thought from an overactive imagination. True intuition is brief, immediate, spontaneous and not under our conscious control.

I have also found that intuitive messages can come via our subconscious minds from celestials and masters during meditation when we are connected to the Collective Mind. This is sometimes called *clairaudience*, as we can actually hear words of guidance in our own language. It seems that our minds are also able to translate impressions into words using Synesthesia.

Finally, it is said that this sense of intuition is highly developed in animals, but I believe that this is probably more instinctive. But it is not difficult to imagine the power that it may bring into our lives if we can use it properly. Methods to develop intuition have been fully described in my earlier publication *Multi-Dimensional Thinking*.

INTUITION CAPTURED IN MOMENTS OF INSPIRATION

Many of my best ideas have come to me during those moments immediately before I fall asleep in the late evening. This has been quite disruptive for my wife, as I often rise at odd times to jot down ideas that come to mind which I later include in my books. Usually, using my intuition involves priming my subconscious mind by setting an intention and introducing specific questions. However, in most cases, I simply spend a few hours beforehand reflecting on new and exciting ideas and during my later quiet moments, my subconscious merely re-arranges these thoughts into inspirational ideas. In other words, inspiration is similar to intuition.

USING YOUR INTUITION

The easiest way of using your intuition is during meditation, but you can try simply quietening your mind, posing a question to yourself and waiting expectantly for an answer. The problem is that unless you have a good working relationship with your subconscious mind, the answers may only come in your dreams. Practising with intuition is an excellent way of building your relationship with your subconscious mind.

THE ABILITY TO CHANNEL ONE'S HIGHER SELF

Channelling takes place when we open our minds and thinking to our higher selves or souls, or the influence of a celestial or spiritual master.

Some persons can even go into a trancelike state and not know what they are saying. Many people would say that this is taking a chance, as you could end up being influenced by some or other 'being'. It is true that we have to be careful and so I would not recommend trying to channel archetypes unless you are sure of their good intentions. I think this is what puts most people off *channelling*.

Channelling our higher selves is probably the best way of channelling, as the words and insights come from your own subconscious minds. This is what happens most of the time when we get inspiration for our art or creative writing and the words just flow without our even thinking of them. In these cases, you need to stay sufficiently lucid to write down what you are saying and interpret it later. My first book *In Search of the Oracle* was written in this way many years ago, and the character of the 'old man' is actually a metaphor for my higher self.

Channelling often occurs when metaphysical practitioners come together in groups, (or circles), and one or more of the group get messages from celestials, cosmic personalities, or deceased family members which they then pass on to the others. However, we also need to be aware of tricksters who give out false messages.

Channelling can also happen during meditation, even when we do not ask for it. Always set up a powerful intention before meditating that you only work with celestial light-workers or masters, otherwise you could end up channelling a lower personality that does not have your best interests at heart.

SPONTANEOUS CHANNELLING

I used to do volunteer crisis counselling and one day, as I was counselling someone who had come to the counselling centre, I found myself going into a semi-trancelike state. Fortunately, it was a higher-self (soul) channelling and I found myself giving the client guidance on the true meaning of the events in his life, much deeper insights than usually take place with counselling. I do not normally do 'readings' for clients, so this was a first for me. Fortunately, he was open to this sort of thing and was amazed at the depth of guidance given and very grateful.

OUT-OF-BODY EXPERIENCES (OBES)

Your inner development through regular contact with your subconscious mind and the collective mind will also increase your chances of '*out-of-body experiences*' (OBEs). This phenomenon has been researched for many years, but only anecdotal (case) evidence can be found to support the idea that our consciousness can leave our bodies under certain conditions, while still remaining connected. Some cases of OBEs have been reported resulting from brain trauma, near-death experiences, drug use and electrical stimulation of the brain. However, mainstream science still considers spontaneous OBEs hallucinations caused by psychological and neurological disorders.

In metaphysical practice, OBEs are acknowledged. I have personally had a few experiences in the past, but only under ideal conditions. What I find easier is the projection of my consciousness, as shown in several later examples. These examples will show that consciousness can be projected during enhanced states of mind, (deep meditation), and combined with imagery to create a thought-form (etheric body) to house one's consciousness as it moves around within the realms of the collective mind. As this is a very advanced skill, it will be discussed later in greater detail.

THE ABILITY TO INTERPRET OMENS

I am sure that most of you have found feathers or strange objects in places where you did not expect them to be. In South American shamanistic wisdom, these are called *omens* and can include the sudden, strange appearance of animals, birds, reptiles or objects. All have a special message or meaning for the one who can see, recognise and interpret them. These messages are usually from one's spiritual guide, especially those that lived close to Nature when they were alive, (such as shamans), and now use this as a symbolic means of communicating with you.

THE OMEN OF THE HAWK

During a lucid dream, I saw a small hawk flying overhead. I had enough awareness to make the decision to hold up my left hand. Unbelievably the hawk settled on my arm and fell asleep. I think at that time I also resumed my sleep and when I again entered the lucid dream, the bird was gone. I gave thanks and woke up to do the interpretation.

COMMENT

In South American teachings, seeing a bird of prey is a good omen, and when settling on my left arm, would signify a gift of spiritual power from a higher source, as in terms of these teachings, the left side is the spiritual side. When I looked deeper I noted some more characteristics. The hawk was small and placid and settling down to sleep on my arm suggested contentment, trust and gentleness, possibly an angelic presence, or a gift of the powerful, but divine feminine energy. The study and interpretation of omens is a fully comprehensive study on its own and does not form part of this book. If you are interested, I urge you to read some of Théun Mares' books.

CHAPTER TEN

INITIATIONS

'The disciple who feels that one needs to rise should follow the process of initiation and intuitional science with all sincerity, perseverance and passion with regular and sustained effort.'

Maitreya Rudrabhayananda: Spiritual teacher, author

THE POWER OF INITIATIONS

There are guidelines and requirements when it comes to moving to new levels of consciousness. This chapter deals with rituals and initiations, as well as the type of trials, tests and experiences you can expect further along your journey of metaphysical development. We look at some issues relating to rituals and initiations, their importance, what they actually are, what they do and how they are put together.

In this chapter, we look at these important milestones which you can request or do for yourselves during a meditation. We also consider the proper procedure when it comes to asking for initiation.

Sometimes we may attempt a self-initiation for which we are not ready. A certain level of brain and mind development is necessary to move to a higher level of consciousness and in this case, it will simply not work or else we will be emotionally 'dressed-down' by the experience. There are rules for progress along the metaphysical path and forcing the issue is certainly not a good idea.

Ideally, we should consciously petition, pray, or ask for the privilege of a true spiritual initiation. This is probably the safest method, as it will not happen unless we have reached the proper level of consciousness and emotional and psychological readiness. We will also then be supervised and directed by inner guidance as to what to do and so not overstep the rules given to us.

SYMBOLIC RITUALS

Rituals are an elaborate and powerful symbolic form of instruction. The ceremonies are similar to theatrical plays in which metaphysical principles are presented in a dramatised form with ritualistic scenes and movements. As is the case with theatrical dramatisations, each ritual has a script as well as many different dimensions in which the sacred truths, lessons and symbolic messages are concealed. These dimensions include the actual setting of the ritual, the backdrop, layout, lighting, positioning of the props, background music and the meaning of the movements and gestures themselves. All have a symbolic meaning and work together to fit the purpose of the ritual.

However, to fully appreciate a ritual and get the most out of it, we need to be in a state of emotional and psychological *'readiness'*. This readiness is usually induced during the ritual by the use of music, lighting and chants to create powerful emotions such as expectation, awe or excitement. These emotions then prime our minds for deeper experiences and can bring about an enhanced state of consciousness. In this state, the symbolic meanings of the objects, movements and gestures become subconscious *cues* to allow us a deeper realisation and understanding of the hidden laws and principles.

Most real-life rituals are organised by different brotherhoods or spiritual groups, as they are quite colourful, complex and need many helpers or participants.

However, when working alone, we can create our own rituals during meditation using spontaneous imagery. The idea is to create an imaginary scenario to open the mind, (establish readiness), bypass our psychological barriers, and engage directly with our subconscious minds ('lover'). Our subconscious mind, in turn, will help by changing the scene, according to our needs, and allow us to see and understand the deeper symbolic significance of the movements.

Real-life examples of self-induced rituals are given in the next section.

TYPES OF INITIATIONS

WHAT ARE INITIATIONS?

An initiation is a graded introduction to the mysteries of the self, the universe and reality, usually done by a master metaphysician or by unseen masters working from the Universal Collective Mind It involves a ritual with symbolic processes, lessons and sacred objects in which one has to make new commitments, Although it is far better to request an initiation to ensure you are ready, an initiation can happen spontaneously if you pass into a new level of understanding and service.

Initiations are there to make sure that you are not moving or evolving at a pace which can damage your mind and consciousness and ideally, 'permission' should be given before you go-ahead with any action. In other words, during advanced meditations and true initiations, you will probably be 'invited' to proceed, especially when working within the higher realms of the Collective Mind.

SELF-INITIATIONS

We have the ability to do self-initiations without elaborate décor and objects using meditation, visualisation and spontaneous imagery. In this case, we mentally create ritualistic settings and perform the ritual in our minds. As seen in previous chapters, this is still quite powerful, as self-created imagery has a very real effect on our subconscious minds and they will usually cooperate.

However, always ensure that you are ready for this initiation, as, if not, you could find yourself at odds emotionally. Sometimes if you are not fully prepared the ritual will simply not work at all, but if you are in regular contact with guiding personalities you will be told what you need to do. Always follow your inner guidance or your celestial 'advisors' to find out when you have reached the right level of readiness for your next initiation.

All you need is an enhanced state of consciousness and the full cooperation of your subconscious mind. Some cultures or holistic groups use drumming, repetitive chants, or even drugs, to achieve this state, but meditation together with spontaneous imagery is all that you need. I personally do not believe in drug-use for metaphysical development, as it encourages dependence and can also force open your mental pathways when you are not ready and you could end up with some or other mental disorder.

Remember that the rule is, during an enhanced state of consciousness, your subconscious mind is open to suggestion and will accept your actions and enactments as real, or at least sufficiently real so as to bring changes to your mental state and consciousness, moving you to the next level.

HOW TO CREATE A SUITABLE SCENE

Set up your ritual by asking guides, celestials or masters from the collective mind to assist you. If you engage spontaneous imagery and are actually ready for this initiation, you will find that your subconscious mind will respond well, with archetypal figures revealing themselves and assisting in your initiation. If the time is not right, your archetypal helpers will warn you at the start of your ritual.

For your initiation, you need to visualise a complex three-dimensional image of a sacred site, or a special location such as a sanctum, a temple or a natural site. If you can recreate a good representation of a well-known sacred site such as *Stonehenge* or the *Temple of Athena* you will feel the energy of the actual place. This is because your visualisation, if accurate, will, through the interconnected collective mind, resonate and link up with the actual site, according to the Law of Affinity or 'sympathetic connection'.

Now try to *superimpose* the image of the temple or holy place on your normal view of reality in the room where you are. This is done by opening and closing your eyes slowly during the meditation and imagery until you feel you are actually at the sacred site and the experience becomes more realistic. Although you may feel like you are actually there, it is only a shift in your perception which is allowing you to recover the energy impressions and feelings relating to these sites.

You may walk and carry out the movements and gestures with your body and hands, while the décor and surroundings shift and unfold in your minds under the direction of your subconscious 'lover' and any helpers present. However, if you have engaged spontaneous imagery correctly, the ritual will unfold of its own accord and involve situations in which you have to consciously make choices, decisions and commitments. The figures present may include powerful archetypal figures, guides or masters who will ask the questions and expect commitments from you. Always follow the guidance you receive during your initiation.

SPONTANEOUS INITIATIONS

When due, initiations are usually set up for you by celestials, powerful archetypal personalities, or unseen masters within realms of the collective mind and usually come in the form of lucid dreams, or unexpected changes to your scene while you are meditating. As is the case with the self-initiation, a complex ritual will spontaneously begin to unfold in your mind during a lucid dream or meditation in which your readiness, intention, commitment and courage will be tested. You will have the power of choice, as you have to make new commitments.

Initiations differ in form and content, but they share common characteristics or requirements. For instance, they all involve a situation where you have to consciously take certain actions and make a choice, comittments or a decision. In the case of a lucid dream, your ability to choose and act distinguishes it from a normal dream or vision, so this is the most suitable for an initiation.

Initiations could also involve a challenge in which you will have to overcome certain obstacles and could even include a dramatised battle with protagonists representing different aspects of yourself. Remember that your most important battle is 'within'. Finally, initiations all need you to make new commitments and dedicate your gifts to the service of mankind. You will need to be prepared to do this to receive the gifts that come with initiation.

LUCID DREAM INITIATIONS

THE INITIATION OF COURAGE/ THE SANGOMA

In a lucid dream John had while on holiday in the mountains many years ago, he was approached by a black sangoma (witch-doctor) who asked him if he was prepared to undergo a few trials. He was a bit concerned as sangomas often use blood from the killing of animals as part of the ritual. John was not prepared to do this but decided to agree to the initiation, as a sangoma works closely with *ancestral and earth spirits* and this was a side of metaphysics he had not yet explored.

The trials all had to do with testing courage and demonstrating strength and a lack of fear. For example, the first was to battle a number of tribesmen simultaneously and the second was to face a raging sea and put his hands into a dark hole. He succeeded with both of these trials, calling for help when he felt he was going to be overcome as the fight was very intense. However, John refused the third, which was to drink from three different containers. He felt that one of them may contain blood or a concoction which would bind him to the earth in some way. The sangoma seemed satisfied with his decision and they parted ways with mutual respect.

COMMENT

John was actually exhausted after he woke up, which showed that his trials had been demanding. The area in which he was staying had plenty of traditional African huts and sangomas worked in these areas, so this formed the backdrop to the initiation. He knew this was an initiation because in all the trials he had to make conscious choices. However, at the time he was also not sure if it was a genuine visitation from a real sangoma in a projected thought-form, or just a scenario put together by his own subconscious mind to test his courage and conviction. He believed it was a true visitation, as there was frequent and spontaneous interaction between him and the sangoma in the lucid dream, and in his experience of lucid dreams, symbolic characters do not interact with the dreamer that much. The responses of characters created by our subconscious minds are more programmed and 'robotic'.

The following is another example of an initiation into the old traditions during a lucid dream.

THE TEST OF SACRED TEACHINGS

Sometimes initiations can come as a result of new knowledge and insights from sacred books, and become almost like an exam to see if we have learnt and taken in what we have been taught. Many years ago, Joan made an extensive study of South American sacred wisdom (Toltec) and soon after that had a lucid dream which tested her knowledge of what she had learnt. To master these sacred teachings one has to show courage, fortitude and powerful perceptual flexibility and all the tests involved these attributes.

In this case, Joan had a lucid dream in which a South American shaman appeared to her and with her permission, proceeded to give her a number of tests. He first threw Joan into a cage with a lioness, and she was to show no fear. He then shocked Joan by transforming a branch into a snake, which she had to accept without concern. These were all tests of inner courage and deeper understanding.

However, after this, he told Joan that she was not suitable for some obscure reason she did not understand. She remembers pleading with him for another chance. Perhaps he just wanted to see how she would react to failure and if Joan was committed enough to fight for what she wanted. She then found herself facing a third test, battling a number of shadowy opponents with her hands tied behind her back. In other words, he tested her by giving her a handicap.

Perhaps she had taken a shortcut with the other tests. She couldn't say, but she finally convinced him, as, after the initiation, the principles she learnt from those teachings began to manifest in her life.

INITIATIONS INTO HIGHER DIMENSIONS OF REALITY

Apart from initiations into the sacred teachings, one can also be initiated into higher dimensions of the Collective Mind. This is one of my own personal experiences.

THE TECHNOLOGICAL DIMENSION

During a lucid dream, I found myself standing outside a large underground building. The dream was sufficiently clear for me to able to make a conscious decision to enter, at which time I saw some humanlike figures operating what seemed to be strange machines. I found that I was able to consciously talk to them telepathically, although the dream was so powerful that it appeared as if I was actually speaking.

The machines were busy with scientific feats, unlike anything I had ever seen before. For example, in one scene, I saw an array of electrical apparatus holding back a mountainous wall of seawater. The workers appeared very secretive and the underground location seemed to be within the Earth itself. None of the figures seemed to be particularly friendly or concerned and I got the distinct impression that I was more of a nuisance to them. As the scenes continued to unfold eventually one of the beings asked me if I wished to join their group. Due to the clarity of the dream and my high awareness in the dream, I was able to make a considered decision to reply 'yes', at which time the dream faded. The fact that I was able to make decisions and agreed to join their 'group' means that this was probably an initiation which allowed me access to cosmic intelligences as well as celestials. This is now indeed the case.

COMMENT

By answering 'yes' to their question I felt it was an initiation of some sort. But this was a complex lucid dream and we will have to look at the symbolism involved in order to make any sense of it. In this particular case, with the level of technology present, during my dream travels in the collective mind I may have stumbled upon cosmic intelligences rather than celestials. This is probably due to the fact that I also have a background in science and technology. A 'cosmic intelligence', in this case, could be a member of a much earlier race of mankind who has advanced to the point of living and working on a plane higher than ours. However, I do not exclude the possibility that these beings may also have been from elsewhere in the cosmos.

My idea of 'complexity' was represented by the advanced machinery and complicated mechanical structures that I saw. In fact, my intention before the lucid dream was to more fully understand the nature of reality. And what was revealed very clearly in the dream was a detailed tightly–packed collection of pipes and tubes feeding into each other which gave the distinct impression of an engine within a huge factory. Obviously, this is a metaphor for the complexity of the underlying matrix of reality that is formed in our minds.

In interpreting this symbolic scenario, it could be said that the underlying structure and foundation of physical reality was shown to be a highly complex and yet organised collection of interacting energies and energy-matrices, which, due to the limits of human vision and perceptual processes, are simply not visible or accessible to us.

This message is easy to understand, as a similar principle applies to any complex machinery in everyday life. For example, when driving a motor car we don't need a complete understanding of all its internal workings. This idea of the underlying structure of reality being hidden from us is due to the limits of our human perceptual processes and the good (evolutionary) reasons for this. Imagine driving around in a totally transparent motor car in which we could see all the moving parts, or even worse, being able to feel, see, hear and smell absolutely everything taking place in our immediate vicinity on all levels simultaneously. The fact of the matter is that with our present mental processing abilities, we would very quickly have a complete total sensory overload and not be able to cope. Apart from anything else, we certainly do not need this level of information to live effectively and experience love, joy, fulfilment and enjoyment in our lives.

Let us look at another example of the direct involvement of cosmic personalities in an initiation.

BRAIN STIMULATION BY COSMIC INTELLIGENCES

Sue's relationship with cosmic intelligences was cemented during a later deep meditation and spontaneous imagery during which she was approached by humanlike intelligences who offered to use scientific means to enhance her brain functioning for greater perception and clarity.

One has to be careful when approached in this manner, as I have been told that there can be some cosmic beings that may not have our best interests at heart. So what Sue did was to consult with her unseen spiritual master as to whether it was safe. Only after she received an intuitive go-ahead did she agree to the procedure.

After that, she saw some sort of energy apparatus being placed over her head and was told that it would stimulate specific areas in her brain for improved perception and understanding. What she experienced was flickering images and mathematical formulae being downloaded into her brain at great speed. After this, the apparatus was removed and the beings departed with her thanks.

COMMENT

You must remember that images were being formed in her mind, according to her own personal set of schemas. Sue also has a scientific background, so it would not have been unusual for her to see a technologically advanced machine being placed over her head. In fact, the whole process may or may not have been only a symbolic representation of the actual transfer of knowledge through a mind-link. What is clear from this case study is that some cosmic intelligences are willing to share knowledge with us, and you will have to decide for yourself if you want this knowledge.

TRIALS AND TESTING AT HIGH LEVELS OF THE COLLECTIVE MIND

'The more willing you are to surrender to the energy within you, the more power can flow through you.'

Shakti Gawain: Personal development author

After many years of metaphysical work, visions choreographed by my subconscious mind were beginning to regularly unfold during my meditations. These scenarios are designed to expose my deepest doubts and fears and become a testing ground for the power of my mind and to establish whether I possessed the necessary attributes of courage, fortitude and conviction to continue my development and work within the collective mind.

I belong to an ancient order dedicated to spiritual study and often have spontaneous visions or ritualistic scenes appearing during my meditations or lucid dreams. Some of these scenes are of places such as forest glades, medieval castles and Egyptian temples, all places sacred to the Order. During these times, I simply allow the images to unfold naturally, while I keep my eyes half-closed, as this increases the definition of the images which unfold like daydreams in my mind. Some of these visions are accompanied by spontaneously choreographed rituals or challenges during which I have to use my will-power and intent to make conscious decisions to act. I remember a number of these tests which I will share with you to show you what to expect at the higher levels of the Universal Collective Mind. Some of these dramatisations are quite complex and challenging.

MORE SPONTANEOUS INITIATIONS

THE ANALOGY OF THE MOUNTAIN CLIMB

During one such meditation, I suddenly found myself transported to the base of a mountain and had to make a decision to climb, although it was dangerous and the path had many obstacles, such as boulders and precipices. Each obstacle was a metaphor for a particular challenge relating to commitment and fortitude. What was interesting was that after making the decision to continue and overcome each of these obstacles, I actually felt mentally exhausted in real-time.

If you are interested in this kind of inner development process using a mountain climb as an analogy, read my earliest publication *In Search of The Oracle.*

THE METAPHOR OF THE CAVE

During another meditation, I found myself in front of a dark cave and had to make the decision, without fear, to enter and pass through. This is often an invitation to enter one's own subconscious mind. After passing through I found that there was actually nothing frightening in the cave, but it still took quite a bit of nerve. The initiation was to have the courage and commitment to face the unknown with blind faith and full confidence in your abilities.

THE CHALLENGE OF THE TIGERS

During a later meditation, the scene changed spontaneously and I found myself walking towards a group of tigers. I knew that the challenge was that I had to pass by without fear. This reminded me of the legend of the Sphinx with the body of a lion which one had to pass by to enter the ancient city of Thebes in Greece. Once again, this task requires courage and belief in oneself.

METAPHORICAL BATTLES

I have also had many spontaneous scenes during meditations and lucid dreams which involve battling a series of opponents. These battles challenge your inner strength and will-power and are designed by guiding personalities within the collective mind to ensure that one has the necessary readiness and mental stamina to enter deeper into its power and mystery. If you can't overcome these easy challenges, it is not likely that you will cope with the more powerful experiences waiting within higher realms of the Collective Mind.

CHAPTER ELEVEN

MENTAL CREATION

'All things are created twice. There's a mental or first creation,
and a physical or second creation to all things.'

Steven Covey: Author and motivational speaker

HOW TO CREATE WITH YOUR MIND

In this chapter, we will specifically be looking at the power of our minds to create the mental images and thought-forms that we use during visualisation and imagery. This is a very important chapter, which unpacks the principles and methods of creating powerful etheric thought-forms such as the '*avatar-body*' and shows you how to project your consciousness into this body, as well as different dimensions of the collective mind to have a variety of experiences. These exercises are not recommended for novices as they are quite demanding.

This chapter also deals with advanced work such as the movement and *transmutation* of energy through the body and even outside the body using the mind and intention (will-power).

This is not fantasy, as I show how it is based on sound scientific laws such as the *conservation of energy*, which means that energy is never created or lost, but transformed from one form to another. Add to this the well-known metaphysical principle of *energy follows thought* and we can see how the energy of the mind can be used to direct other forms of energy.

MENTAL CREATION

'And we're seeing a higher level of consciousness and many more opportunities for people to challenge their present ways of thinking and move into a grander and larger experience of who they really are.'

Neale Donald Walsch

CREATING PORTALS AND MEMBRANES

Earlier I showed you how to create simple stairways and doorways to your subconscious mind, or higher states of consciousness, using the power of meditation and spontaneous imagery. This skill can also be built on and used for more advanced work to create more powerful energy-portals and membranes to act as gateways into higher realms or dimensions of the Universal Collective Mind. Visions of 'portals' and 'membranes' seem to have more of an effect on our subconscious minds and as a result, offer a more powerful experience than a stairway or door, as it feels as if you are actually being transported to higher realms of the Universal Mind. Such profound experiences can implode your old schemas and scripts for self and reality and change your whole view of reality overnight.

You must remember that our subconscious minds respond quite well to language, in this case, *metaphors*, which act as word-symbols for the real thing, and the idea associated with a 'portal' is that it can transport one to unknown parts of the universe, or in this case, of the collective mind. Likewise, the concept of a 'membrane' or 'veil' is that it hides a 'mystery', an idea which is also taken into consideration by your subconscious mind when it shifts your consciousness. You can now see how, by using word-association, these two metaphors are so much more powerful to your subconscious mind than a simple 'doorway' which is only supposed to take you into another room.

However, the question now arises of whether we are actually stepping outside of this reality, or are these experiences of passing *through portals and membranes* only illusions brought about by changes in our perception.

I will now discuss a few examples which may help to answer this question:

'PIGGYBACKING' THROUGH A PORTAL

One evening during a lucid dream, I took control and passed through a portal which spontaneously presented itself into a dimension of the collective mind which was inhabited by an advanced race of cosmic personalities who appeared to look very much like us, but I intuitively knew that their technology and consciousnesses were far higher. As a result, the whole scene was very 'bright' and I could not see clearly. I had the idea of *channelling through one of them* to match their energy level and set the intention to enter one of their bodies. When one is working within the collective mind during deep meditation, reality is more fluid and we can do things with our minds which we can't normally do on this sphere. Connecting with other 'bodies' or archetypal forms in the collective or universal community of minds is one of those skills.

But I had no success, as their consciousness was simply too high for me to match, and I was effectively blocked. After a few moments, I did find myself seeing better for a few brief seconds by 'piggy-backing' on the body and mind of an infant or small child. My consciousness was simply not enough to activate the neural circuits of an adult. The infant appeared agitated by my incursion into his mind and within a few moments he simply expelled my consciousness. However, during this time, I did see more clearly and was convinced that this was a race of very advanced 'humans' who were far ahead of us in terms of mental and moral development. It seems we are not alone on this journey.

COMMENT

I have been meditating and working with mind and consciousness for many years and have gone as far in my studies as is academically possible. Yet in this dimension, I could not even match the consciousness of an infant for more than a few seconds. The problem is that our present human brains and minds have only evolved to a point of seeing and thinking in three dimensions, while cosmic intelligences on higher planes of the collective mind are more evolved and should be able to think and reason in many more dimensions, much like a quantum computer.

This example shows the massive potential for growth of our minds and consciousness that is there for us within the levels of the collective mind. This experience also possibly speaks about our future, when our souls will no longer be born into this sphere of reality, but into higher levels.

Let us look at another interesting example:

STEPPING OUTSIDE OF REALITY

David combined his skills of meditation and visualisation to create an imaginary membrane in front of him with the set intention that everything inside this membrane was reality as he knew it. This idea of a membrane came to him spontaneously during meditation, so he believed it to be an 'upgraded' method of moving between realms of reality given by his guiding celestials. This was confirmed by the fact that the membrane actually appeared spontaneously out of nowhere during the meditation.

During the meditation, David asked the collective mind for the borders of reality to be represented by this large membrane. Immediately following his request, the membrane spontaneously sprang up and took up the entire space in the visual screen in his mind, almost like a wall. He consciously stepped back out of the membrane and opened himself to images or impressions that would spontaneously present themselves. He remembers touching the membrane which was almost tangible and looking inside, he noticed that it was spherical and inside the sphere was the form of a gigantic human embryo.

COMMENT

This was a very powerful experience for David. If I were to attempt to interpret his imagery, I would say that the spherical form of the earth membrane matched the round shape of the earth itself, suggesting that the most perfect balanced universal form (or system) is spherical.

To me, the human embryo inside the membrane meant that, in this sphere of reality, we are not yet fully evolved and are still in the process of growing and unfolding, an idea which may bring hope to those who feel overburdened by this life.

CREATING MENTAL AND ETHERIC FIELDS

As a result of the effort needed to keep one's connection to the Universal Collective Mind, by doing this regularly you should now find that your will-power, focus and intention have improved. This means that you should be able to create mental fields, etheric envelopes and thought-forms using only your mind and imagery. This is a powerful upgrade to your consciousness, as, although it is only imagery, you are applying the principle of *energy follows thought* and creating mental templates (the potential) for the shaping of real energy with your mind.

Let us begin with a few simple exercises:

THE PROTECTIVE ENVELOPE

By now you should know that your subconscious mind is always open to impressions or energies from outside of your own body and mind. You can now use this ability to create an early warning system for yourself. You will need a relaxed state of mind and use spontaneous imagery to create an etheric field or 'bubble' surrounding you. In this case, your body provides the energy for the focus and intention and the imagery directs your mental energy to shape the etheric envelope around your own body.

However, this is a 'passive' envelope which you have to program with intention for what you want, in this case, to warn you of physical or 'spiritual' threats. Simply use spontaneous imagery to create the envelope (or bubble) around you. Give it a colour, (usually silver, which is a protective colour), and use will-power and intention to keep it superimposed around you for a few minutes.

Program your envelope with affirmations and intentions to the effect that you are surrounded by this protective envelope which will warn you of any danger, consciously reinforcing it every day until it becomes a conditioned response. In the presence of a threat, you should immediately feel a 'bump' or change in your etheric field, and if you have used a protective colour in your field, see this colour spontaneously rise up to warn you of physical and energy-threats to your well-being.

THE INNER VISUAL SCREEN

By now, you should be familiar with your own *'inner visual screen*, on which your visualised images and interactions with celestial archetypes are projected. You can also create another visual screen specifically relating to your 'state of self', almost like a *spiritual notice board* on which you can see messages or changes to your state of mind, emotions and consciousness revealed in the form of colours, light or specific symbols in the space you create for this purpose. A 'state of self' refers to one's changing levels of consciousness, mental states and clarity, like bio-rhythms for the mind.

The process will be easier to understand if I use another real-life example:

THE SPIRITUAL NOTICE BOARD

One evening during a meditation Paul mentally created a small visual space about a meter in front of his forehead and set the intention that this will be a 'notice board' or visual screen to show him any problems with his 'state of self' and personal life on a daily basis. One must remember that the stress and anxiety of everyday life also affect our consciousness and openness to the collective mind.

Paul affirmed this visual field for a few days. Eventually he began to see different symbols placed there by his subconscious mind as *feedback*, and began interpreting the meaning of each image in terms of his past experiences and paradigm of thinking. Sometimes they appeared as different forms, balls of light, colours, geometric shapes and sacred symbols representing his bodily, emotional and consciousness states which he was able to interpret. They changed every few days as his inner states shifted and he found that the brighter the light in this space, the clearer was his consciousness. Dark colours represented illness and other strong colours such as red or pastel, his changing emotional states. The 'Om' or 'Aum' Sanskrit symbol would normally appear in the middle of the screen following a particularly deep and fulfilling meditation.

The outside of the screen normally represented the outside conditions in the global *'astral cloud'*. If it was dark around the screen, he knew it was not a good time to meditate.

COMMENT

This type of feedback is useful if you are concerned about your mind being too full of unnecessary baggage, your state of consciousness, or your mental and physical health. This also helps one to know the best time to meditate and when to avoid meditation due to unfavourable conditions.

CREATING THOUGHT-FORMS

'Our mind is capable of passing beyond the dividing line
we have drawn for it. Beyond the pairs of opposites of
which the world consists, other, new insights begin.'

Hermann Hesse: Swiss novelist and painter

From visualisation we know our ability to create images and entire moving scenarios in our minds using only the power of thought and intention. What is less well-known, is that we can also create and project powerful etheric thought-forms which become quite real when working within the collective mind. However, this takes a lot of mental focus and energy.

When focussing and concentrating intently on a particular spot or image, we transform our physical energy into mental energy (willpower and intention), which, in turn, can be used to shape and mould our etheric energy (Qi) into a variety of forms. I showed you earlier how you can use your etheric energy to create a 'spiritual' notice board. However, if you concentrate your Qi even further, it can be used to strengthen your body (as in martial arts) and even to make protective shields around your person, home or property.

HOW TO MAKE A PROTECTIVE ETHERIC BARRIER

To work with etheric energy you need a quiet and fully confident state of mind, (not necessarily meditation), such as you would use to set intentions. The next step is to visualise the colour silver, (associated with protection), and apply your will-power and intent in a continuous flowing manner to 'paint' or superimpose this colour on your walls or fences. When using imagery in this way you are using mental energy, (focus, concentration and intention), to mould your etheric energy to form the essence of the silver 'coating'.

It helps if you have mastered the use of programmed gestures and are able to move your hands around, 'applying' the silver coating to your perimeter walls. In the beginning, it is better to keep your eyes closed and simply visualise the walls and the silver colour on the walls. Later, with more practice, you can concentrate on the walls and superimpose the silver protective coating on them while you keep your eyes open. The stronger the silver barrier, the more it will extend above the wall and the more real it will seem. You will clearly see this barrier when you meditate and use spontaneous imagery, but will need to re-do the exercise from time to time to keep it going. You may see it changing colour or form, as your state of mind and 'self' affects it as well. Sometimes after a good session of meditation it will seem higher and stronger.

The following is a real-life example which clearly shows the steps involved:

SUE CREATES A PROTECTIVE ETHERIC FIELD

Sue began engaging spontaneous imagery and used her focus and intention to create a silver colour and used sustained focus and intention to put the silver coating on a visualised outline of her perimeter wall, using her hands to support her intent in practiced symbolic gestures. In other words, while holding the image of her perimeter wall in her mind, she ran her hand along from left to right, following its outline one section at a time, until she had succeeded in superimposing the silver colour on the entire wall. She then held it like that in her mind for about 30 seconds. One usually has to take a 'step back' and distance oneself during the visualisation to see the perimeter.

The power of the will on etheric energy became clear when she noted that, by just tensing the muscles of her (right) hand, the silver suddenly took on a more definite and solid-looking form. She did this every night for a few weeks and soon noticed spontaneous changes taking place in the superimposed etheric protective field. For example, the field became denser, changed colour automatically from time to time, and even took on a different appearance on its own, changing from a flat colour, to realistic-looking metal protective spikes. It seems that once your subconscious mind responds to your intention and persistence, it sets about improving the protective barrier on its own. After many weeks of practice, the barrier should become noticeable to your inner 'mind's eye' if you walk around your yard with a quiet, open, reflective state of mind.

HOW CAN THIS BE EXPLAINED IN TERMS OF SCIENCE AND PSYCHOLOGY?

From a scientific point of view, the barrier is obviously invisible to the untrained naked eye, but metaphysically, it will be seen by clairvoyants. But what of the criminal mind? Psychologically, we know that our subconscious minds can pick up impressions and sensations from etheric energy and I believe that a person with a bad motive coming close to the barrier should begin to feel uncomfortable, or sense something akin to danger. I have no doubt that these feelings should, at the very least, create doubt and uncertainty in the mind of the criminal, being something they do not understand and will best leave alone.

To support this conclusion, I remember doing an experiment with a group of gifted people at a talk I gave a few years ago, at which time I created a silver protective shield around the room *without telling them what I had done.* A number of those present were able to pick up the colour silver surrounding them, and some even saw it in the form of a wire fence, obviously as a result of their own internal schemas, (a wire fence would signify protection).

PROJECTING CONSCIOUSNESS

'Within us are powers and abilities that are like invisible sparks waiting to be fanned into brilliant flames.'

H. Spencer Lewis: Rosicrucian author and mystic

If we combine meditation with spontaneous imagery and the use of sustained intention, we can actually project our consciousness anywhere, including into the higher realms of the collective mind. If our consciousness is high enough and our intent strong, we will be able to shape and project our etheric energy envelope to create an almost tangible form. For example, earlier I showed you how a visual field of etheric energy can be formed in front of your forehead and become a screen for your subconscious mind, as well as for cosmic and celestial personalities to imprint messages, figures and symbols in the mind-space you have provided (the spiritual notice board).

However, this is only a passive use of consciousness. There are far more advanced methods of projecting your consciousness, such as when you encase it in an *etheric protective thought-form*, and send it forward into deeper realms of the collective mind to bring on more lucid and powerful inner experiences. In this section these processes are revealed.

CREATING AN AVATAR THOUGHT-FORM

An avatar is an accumulation of etheric energy able to house our consciousness which has been shaped and projected as a humanlike thought-form.

THE ANALOGY OF THE GAMING AVATAR

This is not the avatar mentioned in esoteric teachings as a great spiritual master who incarnates through the ages, but the idea is more in line with the illusion of *remote embodiment* as used when playing video games, in which a player takes control of a heroic figure in the game (an avatar) and acts through the eyes and body of this figure.

As this is a simple and suitable analogy, I will use this concept of a *gaming avatar* in my examples to explain what a projected humanlike thought-form looks like and how it works.

What I find interesting, is that this concept can likewise be used as an analogy for the way in which our soul consciousness expresses itself in this sphere of reality, *by using our body as an avatar*, a body formed from an etheric template provided by the collective mind.

This method of channelling our consciousness through a created avatar is quite demanding, so let us begin with the simpler task of projecting consciousness without creating this thought-form.

PROJECTING CONSCIOUSNESS WITHOUT AN AVATAR

If we accept the idea that everything is formed in the collective mind, we can simply move our own consciousness through the interconnected matrix of consciousness to any sacred place or site around the world.

THE SIMPLE PROJECTION OF CONSCIOUSNESS

One day, whilst in a connected state, I was looking at photographs of the sea and country scenes. I set my intention to connect with these places shown in the pictures and within a few seconds was able to pick up sensory cues in the form of subtle scents of seaweed and *fynbos* (a sparse rural vegetation). Both were shown in the pictures.

COMMENT

A SCIENTIFIC VIEW OF THIS PHENOMENON

Psychologists will argue that the scents were created in my imagination from memory by looking at the photographs. This may well be, but during my earlier example, in which I projected my sense of smell over 15 meters to the rose in my garden, I was able to confirm the scent as identical. You must also remember that time and space have already been shown by Einstein to be relative, and later on I will show you how space, (distance), is relative to our field or level of consciousness.

Finally, if you read more widely, you will find that the experience of distant sensing or the projection of senses is not unusual in metaphysical circles and you really only have to test it for yourself with photographs or mental imagery to be convinced.

Let us now look at even more advanced cases of the projection of consciousness, this time using an avatar-body.

PROJECTING CONSCIOUSNESS USING AN AVATAR

I mentioned earlier that we all have an etheric envelope surrounding our bodies which comes from the electrochemical activity in our bodies. This envelope can be shifted, shaped and even *extended beyond the body* by the use of will, intention and the principle of *energy follows thought*. This is shown in the following practical example:

MARY CREATES A THOUGHT-FORM 'AVATAR'

After many attempts over the years during advanced meditation and spontaneous imagery, Mary eventually succeeded in projecting her senses into a thought-form, an etheric replica of herself (an avatar).

How she did this was to set the intention to shift her etheric body and consciousness and using the first-person perspective, move it away from her body. Many will say this only happened in her imagination, but the fact is that her perspective of the layout of the room changed spontaneously, and she was also able to see her seated body in her peripheral vision (imagery) about a half a meter behind her.

In her imagery, she now saw a cloudlike mass forming in front of her about 30-40 cm from her body and her second task was now to use her visualised hands to shape this into a body. Mary started shaping herself some feet, moving her hands up and around in practised gestures, forming an outline of a body, ending with the head, Fortunately, she had the cooperation of her subconscious mind which kept the rest of the thought-form body together while she was busy moulding it. It was a tedious and difficult process as it took a lot of sustained focus and concentration (intention) and many minutes to do this.

Her third and most important task was to transfer some of her consciousness to the thought-form, at least enough to let her move its arms and hands independently of her real body. Although this was all taking place in her mind, she could feel the etheric energy extending and even saw a connecting cord between her body and the etheric avatar body. Eventually, she felt that enough of her consciousness had been projected into the avatar for her to move to the next phase, which involved passing through a *portal* she had also created with the intention that it would lead from her meditation room into her back yard.

Mary used sustained intention to move her avatar thought-form through the portal and immediately found her vision shifted to her backyard. She was amazed to find that she was seeing through the eyes of the avatar, although it was not clear, a bit like a misty dream.

Once in this state, she found that her subconscious mind had taken over and was automatically loading background surroundings such as images of her driveway and the back of her home. This freed her up to consciously create a *second level of imagery* within the first, in which, using her etheric avatar or thought-form, she moved around in the scene and actually saw the scene shift as her perspective changed.

Once she had grown accustomed to the situation, she remembers consciously making a decision to stand on the driveway and was actually able to have the sensation of ground beneath her feet, see clearly through the avatar's eyes and touch (and feel) walls through the hands of her avatar.

What was particularly interesting was that, using her will and sustained intention, she was able to do other things that one would normally not be able to do in real life, such as passing her avatar's hands through walls and even raising her avatar-body off the ground and seeing the roof of her house come into sight, still viewing through the 'eyes' of her avatar. However, as soon as she began to tire, she took control of her avatar-body once again and retraced her steps through the portal back into her meditation room and returned her etheric thought-form to her physical body.

COMMENT

This type of advanced meditation and imagery using many different levels of visualisation is very demanding and needs a huge amount of focus, concentration and mental energy. Forming an etheric avatar is similar to creating a first-person perspective in spontaneous imagery, but one has to use greater focus and concentration to shape the etheric energy into a humanlike form and keep it that way. The benefit of this process is that you can *move your consciousness outside of your body* into the avatar and have experiences from different visual perspectives. Channelling through an avatar body, or mental thought-form, makes the experience more powerful and allows us access to even higher realms of the collective mind.

It is important to note that Mary's body didn't actually re-locate during this case study and these inner experiences took place as a result of her successfully projecting her sensory awareness and consciousness into the avatar, and at the same time, working through different levels of imagery.

What happened here also shows us the potential that exists for us to enter deeper realms of the collective mind where the normal laws of physics do not apply, as shown by her being able to lift her avatar-body off the ground and pass her avatar-hand through a wall by a mere act of will.

However, as you have seen, there are some real challenges to this advanced technique, the first being able to sustain the high level of focus, concentration and mental energy needed to create and hold the thought-form or avatar together and at the same time, embody it with senses. Secondly, she was lucky to have had the full co-operation of her subconscious mind in supporting the background to her imagery, as well as holding her avatar-body together, allowing her to act with more freedom in controlling the thought-form and passing through the portal. Another lesson that she learnt was the fact that the deeper we go into the collective mind and the more complex the process we use, the greater are the demands on our body and mind. This particular technique was very draining for Mary.

Finally, Mary found that being too long in such heightened states of consciousness brought her to begin to question the veracity of the mundane world, which felt a bit jaded and meaningless after her powerful experience. Using an analogy, these powerful inner experiences can be compared to a climb up a great mountain and being able to see the world in all its beauty from above, and then having to return to a relatively dreary life and existence. This is why intense periods of meditation with advanced techniques such as this should be *balanced* by grounding regularly with exercise or physical work.

CONCLUSION

This is the last of the advanced skills to be included in this book. These techniques have to be practised regularly if you wish to advance mentally and spiritually. The final chapter deals with new perspectives on life, death and reality gained by the author whilst engaging the collective mind.

CHAPTER TWELVE

NEW INSIGHTS

'Sit down before facts like a little child, and be prepared to give up
every preconceived notion, follow humbly wherever and to whatever the
abyss of Nature leads, or you will learn nothing.'

T.H. Huxley: English biologist and educator

COSMIC WISDOM

During my many engagements with the Universal Mind as a *community
of minds*, I have been privileged to receive greater guidance as well as new
visions being presented to me, inspiring me to continue my metaphysical
journey. As a result, I have been able to identify *three important shifts*
in consciousness and understanding necessary to discover who and what
we are, as well as the true nature of reality and the collective mind. These
are given as follows:

A shift to a new understanding of reality (which includes notions
of time and space)

A new perspective on creation

And a more in-depth view of self

Much of this information has already been presented in the book, so this chapter will be more of a wrap-up and summary of these earlier insights.

However, in this chapter I will also present some new revelations to answer questions such as 'What is consciousness?', 'What is the essence and power of love', 'Is there really meaning to life?' and 'What happens after death?'. I also introduce the idea of world-service as a means of meeting your full potential (reaching the point of self-actualisation). Some of these explanations are quite complex, so I will do my best to simplify them by again using analogies, metaphors and the process of *multi-dimensional thinking*.

I hope you will enjoy this final chapter.

A NEW UNDERSTANDING OF REALITY

'Everything we see is a shadow cast by that which we do not see.'

Martin Luther King, Jr.

In projecting my consciousness to many dimensions of the collective mind using the technique of 'membranes', I found myself better able to communicate with cosmic intelligences. During these times of conscious contact, I asked what I believed to be important questions and found out as much as I could about the universe and the formation of our three-dimensional sphere of reality.

IT ALL BEGAN WITH A SINGLE 'MOMENT' OF CONSCIOUSNESS

The answers I got from these intelligences were to the effect that the physical universe is only the outer shell of an inner universal reality made up of different spheres of consciousness, each of which can be likened to a *'mind-cluster'*, eventually forming a single, collective Universal Mind.

This fully-conscious, multi-cellular, mega-system of consciousness is busy with a process of expansion and emanation, and as it expands and unfolds, *it brings order to what is an underlying chaotic, formless, state.* This activity results in changing patterns which have a ripple effect on the lower levels and leads to the 'creation' or forming of a hierarchy of sub-personalities (archetypes) with the purpose of bringing structure and order to this expanding, universal consciousness.

WHAT IS OUR WORLD?

This collective mind emanates a *hierarchy of different spheres or levels of consciousness.* To use an earlier metaphor, this can be likened to a very deep ocean of conscious energy with different living creatures adapted to living in each layer of this ocean. The reality in which we live as people is deep and close to the bottom of this great sea of conscious energy. By analogy, we experience this reality as 'solid matter' due to the depth and concentration of the water (energy) around us. However, I have experienced an even lower, more un-evolved state closer to the state of chaos. This would be like the 'muck' or sediment at the bottom of the ocean.

You will have to make up your own minds on this issue, but perhaps another example will help.

A WIDER VIEW OF REALITY

During a lucid dream, I saw myself as part of a small group of children. However, when I started thinking and playing by myself, I was immediately excluded from the group and chased away. I then decided to go further into the world and found a well with water and reached a high precipice. I saw many strange animals and people on the other side. The next moment I found myself in an "aeroplane' high above the clouds looking down and saw how small my earlier view of the world was compared to what I could now see. I also saw that my previous view was bounded by rocky walls; I suppose to keep people in.

I believe this was a vision pointing to the greater extent of reality. I gave thanks for the revelation.

COMMENT

When I took the time to interpret this lucid dream I gained the following insights:

The issues arising in the dream are typical of the everyday world today. While we follow the norms and values of the majority of people, we are accepted, but the minute we begin to question these norms, standards and behaviours and follow the metaphysical path, we are excluded. However, this is no reason for giving up. In fact, it is one of the tests of true metaphysical commitment that we are prepared to think and act independently of the crowd.

Being one of a group of small children suggested that our present understanding of the world and reality itself is like that of a child. In other words, we do not have much maturity or insight at all, compared to those who have passed into the higher levels of the collective mind. Then, the minute I started thinking for myself and seeking the metaphysical path, the other children chased me away, which meant that I was excluded from society. To an extent, this is true, as metaphysical thoughts and ideas can be radically different and confuse others who may end up avoiding us. For this reason, I normally wear a 'mask' of normality when I engage with people in the everyday world unless I meet someone of a like-mind.

My journey alone into the world is a metaphor for the metaphysical path, sometimes lonely. However, on this journey I was able to find a well-spring of life-giving water (inspiration and support).

The precipice is the point in our lives where we stand and can see a different world on the other side. This can be scary, as this other side is unknown. Behind us is the world as we know it and beyond the chasm, the great mystery of the depths of the collective mind. However, this is only another test of dedication and commitment, as once we reach the other side, we discover a new world of excitement and wonder.

Finally, the view from the aeroplane signifies a few moments of higher consciousness that were given to me in the lucid dream, during which I was able to see a far larger reality and note how my previous view of the world had been only a small, cut-off section of reality (surrounded by rocky walls). It was a very powerful experience.

A NEW PERSPECTIVE ON CREATION

'The awakening of consciousness is the next step for mankind.'

Eckhart Tolle

THE 'BIG BANG'

In terms of creation, science accepts the *Big Bang Theory*[1], in which a giant explosion is said to have taken place, giving rise to the cosmic dust which later formed the physical universe as we know it. This is largely based on astronomical observations, which show that the universe is expanding out from a central point. Perhaps there is another even simpler possibility.

Personally, I do not subscribe to the idea of a great mass of 'matter' undergoing a sudden once-off explosion to form the universe. Why would 'matter' explode just to form 'matter' again? And why would it explode at all? And where did the original matter for the explosion come from? There are just too many unanswered questions.

I think metaphysics would support me in this, in that I believe in a gradual formation of matter from *a central point* in which the power of the intent of a Universal Mind gave rise to a form of energy with dual polarities, (positive and negative), which form the energy-basis for sub-atomic particles to combine to form matter in a natural, logical process of expansion.

These two ideas are not that far apart, as an *'explosion'* is, after all, only rapidly outward-moving energy and substance from a central point, which still links up with the symbolism of the triangle. So only one question now remains. Was it a sudden once-off explosion (a *Big Bang*), or a gradual formation of matter from a central point and expanding outwards, which in fact, is still ongoing?

I believe that metaphysics, (and good reasoning), would agree with my explanation. Let us look at an interesting real-life example which supports this view.

A VIEW OF CREATION

Creation was the focus of a meditation during which Dorothy asked for a vision of what came before the creation of the physical universe (the cosmos). Engaging spontaneous imagery, she used sustained intent to pass through a membrane she had formed in a darkened outer space background and found herself in an area which was completely open and unstructured, something like the eye of a storm, but surrounded by images of outwardly spiralling clouds (of cosmic dust). This scene unfolded further, during which she saw the dust clouds merge to become planets, solar systems and galaxies which formed gradually around this centre of pure mind and intent. Dorothy was extremely excited, as she felt she was privy to a vision of the creation of the universe from a centre of pure thought and consciousness.

Dorothy felt very privileged to have experienced, if only for a few moments, a vision of the power of the Universal Mind, a state of consciousness which could in religious terms, be equated with the *Logos*, the 'Christ' or the 'first thought' (Word) of God as mentioned in sacred scriptures.

COMMENT

EXPLAINING DOROTHY'S VISION IN TERMS OF METAPHYSICS

So much is lost in the translation of this kind of deep personal experience that I will have to once again use *multi-dimensional thinking* to try to explain it. During this time, I will once again be crossing the lines of different fields of knowledge and comparing ideas from each of these fields. In this case, I will draw mostly on the power of symbolism. A symbol, as you may remember, is an image, shape, or pattern, which hides within its form and structure, metaphysical principles as well as different levels of symbolic meaning.

So let me try to explain Dorothy's experience as best I can using the characteristics of a triangle.

The triangle is a very powerful metaphysical symbol which often pops up spontaneously during deep meditations or initiations. Let's look at this symbol further and unpack its many levels of meaning and see how it can be applied symbolically to this vision of creation.

In metaphysical philosophy, the apex of a triangle represents *oneness or unity*, a situation in which the two sides of the triangle come together at a single point (become one). If applied to Dorothy's experience, the apex of the triangle would symbolically represent the centre from which everything seemed to be emanating, a state of perfect balance, but as yet having no real form.

To continue, we see that the tip of the triangle divides and becomes two equal sides as it extends downwards in different directions, eventually forming the two angles at the bottom. In metaphysical philosophy, these two lower points or angles represent the *duality of two opposites* which are said to emanate from a *singularity* (the apex). Returning to the vision, it was clear that the outwardly spiralling clouds were being created from the centre, although Dorothy could see nothing there.

This relationship between the apex and the two angles symbolically means that the apex, (the singularity), initially holds *two opposing polarities in perfect balance,* until something causes them to separate. If we use this symbolism to explain what Dorothy saw in her vision, it means that, under the right circumstances, a unified state of consciousness or conscious energy can separate to form two opposing principles, active and passive (positive and negative), or, in this case, *unity* giving rise to *duality.* But what gives rise to such a separation?

In the symbol of the triangle, the process applied is a *two-dimensional extension,* in which a single point, (the apex or single dimension), extends to form two dimensions (the sides or two angles).

If we now apply these metaphysical principles to her vision, we can interpret it as follows: To unfold (extend) fully, *pure consciousness,* (as a latent single-dimensional state), became active, extended and separated within itself to form *duality,* or two opposing principles (a two-dimensional state). This duality, in turn, led to a dynamic interplay between the opposing forces (polarities), ultimately giving rise to the bonding, (coming together), of active polarised energies and a process of *three-dimensional* creation as we know it, seen by Dorothy as the forming of (dust) clouds, planets, solar systems and galaxies.

A COMMENT FROM THE STANDPOINT OF SCIENCE

At first, this seems very complicated, but all that it is, is a representation of the physical creation of the universe from positive and negative principles of attraction, (duality), created, (or separated), by a single act of intent from the Universal Mind (the 'singularity' in this case). This is well-documented in science, in that bonding of sub-atomic particles of different polarities is necessary to form matter. In other words, duality gives rise to creation as we know it, but within the Universal Mind, there is only a unified consciousness as the source of it all.

A NEW VIEW OF SELF

'You are not IN the universe, you ARE the universe, an intrinsic part of it. Ultimately, you are not a person, but a focal point where the universe is becoming conscious of itself. What an amazing miracle.'

Eckhart Tolle

WHAT ARE WE?

As living, conscious, archetypal beings, we are all part of this creation, unfoldment and expression, and likewise have the task of bringing order out of chaos, or to put it more simply, introducing rationality and moral development into what would otherwise be a chaotic world without understanding. Once we become self-aware, we take on this great responsibility, and as a result, have a great potential to expand our own individual consciousnesses to encompass more of the whole. In this way, the intent of the collective mind is to express itself through its conscious imagery, (creations), and to unfold its full potential. With the high levels of chaos and ignorance in the world today it is clear that we are not fulfilling our mission and potential.

AN EXPRESSION OF THE SOUL

Let me summarise what has been revealed in this book thus far. There is a Universal Soul, as part of the Creator Source, a Universal Soul which becomes many individual souls or soul-essences for the archetypal forms of mankind. According to metaphysical laws, when these souls enter bodies they bring with them consciousness, life and other aspects of the Creative Source (the Universal Mind). Unfortunately, this means that at this time there is a loss of consciousness, as our bodies have not yet evolved to express this consciousness fully at birth. Using a metaphor which relates to life and reality as a dream, our souls simply *fall asleep* when entering our bodies and a veil of forgetfulness covers our minds. As a result, we forget our true source, its aspects and perfection, and this leads to our forming a separate sense of self, (the ego), which is more closely linked to our bodily drives and desires and formed also from our experiences stored in our minds in schemas and scripts.

Due to the limitations of our consciousness, what we see with the eyes of the ego is not a true reality, only an image or scenario formed in our minds from our own thoughts and coloured by our perceptions. And as we know, perceptions are not always accurate.

SO WHAT IS OUR TRUE PURPOSE?

We have quite a few tasks to complete successfully before we can fulfil our true purpose, which is to allow the Universal Collective Mind and Universal Soul of the single Creative Source to expand and express fully through us.

- Our first task is to come to the point of self-awareness.

- Our second task is to clear a path to the soul through our subconscious minds.

- Our third task is to awaken our soul, (metaphorically awaken from the dream) and bring consciousness (rationality) and moral awareness (heart) to this sphere.

- Our final task is to fully express all aspects of the Creative Source, as Universal Collective Mind and Universal Soul on this level of existence.

The world then becomes the stage for us completing these tasks as well as for our awakening.

When it comes to the new view of self, with all the research and anecdotal evidence presented in this book, let us now see if we can add anything to our earlier view of consciousness.

CONSCIOUSNESS AS ETERNAL

We know that consciousness gives us the experience of '*being alive*' and without it we would not be able to feel, think or reason at all. To add to this, my personal experiences with consciousness, as well as information about life after death given to me by higher cosmic intelligences, all point to the fact that once we have become self-aware, our consciousness can never be lost again. It will continue on in another form or avatar 'body', even after the passing of the physical body. This will not be a material but rather an etheric body held together by our consciousness, bringing with it an eternity of new experiences in the higher realms of the collective mind.

It is interesting how this metaphysical idea links up with religious concepts of our gaining a 'new body' after death.

CONSCIOUSNESS ACCORDING TO SCIENCE

Available scientific evidence points to the idea that we achieved self-consciousness after a long period of evolution of the brain and neural systems which took place over millions of years. In science, the issue of consciousness after death is not specifically addressed or considered at all. Hard-line scientists still believe that our consciousness will simply disappear with the passing of the brain. However, let us look deeper into some scientific laws and principles and see if we can't find some hidden messages or principles that may point to life and consciousness being eternal.

For example, our human physiology points to electrochemical operations underlying thinking and consciousness, and as we know, different states of consciousness, (from wide awake to deep sleep), can be measured on an E.E.G, an apparatus designed to measure electrical brain activity. This tends to support the metaphysical notion that consciousness is actually a very *high form of conscious energy,* and if this is the case, the scientific law of the *conservation of energy* would apply. This law states that *energy is never lost, but transformed from one type to another.* In other words, in line with this law, our consciousness would change after the passing of the body but should continue on in another form.

Secondly, the metaphysical idea of consciousness simply being conscious energy, lends itself to another scientific analogy, that of an electrical circuit. We know that an electric circuit will not work unless the circuit is closed (complete). In other words, if there is any break in the circuit, electrical current will never flow at all. If we then compare our present consciousness to the flow of electrical energy in a closed, (conscious energy) circuit, any break in this circuit would rule out the possibility of us ever becoming self-conscious or self-aware. In other words, we would never have become self-aware if there was no continuity in our cycle of consciousness, continuing even after death.

Let me put it another way. For us to have become conscious in this life, our circuit, (circle) of consciousness would have to be complete and continuous, even after death. This suggests that our present consciousness is part of a *continuous, (eternal) cycle of consciousness* in which only its form changes as we enter or leave this life, in the same way as when we awaken, fall asleep, dream and awaken again. This dream metaphor keeps popping up and is quite important, as you will see.

WHAT ABOUT THE EVOLUTION OF CONSCIOUS-NESS?

Can the law of evolution, another scientific process, also not give us a clue to our consciousness being eternal? Let us consider this philosophically and ask ourselves, from a purely evolutionary point of view, would such a hard-won faculty, (consciousness), which has taken millions of years to emerge in a human body, simply disappear into nothingness with the passing of the body? Surely in terms of evolutionary principles, it should progress to a higher form of life?

WHAT DOES PSYCHOLOGY SAY?

The psychological view of consciousness is the same as science, in that it maintains that our consciousness will disappear at death and is only the result of having a brain. However, this is unacceptable from a *psycho-spiritual* standpoint, which supports the idea that consciousness comes from a higher source (the Universal Mind) and can never be lost.

Let us look more deeply and carefully and see what else we can infer. You will remember that in the systems approach in psychology, one of the main principles is that everything is composed of 'systems' which are interconnected and do not stand alone. Here we are talking about biological, ecological, family, societal, national and global systems being part of a universal mega-system. If consciousness is seen as a *sub-system* of the human psychobiological system, it would then link up with a larger global consciousness system, and ultimately the mega-system of consciousness, (the Collective Mind). It is unlikely that any part of the mega-system would simply cease to exist, leaving gaps in the matrix of universal consciousness. This is not a characteristic of systems at all. They evolve to become larger systems. And this should apply to our consciousness as well.

IS IT REASONABLE TO BELIEVE THAT WE SIMPLY CEASE TO BE?

Finally, let us look at the reasoning and logic behind the idea of us totally losing our consciousness at our passing. From a philosophical point of view, can we really accept that death swallows up complete human lives and the collective history of mankind, having so many memories and a level of self-consciousness which has evolved over millions of years? Are we really supposed to accept that we are born, and live, love and laugh merely to pass away forever into some sort of oblivion?

It really seems unreasonable to suppose that a highly-developed principle such as *consciousness*, having evolved in different forms for millions of years and eventually expressing itself in a sentient human being, would simply be extinguished forever after a few short decades. Is it really logical for an evolving process such as consciousness to continue along a route that will lead it to a point of nothingness?' An even bigger question is, using the metaphor of life as a theatrical play; would the principle of 'life' itself participate in such an ill-fated drama that would leave it with nowhere to go? These are important points to consider.

SELF AND SOUL

'most humans see only the outer forms, unaware of the inner essence, just as they are unaware of their own essence and identify only with their own physical and psychological form.'

Eckhart Tolle

If we truly wish to know all the aspects of our being, we have to travel back to our beginnings in the Creative Source which gives rise to all. In this book, I have used the law of 'As above, so below' a few times. This law points to a direct connection between us and this Creative Source.

Applying this principle, in metaphysics we can be seen as dual beings, having an earthly existence on this plane, as well as a source on a far higher plane of existence. This source is called our soul and is derived from the 'heart', (Universal Soul), of the Creative Source. This soul, in turn, can be thought of as the heart of the human being, in which we represent the perfection of the Creator as closely as we can. This heart of the Creator is obviously not a physical heart, but rather a *centre of perfection and power* from which we, on a lower level, derive our higher emotions of love and compassion. However, the Creator is still ONE in essence, as our souls bring both consciousness and life and we become a unity of self-realisation and feeling.

OUR CREATION

To explain our coming into being I will have to go back to my analogy of the *human biological cell,* where I showed how a natural process of growth and expansion begins with an initial process of splitting into many cells and later, these mature cells come together to form functioning organs and ultimately one body. This process mirrors in some small way the unfoldment and expression of the single Creative Source in its aspects of *Universal Mind/Universal Soul* into separate human seeds or souls which give rise to each of us, and our first task as human beings would be to recognise this, and work to fully unfold our souls, bringing both mind-consciousness and soul-consciousness into this sphere of reality.

I was informed that this normally happens slowly during our lifetime, or if you accept reincarnation, over many lifetimes, and involves a *number of stages* in growing our consciousness, from first being asleep, to a partial awakening, to full awakening. I also described this in my analogy of the caterpillar and the butterfly, in which the un-awakened person is the ego (larval) stage and is only concerned with its own needs. Only when it emerges from the chrysalis (metaphorically, a time of self-reflection and inner transformation), will the shell of ego burst open and reveal the new being (person) in an exalted state of consciousness.

In everyday life, this transformation normally only happens after the passing of the person and the body, which falls away to reveal the authentic self and soul. However, with sincere commitment and a willingness to change, this soul-connection can be achieved while we are still alive, bringing with it a radical transformation and a feeling of inner peace and great joy.

TIME AND SPACE

'Time and space are not conditions in which we live,
but modes by which we think.'

Albert Einstein

The question often arises. Do time and space really exist and if so, how do they fit into our view of reality and the grand plan of creation? Let us, therefore, examine them using some more analogies.

THE ANALOGY OF THE DREAM

It seems that I keep coming back to the analogy of the dream and there is a good reason for this. Time does seem relative to our state of perception and consciousness, as seen by the differences in the time passing in 'dream-time' as opposed to real life. An event which seems to last only a few minutes in a dream, ends up being a half-hour in real-time. This also explains how different the passage of time feels during meditations when we engage higher states of consciousness. This is important, as it points to the possibility that our sense of time is relative to our conscious state.

THE ANALOGY OF THE TWO FRIENDS

Space can be linked to our conscious state or level of consciousness as well. We can see this using a simple analogy. Imagine a situation where two friends are parting after a meeting. As the one friend moves further away, he eventually reaches a position where he can no longer be seen by the other. He is simply too far away in terms of space. However, from another vantage point a few hundred metres above the ground, both friends are still clearly visible, although they are a few kilometres apart. Theoretically then, to someone with a higher 'view' (consciousness), space will differ, and to someone with an infinite view, nothing is ever out of sight. In other words, we could say that 'space' depends on our perspective, and our perspective depends, in turn, on our depth of perception, (consciousness), of the issue at hand.

As a result, we metaphysicians would not be far wrong is assuming that time and space do not exist, or at least exist in a different way in the highest realms of the Universal Mind, as this would be the highest possible sphere of consciousness.

DO TIME AND SPACE EXIST IN OUR MINDS?

So if space and time are linked to our level of perception and consciousness, we could, in fact, say that they are both put together in our minds. This idea goes back to 1787 when the philosopher Immanuel Kant wrote that space and time are not scientific absolutes, but rather '*categories*' of our minds which allow us to structure and manage reality. What is interesting is that recent thinking in quantum physics now also supports this view, by suggesting that both time and space are only mental formulations (existing in the mind) which allow us to make sense of our physical universe.

THE TRUE NATURE OF LOVE

'Someday, after mastering the winds, the waves, the tides and gravity, we shall harness for God the energies of love, and then, for a second time in the history of the world, man will have discovered fire.'

Pierre Teilhard de Chardin:
French idealist philosopher and Jesuit priest

In some of the earlier chapters, I mentioned the power of the enigmatic emotion we call 'love'. However, I think we get so easily caught up in the sentimental aspects of love and fail to see the universal principles at play in this powerful state of mind and emotion. Let us examine what has been revealed during my engagements with personalities within the collective or community of minds and use a *multi-dimensional approach* to see how this changes our view of love.

Religious persons will simply say 'God is Love' and inspirational speakers often mention that the 'universe revolves around love'. But let us *go beyond* these figures of speech, fancy words, analogies and metaphors and try to understand what this powerful state of mind really is.

I believe that most common descriptions of 'love' are only simplifications of a much more complex *existential experience* which we come to know as love. If we probe deeper, we will find that it goes back to the beginning of creation and embodies metaphysical principles of the Universal Soul itself. So let me apply a balanced, scientific approach in unpacking this nebulous idea and see how it ends up as a '*golden thread*' able to connect many different fields of knowledge.

LOVE AND THE SCIENTIFIC NOTION OF DUALITY

My recent meditations have revealed how closely love and science are related in specifically the notions of *duality* and *polarity*. In physics, duality refers to polarities of positive and negative and in biology, male and female. According to physics, both polarities are necessary, in that they combine to form sub-atomic structures which give rise to matter and physical structures.

In metaphysical philosophy, the notion of duality is more complex. Duality in metaphysics points to an original state of oneness which separates into two opposing principles. You may remember the symbol of the triangle I used earlier. Metaphysics accepts the concepts of positive and negative but now extends these to include two opposing processes, notably 'activity' and 'passivity' as I discussed in the section on the concept of energy in metaphysics. Let us try to see how this works within the framework of a Universal Mind and a Universal Soul.

Metaphysics supports the idea that the highest state of the single Creative Source is a Universal Mind comprised of pure consciousness and a universal soul as a state of pure perfection, forming together, a state of *absolute unity*. Within this state, there is no duality or polar opposites and it can be seen symbolically as the single-dimensional point, (apex), of the triangle. However, in moving from a passive condition of pure potential, to becoming active, creative and expressing itself, this consciousness/soul enters a new condition which includes the principle of duality and with this comes a *new state of activity* which, by analogy, in the case of the Universal Mind, we could liken to 'thinking' or 'imagery', the essence of the Universal Mind and creation itself, and duality within the Universal Soul likened to the affinity brought about by the attraction between polar opposites.

It may seem strange that I am trying to link a real emotion such as love to abstract concepts such as *unity, duality* and *affinity*, but be patient and all will become clearer later on. Allow your mind to flow freely, as we are looking for love's true basis or essence, the fundamental condition in the Universal Soul which gives rise to it. I will return to these principles of duality and affinity and their relationship to 'love' a little later.

THE TRUE ESSENCE OF LOVE

So what is the essence of love? Romantics will snigger at this question and say "Oh you fool, this is so simple. Can't you see that love is a natural feeling, an attraction or emotional connection between people?" That is true, but is this the only true essence of love? Can we reduce love to an evolutionary drive and physical attraction? For instance, what about the related feelings such as empathy, caring, brotherly love and 'agape', the pure, selfless, unconditional form of love? Are these all just old DNA imprints we inherit from past generations? Is there not some other principle that can explain the origin of this powerful emotion?

Let me continue with my *multi-dimensional* approach in comparing ideas from different fields of knowledge until we can hopefully get to the heart of this matter. Here are a few more ideas from theology, philosophy, science and psychology which seem to have a golden thread linking them. Perhaps these ideas will lead us to the true essence of love.

THEOLOGY AND LOVE

If we begin with Theology, we have to include one of the most well-known religious statements, 'God is love'. Although this sounds very tantalising, it does not really take us anywhere, as it means that to know what love is, we have to know what God is and I don't think there is anyone who can stand up and say for sure that they know the true nature of God. So we are actually back to square one.

PHILOSOPHY AND LOVE

We now enter the thinking field of philosophy in which some will argue that the essence of love is linked to moral principles and specifically the idea of '*the good*' (Plato). In other words, love simply means one person treating another in a 'good' or selfless way. But if love just means being 'good' to someone, we again end up in a situation in which love is the moral 'good' and the moral 'good' is love. This takes us part of the way but still leaves many questions unanswered. It does not take us deeper into its more basic principles. It seems that we just can't seem to get past words and concepts to enter the realm of undeniable facts.

With all this in mind, there seem to be two common factors to love and science, namely attraction (affinity) and relationships.

SCIENCE AND ATTRACTION (AFFINITY)

Let us return to science and see what else it has to say about love. Earlier we explored the notion of duality and I offered you a tantalising titbit by saying that I will link it later to the emotion of love. If we look at what is common to both, we can see that love and physics both include the idea of attraction. In science, it is the *attraction* between positive and negative polarities, (remember, this is the basis of duality), while in the human sciences, it is the '*affinity*' between people. So let's keep the idea of attraction or affinity as a starting point and look for more common factors between science and love.

SCIENCE AND RELATIONSHIPS

As a general rule, we could also say that love, as well as the entire physical universe, finds form and expression in *relationships*. Let me explain. In physics, two opposite polarities attract and form coupled relationships, (sub-atomic bonds), which, when brought together, create physical things. We also see affinity, (attraction), between people and relationships, (bonds of love), are the ideal outcome of this affinity. These bonds underlie the coming together of families and the forming of societies. So in this case, we are justified in saying that two principles, namely '*attraction/affinity*' and '*relationships*', seem to be common to both human love, as well as the natural laws of physics.

LOVE IS A RETURN TO UNITY

Now, let us take one step back to the explanation of duality. In physics, the source of attraction and sub-atomic relationships is the principle of *duality*, in which positive and negative polarities are formed as the result of natural laws and inherently attract one another. But how can duality explain love? We normally explain polarity in human relationships as male and female, but in some cases, affinity (attraction) and love, can occur between persons of the same sex. So we have to move beyond 'male and female' and have another look at the notions of *unity* and *duality* themselves.

In physics, when the two polarities of positive and negative are brought together, there is a natural tendency for them to attract, re-combine and return to their original oneness, (unity), through bonding. The question now remains whether we can compare this scientific principle to recombine to a desire to return to *oneness in people, to become one with the other person.* In other words, affinity and a return to unity could be two of the metaphysical principles underlying the emotion of love.

On the surface this seems reasonable, so let's see how well it fits the symbolism of the triangle I used earlier. Applying these principles to the triangle, the apex of the triangle once again denotes unity, which means that the pure consciousness of the Universal Mind is signified as ONE. However, as I said earlier, to bring about a process of extension and expression, the Universal Mind becomes active, (extends), separates and thus introduces the principle of duality, which underlies the principle of attraction, the forming of sub-atomic bonds and the structuring of reality as we know it.

THE METAPHYSICAL IDEA OF A UNIVERSAL SOUL

As I mentioned earlier, the Universal Soul is another aspect of the Creator, the 'heart' of creation, a universal expression of the principles of affinity and ultimately, also of the unity within the ONE. This universal soul also extends to embody the principle of duality and differentiates, as does the Universal Mind, to form individual souls. This process of differentiation and re-integration has been mentioned earlier. We see this duality also existing in human relationships, bringing about feelings of affinity and the desire to unite with someone else and rekindle the original oneness, (unity), between souls which existed before the process of differentiation. At our level of understanding, we could call this a desire to *return to unity*, 'love'.

SO LET ME AGAIN POSE THE QUESTION 'WHAT IS THE SOURCE OR ESSENCE OF LOVE?

On a metaphysical level, this would mean that 'agape' love is recognising one's oneness *with all of creation* and acting accordingly. In releasing duality, (the illusion of separation), we move back up the sides of the triangle, (raising our consciousness), to eventually return again to oneness (unity).

PSYCHOLOGICALLY SPEAKING, THIS IS LOVE

On a psychological (social) level, in terms of this explanation, love would be the *desire to unite* and share one's life with another (person). This will arise in situations where the affinity, (attraction), between personalities leads to a relationship. With our morality also originating with the Creator as a Universal Soul, this pull towards oneness points to an underlying unity and brotherhood of man. While not always openly acknowledged, this would explain the unselfish emotions of compassion, empathy and brotherly love and at the same time explain judgment and hatred as not realising our brotherhood and oneness with others.

LOVE IN TERMS OF THEOLOGY

Finally, in religious terms, love would be the soul's desire to return to union with God as its Source.

In fact, the saying that 'God is love' would not be far wrong if the source or essence of love is first in the duality and ultimately in the unity of the Creative Source (God). It certainly makes more sense now that we have 'unpacked' it. It would also not be wrong to say that 'love is central to everything', as creation itself is founded on the same principle of duality. This would explain the higher and more pure form ('agape') of love which does not involve physical love but rather a feeling and realisation of oneness.

If we go back to symbolism and read it together with theology, we could compare the idea of the single source of creation (God) to the apex of the triangle, which includes the principles of unity and perfection, attributes we assign to God.

THE POWER OF LOVE

This is the reason why love is so powerful, in that it shares the same essence, (principles), as the *power of creation*. When we radiate love, we are actually accessing this essence, which is very real energy, channelling and sharing it with others. As I showed you earlier, during my interaction with the elementals, love can be seen as the *'gold standard'* when it comes to emotional energy.

AWAKENING TO THE NEXT LIFE

'If consciousness can function independently of the body during one's lifetime, it could be able to do the same after death.'

Stanislav Grof: Czech psychiatrist

After my experiences within the collective mind, certain issues around life and reality have become clearer and perhaps these experiences can provide us with a clue as to what happens after death. In this section, I will be using two metaphors, *'the light'* and *'moving into the light'* to represent entry into the highest and most sublime regions of the Collective Mind. I will also be using *'personality'* instead of *'person'*, as the deceased is no longer a 'person' in the normal sense of the word.

PREPARING FOR YOUR PASSING

If we can prepare consciously for our passing while we are alive, our transition into the *'light'* will be so much easier. Our biggest concern will be to try and bypass the shadow layers of the collective mind surrounding the earth sphere, as, if we get stuck there, it could be quite distressing. You can now see how the religious concept of *'hell'* was formed, as those with a troubled consciousness and a mind filled with hatred, doubts, fears and mental anguish could find this a difficult journey, as they will immediately be faced with images of their own lives, past failures and ugly memories.

As a result of the shadow layers, the 'official welcome home' from late family and friends may be delayed and only happen after the deceased has passed through these layers, although I could be wrong about this, as it is possible that there may be some immediate help from the deceased family, friends, guides and celestials to help the personality get through. Although in some cases I have worked with, this did not always happen. I have encountered several personalities in distress in the lower regions of the astral.

On many occasions, I have also received requests for help from a deceased relative, friend, or even strangers, and have assisted where I could. You must understand that engaging these personalities is not the same as '*calling up the deceased*' using occult board-games or rituals, as here we are merely working with '*projections*' of their consciousness and personalities on the inner visual screen we create in our mind, so there is no judgment in this.

However, I would not advise you giving long-term guidance to deceased personalities, unless they are special cases, as you could end up attracting others that you do not know or are not able to help and they could end up being a nuisance. This has happened in the past. The easiest way to respond to these requests is to engage the Collective Mind during meditation and ask a celestial or spirit-guide to assist them on their way, otherwise, a prayer will suffice.

The following real-life example will explain this problem.

CONTACT WITH THE DECEASED

On one occasion, I had just woken from a slumber in the early hours of the morning and suddenly entered an enhanced state of consciousness, (possibly a very lucid dream), in which I found myself walking past a set of apartment buildings in a low-income area of a town. I suddenly found myself in one of the apartments and was confronted by an old man, (deceased), that I had known many years ago. The apartment was dark and dingy and he reached out to me in desperation, shouting something about what others had done to him in the past. There was nothing I could say to him and just felt very uncomfortable.

However, a few seconds later, the figure changed to that of a close friend who had also died many years ago. This personality was more relaxed and the apartment was lighter and better furnished. When I asked him how he was I received a short answer 'It's ok', after which the visitation ended and I returned to normal consciousness.

COMMENT

This vision should be interpreted symbolically in the same way as a dream, although I was fully conscious. The first figure, the old man, clearly had many unresolved issues. Even though deceased, he was still complaining about the past and this obviously was holding him back in a rather low state of post-death existence, (represented by the dingy room). The fact that he had so much past emotional baggage, made it impossible for me to offer him any help, as this would take many years to resolve. I know this because I have worked previously with a close deceased family member and it took seven years before he was able to pass into the light.

In the case of my deceased friend, his response ('it's ok') suggested a more restful and slightly higher realm of existence, (the lighter, neater room), in which he appeared to be biding his time waiting for things to improve, (possibly to finally release his past). These experiences are very useful for anyone trying to come to terms with death and to construct a workable framework of life after death. But I do understand that these are my personal experiences and are not proof, so let us look at other fields of knowledge to try and find more factual answers to this important question.

WHAT HAPPENS WHEN WE ENTER THE COLLECTIVE MIND AFTER OUR PASSING?

I am sure that by now, from the examples presented, as well as your own experiences, you will have seen that the collective mind has dimensions, levels or realms housing different communities of minds (personalities). Metaphysically, the realm in which each personality will settle after death will be determined by the level and quality of their consciousness and the contents of their minds at the time of passing. It seems to me that after death we still keep the energy-signature of our past personality, as well as what *Elizabeth Kubler-Ross*[2] called our '*unfinished business*' until we are fully cleansed and only our pure soul remains.

A DREAM-LIKE SCENARIO

The metaphor of a dream I gave earlier, is probably the best description for our present sphere of reality, and in line with this metaphor, passing through the veil of death should at first also seem like a dream, with our consciousness slowly crystallising until it re-asserts itself and recreates a semblance of reality with which we are familiar. However, as is the case with dreaming, at some time or other we will have to begin to slowly awaken to things as they really are.

THE QUESTION IS NOW, EXACTLY WHAT ARE WE LIKELY TO EXPERIENCE AFTER OUR PASSING?

The following paragraphs may read a bit like the *Egyptian Book of the Dead* and I admit that it is based mostly on my experiences with the deceased and what I have inferred from metaphysical principles. However, it makes a lot of sense if you also look at it scientifically. For instance, I have noted a similarity between what could happen after death and the stages of the *process of grieving* the loss of a loved one as is known to psychotherapists and counsellors. Only in this case, it is the loss of one's own life that causes the responses. Due to this similarity, I will deal with it in stages.

STAGE ONE: ADJUSTING TO THE NEW CONSCIOUSNESS –
ENTERING A STAGE OF CONFUSION AND DENIAL

My excursions into the collective mind have given me some answers as to what we will most likely experience after death when our physical bodies reach the end of the road and disintegrate. If we accept that our present perception and thinking are dependent on our brains and nervous system, this will obviously change with the passing of the body. However, in metaphysics we do not accept that consciousness is a product of the brain and so with its absence, we will enter a different state of consciousness, probably a dreamlike or semi-trancelike state similar to meditation. However, memories do not simply disappear, as metaphysics attributes an energy-basis to them, and so my reasoning tells me that our subconscious schemas and scripts will continue to exist in some form or other, (probably as energy-patterns), in our new consciousness and will create a semblance of our old reality for us, at least until we get used to the new experience.

As for our emotional state, the Collective Mind as a system maintains *order* and *balance* and seeing that our subconscious minds fulfilled the role of a guardian while we were alive, I can only assume that our new consciousness will also have protective measures, so that we will not be badly affected, or traumatised, by the transition. However, as in the case of grieving, one's passing could still come as a shock to those who are not prepared. This means a period of adjustment, during which the deceased either comes to terms with their situation or else enters a state of *denial*, the first stage of the grieving process.

I have personally encountered deceased personalities who were very confused, as they could not understand or come to terms with this new experience. This is why a strong, holistic belief system is so important, as it prepares us for our passing.

Finally, there could also be feelings of anger and blame, as we saw in the example of the old man in the previous section. This matches the second stage of the normal grieving process.

STAGE TWO: LETTING GO OF THIS REALITY – SADNESS AND LONGING

Hopefully the deceased will quickly adjust to their new reality and state of consciousness and will then look at the loss of their family with a sadness we could view as a form of depression, the third stage of the grieving process. They will probably be caught up in the goings-on relating to the funeral and burial arrangements and have concerns regarding the welfare of their families. I have always advised deceased personalities to rather remain with their families for an initial period and offer them comfort through their presence and especially to send them feelings of love. Sometimes family members can sense their presence and feel this love that is being expressed for them.

However, eventually a time will come when deceased persons can release their attachments to their past lives. However, evolution, even on a spiritual level, is a slow, gradual process. In this regard, I have made the following observations:

- I have worked with several cases of helping deceased relatives and friends and noted that they all have the same problem of reaching the point where they are prepared to let go of family and possessions and move on. This does not mean forgetting or leaving their feelings for family and friends behind, as these relationships will remain, but rather turning in a different direction and taking the first step on this new journey which ultimately leads to higher levels of the Collective Mind.

- This usually does not happen immediately, as the natural order demands a state of readiness from the deceased personality. From my experiences, it is not unusual for departed souls to remain in this earth sphere for many years to give support and comfort to their loved ones through dreams and as I said previously, providing an emotional 'presence', especially one of love.

- When they do reach the point at which they are prepared to move on, they will enter a time of self-reflection, during which they have to recall and deal with each unresolved emotion or issue in their lives and learn to understand and accept the particular path they followed in life. This time of self-reflection is designed to bring them to the point of understanding the lessons of their past life. In terms of the different stages of the grieving process, this would be the stage of *understanding*.

- As part of the final stage of *acceptance*, they will have to learn how to release their past pain and forgive those who caused this pain, and find forgiveness for themselves as well, as they cannot move into the light if they are held back by the chains of guilt and self-doubt. Fortunately, by this stage, they should have dealt with most of their concerns and can see the real issues more clearly.

STAGE THREE: THE PROCESS OF CLEANSING

In the previous section, I spoke about the unresolved emotions, pain and guilt that we have to deal with before passing into '*the light*' or the higher realms of the Universal Mind. We separate ourselves from our higher consciousness through thoughts of self-limitation and guilt. This was shown in Sue's case study in which she lost her connection to the spiritual masters within the collective mind as a result of a single thought. This proves the metaphysical principle that to move to higher levels of the Universal Mind, our consciousness needs to be purged of anything negative, destructive, or that which could be an obstacle to our further progress.

This suggests a *period of cleansing* in which we have to let go of any factors which have bound us to the Earth, such as wealth and possessions, as well as any negative emotions, judgements or thoughts that are holding us back. Our relationships will family and friends will always remain, as these are based on *love*.

THERE ARE MANY WAYS THAT THIS CLEANSING PROCESS CAN BE BEGUN WHILE STILL ALIVE

- Firstly, as you have seen in this book, cleansings can be achieved by following a path of love and personal advancement, although in terms of reincarnation this could take many lifetimes. If we do not accept reincarnation, and our cleansing is incomplete in this one life, it will have to continue on a higher level after our passing.

- Secondly, the process of cleansing could involve following the teachings of a master or guru, but this also involves a lifetime of commitment and in these modern times, not many people have the time, or are prepared, or are in a position to do this.

- Finally, we can petition a *karmic lord* for our cleansing. A karmic lord is a highly advanced spiritual master who has reached the highest levels of the Collective Mind and now has the power and authority to release karma, provided we show true belief, sincerity and motivation. As a Christian mystic, I acknowledge Jeshua (Jesus the Christ) as one of these high Avatars.

This process of cleansing, learning and instruction will continue after death until we are cleared of all imperfections. This stage links up with stage four, in which, through the power of imagery and intention, we create new realities along our journey to *the light*.

STAGE FOUR: CREATING A NEW REALITY

Once we let go of the focus on our old lives, we are likely to enter a 'borderland' where we will find that with our new consciousness things manifest rather quickly and we can create any reality we wish, including different versions of 'paradise' or our 'happy place', at least until we wake up to the truth of reality itself. As with our real-life visualisations, relatives and friends who have passed on should be able to enter this imagery and help the deceased in their efforts. From what I have seen, deceased personalities will remain in a self-created illusion until they eventually see it for what it is and are then ready to move further on into *the light*.

Unfortunately, this stage of imagery also means that negative or brutal images, hateful emotions or unresolved archetypes we have stored in our psyche will take on unpleasant forms and we will need to face them. This is why it is important during our lives to purge ourselves of these emotions such as hate and rage and deal with all our violent thoughts, unresolved guilt, traumatic memories and unpleasant archetypes before we pass on, as they will certainly be there to welcome us as we pass through this stage or sphere of consciousness if we have not dealt with them properly during the earlier stage of cleansing.

This experience will not be pleasant for those poor souls unable to move beyond the lower strata of the Universal Mind due to the weight of their guilt and pain. It is even possible that they will metaphorically '*sink into the bowels of the earth*' until they can reclaim their consciousness and composure. In fact, I have, on occasion, seen un-evolved elemental beings descending into the earth as the sun disappears from sight. I suppose this type of experience lends itself to the notion of the 'Underworld' in mythology, or 'Hell' as mentioned in sacred scriptures.

STAGE FIVE – COMMITTING TO A PROCESS OF RE-EDUCATION

The fact is that we will all have to do a review of our lives and assimilate the lessons from this life after our passing. In fact, some of the imagery I experienced when engaging the collective mind shows that we can even create a classroom-type situation for ourselves for this '*re-education*', although it could just as well be any other learning scenario as well, such as climbing a long flight of stairs one at a time. The chosen scenario must have symbolic steps or grades through which the personality can pass and assess their progress in the cleansing and re-education process.

The following real-life example highlights a classroom scenario. Obviously, this was not a real classroom, but merely a façade created by the deceased to provide them with a sense of normality.

THE SPIRITUAL CLASSROOM

Peter recalled a time when he engaged with a deceased relative during meditation and saw his period of 're-education' as a scene of a classroom complete with desks and a teacher. Obviously, what Peter saw in his mind at the time was only a symbolic representation of the process, but it was enough to convince him that we all have the power create some sort of *pseudo-reality* after death. It should also be during this stage of learning that we will be helped by guides, celestials or familiar, comforting relatives and friends we once knew, all trying to help us through the process.

STAGE SIX – MOVING INTO THE LIGHT

Depending on what scenario the deceased personality has chosen to symbolically represent their forward movement during cleansing, their progress will be seen in different ways. For example, experiencing greater degrees of light, or changes to their symbolic scenario, such as seeing and feeling themselves gradually moving up a flight of stairs. Let me use another real-life example to show you how this steady growth happens after death.

THE CATHEDRAL STEPS

In an interesting real-life case I worked with, this personality had chosen as his symbolic journey into the 'light', a long flight of concrete steps going up alongside an old cathedral and past a school he had attended as a boy. These were familiar and loved by him and made him feel comfortable.

Every time I advised him on how to continue the life-review, to let go and find forgiveness, he was able to climb up one step. The steps were many, probably about two hundred at least. What I noticed was that this was not easy for him, as his consciousness was metaphorically *'weighed down'* by all his past baggage and it was a great effort to even move up one step. He often had to cling to the hand-rail which ran alongside the steps for support. This was a great lesson for me as well, as it showed me how we determine our own progress after death.

Over a period of *seven years*, this personality was eventually able to release all the trauma, pain and judgments of his past and one day I noticed that he was no longer on the steps but was moving out on the road at the top towards a light. I bid him farewell, but a few weeks later he appeared to me in a white gown and he had changed into a much calmer, wiser and gentle soul. He had passed into the light. What he found there he did not share with me.

WAKING FROM THE DREAM

'You have to understand, most of these people are not ready to be unplugged. And many of them are so inured, so hopelessly dependent on the system that they will fight to protect it.'

Morpheus (The Matrix)

In the previous section, I showed you how our third task is to awaken our soul, and if at all possible, metaphorically waken from the dream while we are still on this plane. Let us now look at the processes involved in this important task.

IS THIS LIFE ONLY A DREAM?

What if during our conscious existence we are merely passing from one dream state to the next, with each dream bringing us a little closer to a full awakening of our souls as intrinsic parts of the Universal Soul? Seeing this life and reality as a dream is helpful if we are trying to find ways of by-passing the veil of forgetfulness covering our minds and gaining access to the next stage of life.

My excursions into the Collective Mind have taught me that one does not have to actually die to awaken to this higher reality. Using meditation and spontaneous imagery, we can convince our subconscious minds to allow us visions of the next life while still in the body and also remove the aeons of conditioning covering our souls and preventing our awakening. This also prepares us for the next life. However, this takes a lot of effort and many people are happy to simply continue dreaming, as this certainly makes life easier and more comfortable.

'Waking up' to a higher reality is a gradual process, and if it is done too quickly, it can be quite a shock to the system. I am sure that many of you have had the experience of waking up from a dream with a jolt and will understand what I mean. We have to prepare our minds by letting go of the fear of the unknown, as well as the ideas, thoughts and images which support this dream and reach a *state of readiness* before we can hope to awaken. Waking up is also a great responsibility, as we then have an obligation to awaken others as well.

To bypass the dreamlike state in which we now wander, we have to try to remember something of our previous existence. This metaphor of awakening from slumber is very appropriate and quite effective, as seen by my efforts in using the power of my subconscious mind to part the veil into the next life. As before, we have to create imaginary scenarios which all point to an awakening. I have personally tried and had some measure of success with scenarios of myself waking up in an Egyptian sarcophagus, emerging from a chrysalis, (the metaphor of a butterfly emerging from a chrysalis), and a powerful re-enactment of myself waking up from a coma in a hospital bed, which I will now describe.

THE WHITE ROOM

It has lately become quite normal for me to use meditation and spontaneous imagery to create a re-enactment of awakening from a coma in a hospital and then setting an intention for moments of conscious awakening into the next life.

On one of these occasions, I created an avatar thought-form body and saw a white substance leaving the left side of my body and entering the avatar. This was my etheric body extending to form the avatar-body, while keeping a conscious connection to the energy source within my body. My idea was to see through the 'eyes' of the avatar into the higher reality.

As I struggled to open my avatar-eyes, I vaguely saw myself lying on some sort of hospital bed. I could not see very well, as the light was very bright. I realised that this meant I had accessed a higher realm of reality and my mental processes were struggling to form images on this level. It was very difficult, but after many attempts, I was able to focus my avatar-eyes briefly and for a few moments saw an enactment of what I considered to be the next life. I knew it was only a symbolic façade, as I was still alive and my schemas and scripts would be structuring my vision, according to my past experiences and belief system.

I was lying in a white room on a bright white bed surrounded by deceased family members, and they were all calling for me to wake up. Although I tried, I simply did not have the will-power and mental energy to open my eyes completely, apart from the slight view I had for those few moments. I could not sustain this vision for long and had to end the meditation after a few moments.

The next level of life is obviously on a higher energy plane and this is why our bodies cannot enter this state.

THE WHITE FIGURE

The second example is even more important. During a similar attempt, I also managed to open my avatar-eyes a little for a few seconds while in the 'hospital bed' and saw a beautiful white figure reaching out his hands to awaken me and pull me up. The figure was not very distinct but clearly human-like. But the emotions that I felt at that moment were amazing. I normally do not feel much emotion during spontaneous imagery, but at this time I felt great love and benevolence coming from this being. A truly wonderful experience!

COMMENT

I believe that a partial awakening during this life can cause some disorientation, a little confusion and a feeling of detachment from this reality, as we are halfway between one dream and the next.

At this point in time, the veil separating this reality from the next life is very thin and you may find that when you are in a reflective mood, you see clues to this higher reality, such as faces of deceased loved ones or celestials offering you support. Do not discount these visions as they are important for your awakening.

WE HAVE TO RETURN TO INNOCENCE

In preparation for consciously reaching through to the next life, we need to return to 'innocence', the original state and perfection of soul-consciousness that we lost somewhere along the line. In other words, we have to leave behind the influence of our bodily instincts, ego-drives and the conditioning that has robbed us of our childlike virtue. This is not the same as merely clearing out our subconscious minds, but rather goes beyond that to a redirection of our focus and attention to returning to our original state of soul. In practical terms, the easiest way I can describe this is expressing the unity and perfection of the Universal Soul by *giving out unconditional love* to all.

THE POWER OF LOVE

The first step in this return to innocence is setting a daily intention to acknowledge the unity and brotherhood of mankind and see the soul-light in others. We can restore our faith in people simply by acknowledging their souls. If we continue with this diligently, eventually a day will come when we are walking in the street and begin to actually feel this love and acceptance of everyone that we pass by. I can only describe it as a feeling of compassion and harmlessness towards all living things. This feeling of love will make you resilient in the face of difficulties and lead to a profound peace of mind. Love is a *powerful force* which is little understood. You may recall that I went very deeply into the essence of love in the previous chapter.

This love and harmlessness also brings with it a new world of understanding and perception in which we live in the present, the 'now', and learn to view people and situations without judgment. I have learnt that true insight, wisdom and understanding only come when one has vision without judgment. It is our judgment of others and world events that keep us from achieving total clarity of mind, as we end up filling our minds with unnecessary concerns.

A return to innocence also involves a new realisation that, in its deepest essence, everything is perfect, and what we now see as pain and discord, are but the outer layers of a false reality which we have created. To see the truth, we need to learn to look past our limited thought-systems with single-mindedness and see the true world of beauty, freedom and truth that lies beyond this world of greed, fear and mental slavery.

With an innocent mind, you will see a purpose for every act, event or situation. This will enable you to ignore the old ego-promptings and focus only on that which is positive and uplifting.

A CALL TO WORLD SERVICE

'To whom much is given, much will be required.'

(The Bible: Luke 12:48)

The Universal Mind can be seen as the conscious component of the physical universe and the Universal Soul as its 'heart' (the central core of perfection and unity). In line with the expanding universe, the Universal Mind itself is unfolding and in its unfoldment, takes us *'along for the ride'*. As embodied souls in archetypal forms in this Collective Mind, we become the agents of growth and change on this level of reality and so we have a very important role to play in this expansion and expression.

THE CALL

While on your own metaphysical journey, you may have been fortunate enough to have had several initiations, either in ritualistic settings if you belong to a brotherhood, or else during lucid dreams, or your own meditations. During these initiations or dreams, you may have been asked to make commitments to serve and help others as part of your global *world-service.*

Many of the great philanthropists and holy persons in history have either worked to serve others in practical ways on Earth, or on the higher realms of the Universal Mind as 'spiritual' world servers. As the latter, you become part of a global network of metaphysical practitioners who focus either on channelling healing, harmonizing or protective energies through the global energy-matrix, to specific persons or areas of the world in turmoil, or else work at clearing the global astral cloud of negativity. To do this work you will need to be *emotionally* and *psychologically balanced*, have a high degree of empathy and the ability to work with different energies.

LOVE AND NON-JUDGMENT

Once we commit to world service, whether on a material or spiritual level, we have to abide by the principles of love and non-judgment. This means that we serve all equally, the good and the bad, without favouring any person or nation. In other words, as world-servers, we cannot take sides but should be prepared to assist everyone irrespective of race or creed or ideology, with compassion and understanding. Is this not what the great spiritual teachers and enlightened personalities have been trying to tell us all through the ages?

Even if you have been given only a small a degree of understanding and enlightenment, you now have a duty to help others along their path and your goal must be clear, unwavering, unselfish and loving. In practice, this means looking at others with love and an innocent and pure mind, seeing past the errors, misperceptions and limitations of people and their actions, right through to their souls. In doing this, we will come to understand that their negative actions are due to fear and the illusion of separation, when, in fact, we can never be truly apart from our Creative Source and each other. It now becomes your task as a world server to remove the veil from their eyes and the pain from their hearts and minds so that the light will come through. By acknowledging their souls, we help them to express more fully, and in doing so, also acknowledge our own soul-consciousness.

EQUIP YOURSELF FOR WORLD SERVICE

'The best way to find yourself is to lose yourself
in the service of others.'

Mahatma Gandhi

You will find that once you have begun this work, and not before, you will be given the tools or gifts with which to continue. These tools may come in a variety of forms, from motivational energies and passion for the work, to gifts of wisdom, understanding, clarity and insight.

THE GIFT OF ABSOLUTE CLARITY

Once all the obstacles to the reconnection to our souls have been removed and we learn to see without judgment, we may experience *absolute clarity*. This clarity is needed to awaken fully, to truly know the Universal Mind and to follow its flow. It allows us to see more of truth, remain awake to what is needed, and wary of dreaming more negative experiences into our lives. To achieve this level of clarity, we have to raise our consciousness during meditation and keep it free of bodily and worldly concerns. This is not easy, but with practice, it can be done.

Unfortunately, any limiting or negative thought, or any unhelpful emotion such as fear or anger, or any action that leads to guilt, will cause us to lose this clarity and we will have to retrace our steps to find it once again.

HELP FROM CELESTIALS

Appropriate tools or gifts will be given to those who assist in world service. As I said, you will find that the gifts come *as you need them* and not before, which mean that you have to 'show up' and begin the work before they will be given. What you gain is, therefore, the *result of your service*.

Once you have committed to working as a world server your intuition will improve and you should receive guidance and support in messages, promptings and instructions during dreams, visions, meditations and spontaneous imagery. Celestials may also offer you symbolic gifts for your work in this sphere, usually appearing in the form of precious stones, crystals, necklaces and bowls of fruit, books, robes or sometimes even a sceptre or sword. Remember that these should not be interpreted literally, but are symbolic of different spiritual attributes you will need for specific tasks.

For example, you may be given a gift of inner sight when acting as an advisor to others, as you will need to see what is happening in their lives. Secondly, you may receive a raised consciousness, clarity and understanding if you decide to become a spiritual teacher, or find yourself developing feelings of unconditional love and compassion if you have chosen to counsel. Finally, if you feel prompted to become a conduit for channelling healing energy into the world, I have no doubt that your ability to work with energy will improve, and if you find yourself in a position to bring about positive changes to the negativity of the global astral cloud during meditations, you will be given the strength and extra protection you need, as this can be quite uncomfortable at times.

When it comes to understanding the images of the gifts presented by celestials, try to interpret the objects you see metaphorically based on their characteristics and everyday uses. For example, a sword or a sceptre signifies power and books signify knowledge. A specific image of a large ruby superimposing itself on your forehead after meditation (red signifies activity), could mean that you have been given the power of improved imagery or mental creation, which normally involves that frontal part of your brain. However, if the jewel on your forehead is a clear quartz crystal, this could be the gift of understanding or clarity. In another instance, the gift of a robe could follow a profound initiation and signify your graduation to a higher level of the Universal Mind and greater responsibility as metaphorically, one wears a graduation gown when receiving a university degree or diploma.

Always accept these gifts with humility and gratitude and use them wisely.

The following real-life example reveals how this normally happens:

THE GIFT

Spiritual gifts are usually given after a successful initiation in preparation for world service. One evening during meditation and spontaneous imagery, John saw a celestial approaching with a gift of a small bush in a pot which had on it a hundred 'eyes' instead of flowers. Continuing with the imagery, John took the plant in his left hand, (the receiving hand), and expressed his gratitude to the celestial being, after which it faded away.

COMMENT

John believes this to be a celestial messenger as he radiated such a bright light that he could not clearly make out his features. It is always difficult to tell the gender of a celestial being, as this is not an issue for them. They have no need of this in the higher realms of the Universal Mind. We have to infer from their energy-signatures if they are radiating predominantly male or female type personality characteristics and arrive at our own conclusions.

As is the case with all imagery, we have to interpret the items given as gifts for service in terms of our own personal symbols. After meditating on the meaning of the hundred eyes on the bush, John came to the conclusion that it was a gift of *insight and revelation*, (being able to see further and deeper with 100 eyes).

HEALING ON A GLOBAL LEVEL

'Be the change that you wish to see in the world.'

Mahatma Ghandi

The work of channelling universal energy to those in need can also be done on a global level. The technique is basically the same as for an individual, although I would advise using only universal energy when working on a global level as it can be draining if your own etheric energy is being used and directed to a specific area of the world, a country, or the entire globe, especially if the place requires much assistance.

The idea is that, during meditation, set an intention and form an image in your mind of the place to which you wish to send healing, love, strength, comfort, protection and wisdom (understanding). You can use either a visualised map of the world, or else create a specific scenario which will help you to recognise the country or place. The connection is formed in your mind, so as long as you set the right intention, the energy will go to the right place. Once again, this is in line with the metaphysical principle of affinity or sympathetic connection.

Once you feel a connection to the place, (you can generally feel this 'bump 'in the open palm of your right-hand), either petition celestials for help or, if your sustained intent is strong, simply visualise the type of energy you need around you and draw it out from the Universal Mind, the source of all energy. Once you feel ready, (look for changes in your spontaneous imagery such as colours or movements), simply visualise the directed energy or colour surrounding that area you have chosen, or the whole world if you like, and hold it there for a short while. In other words, you are superimposing the colour together with its energy onto a visualised scenario of the country or area in question. When you start to tire, exit from the meditation slowly as before.

THE POWER TO CHANGE WORLD CONDITIONS

'The cleansing of spiritual contamination is accomplished by offering one's talent, resources, and life to the world.'

Lao Tzu

Conditions on this planet are affected by the astral envelope or 'cloud' surrounding the Earth. This is full of accumulated negative thoughts and feelings such as fear and despair which have the power to influence people and ultimately dump the entire world into negativity. It becomes the task of world-servers to try to clean up this mess. For those who are religious, prayer is the safest way of asking for healing or change to take place in the world. The reason for this is that with prayer we leave it up to the higher powers to decide. However, some world-servers are called to intervene directly as active agents for change on this level of reality, and in such cases, their decisions have to be one-hundred-percent spot-on as there are ethical issues and consequences involved.

With initiation as a world-server comes responsibility, and during your visions and meditations you will be informed of the service you must perform, that which has been approved by your celestial masters or helpers. As before, this work will be done during meditation and spontaneous imagery, so that you will see the effects of your intercession and also still be open to warnings or guidance.

LET ME OUTLINE THE PROCESSES FURTHER:

THE ANALOGY OF THE HOSE

As previously shown, there are two main types of energy and two approaches when using energy. The first is the use of the active, masculine, positive 'yang' energy which is activated by pure will-power and intent during deep meditation. By analogy, this would be like taking a hose-pipe and spraying a concentrated stream of water on a fire. Then we have the passive, gentle feminine 'yin' energy which is more 'channelled' and 'released' and not directed. By analogy, this would be like opening the tap and letting the water *flow* to where it is needed.

As seen in the analogy, the approach of using a nozzle or finger to restrict the *'water flow'* in the case of positive energy can be tiring and demanding as it needs a lot of focus and concentration. I have personally found that working only with positive 'yang' energy in this way for long periods is very stressful, as it passes through the body and neural circuitry before being directed outwards. This type of energy will also cause upsets if not used immediately and allowed to build up in your system. On the other hand, the second approach of merely 'opening the tap' during meditation when using the gentle feminine energy, allows one to stand back a little and this does not have a serious effect on one's body.

I would recommend trying both methods, choosing the most appropriate one. For example, in the case of specific areas or problems in the global astral matrix, the positive focus and movement of 'yang-type' energy would probably be best. However, if a more generalised effect is needed, such as flooding the entire global astral matrix with healing, benevolent or compassionate energy, the passive (yin) energy approach could be used. This will allow your body time to recover from the demands of the positive energy approach.

RADIATING ENERGIES INTO THE 'ASTRAL ENVE-LOPE OR CLOUD'

The technique for sending energies into the astral envelope or 'cloud' is similar to that mentioned earlier for absent healing and other energy modalities. However, this time you have to be more careful as the *cloud* has the power to bounce back and negatively affect you as well, and you should not stay connected for long.

- Try using the positive method first by visualising the astral cloud surrounding the Earth using spontaneous imagery and setting your intention for the type of energy (colour) you wish to send, but the moment you begin to tire or feel affected, end your meditation as quickly as possible, as when your etheric energy is weak the astral cloud can bounce back and affect you quite badly. I usually go in under the guidance of a celestial or master, as in this way I am warned when to stop.

- You also need to keep a safe distance from the inside of the cloud and for this reason, I generally visualise a membrane or transparent wall in front of me, which to me represents the astral envelope or cloud, and I only extend my hands and not my whole body through the membrane. This allows me to withdraw my hands quickly and safely if I feel affected in any way.

COMMENT

This is an advanced technique and should only be attempted if you have been given the go-ahead through higher guidance. It is the power of your mind and sets up the barrier and directs the flow of energy, (energy follows mind), and any effects will happen in your mind. However, this could later affect your body as a result of the close link between body and mind.

Another way of distancing yourself from the effects of powerful channelled energies on your body is to create a giant avatar thought-form and use its etheric 'hands' to direct the energy to where it is needed. In other words, the energy will pass through the thought-form and not your body. The other benefit of this method is that the avatar thought-form will keep you at a safe distance from the astral envelope or cloud. Keep a look-out using your spontaneous imagery and if you see something which could be a threat, exit and close your meditation quickly.

As I mentioned above, you can also use the passive method of clearing the cloud and simply 'let' the peace-producing energies flow around you and into the cloud. This is also done by utilising intention, but the work is usually completed by celestials, or archetypal embodiments of the divine feminine energy. You simply have to ask and let it flow around you and into the astral envelope or cloud. As before, monitor your progress with spontaneous imagery.

SUPERIMPOSING THE CHANGE

A final, and even more powerful method, of effecting real change is to see the problem in the astral envelope or cloud using inner sight or spontaneous imagery and create a new reality in your mind and impose this new reality over the old and hold it there for some time. However, this method lines up with the active, positive energy approach and is quite demanding.

There are also other factors to be considered if you use this advanced method of changing astral conditions, as you may unwittingly go up against natural laws and principles. You must remember that when it comes to global issues, many of these conditions are the result of imbalances caused by societies and nations and there are lessons to be learnt. If one takes away the cause of the pain and discomfort, the lesson may never be learnt. This will be like opening a chrysalis to help a butterfly escape and not realising that its struggle to emerge is part of the process of strengthening its wings, and it could end up unable to fly.

Also, there are certain plans for our development under the guidance and control of powerful celestials and masters and you certainly don't want to tramp on their 'spiritual toes'. So the best is to always *ask* before you act, and act only when you get the go-ahead intuitively, or from a celestial or spirit-guide during spontaneous imagery.

ENDNOTE REFERENCES

1. Big Bang theory – the theory that the creation of the universe began with the explosion of a gigantic chunk of matter and the cosmic dust later settled to form the planets and stars. https://www.merriam-webster.com/dictionary/big%20bang%20theory

2. Elizabeth Kubler-Ross – a famous doctor who worked with dying patients and authored the phrase 'unfinished business' https://www.goodreads.com/quotes/660765-lots-of-my-dying-patients-say-they-grow-in-bounds

CONCLUSION

'Do not take life's experiences too seriously. For in reality they are nothing but dream experiences. Play your part in life, but never forget that it is only a role.'

Paramahansa Yogananda

I hope you have benefitted from this book on *psycho-spirituality* and that this has helped you on your own metaphysical or spiritual journey. Once again, some may argue that these experiences are *all in the mind*, but then again, our daily experiences and perceptions of reality are processed in our minds. So does this make our inner experiences any less real than our outer experiences?

The book aimed to first introduce you to metaphysics, then to hidden parts of yourself, and finally to powers of your mind that you have not yet used. I hope that I have been successful in this and that your experiences have been worthwhile and that a new vista of life, as well as your own path, has been revealed to you.

I personally developed most of these methods of connecting and engaging with the Universal Mind, although some concepts and ideas I did take from books and online articles that you will see in my reference section. I also urge you to go online and read these articles using the endnote links I have provided for a better understanding of the information given.

REFERENCES

BOOKS

Bohm, D. (1980). *Wholeness and the Implicate Order. G.B.*: Routledge.

Jung. C.G. (2004). *Dreams*. NY: Routledge.

Jung, C.G. (1991). *The Archetypes and the Collective Unconscious.* London: Routledge.

Mares, T. (1995). *Return of the Warriors The Toltec Teachings*, Vol. 1. C.T: Lionheart Publishers.

Plato.(1987).*The Republic*. London: Penguin.

Schrödinger , E. (1958). *Mind and Matter*. England: Cambridge University Press.

Schrödinger , E. (1958). *My View of the world*. England: Cambridge University Press.

Schrödinger, E. (1992). *What is Life?: With Mind and Matter and Autobiographical sketches*, England: Cambridge University Press

Schrödinger, E. *The Observer* (11 January 1931), also in *Psychic Research* (1931), Vol. 25, p. 91.

Schucman, H. (1990). *A Course in Miracles*. California: Foundation for Inner Peace.

Talbot, M. (1996).*The Holographic Universe*. London: HarperCollins.

The Bible. London: Cambridge University Press.

Tononi, Giulio.(2012). *Integrated Information Theory of Consciousness: An updated Account*. in Archives Italiennes de Biologie, Vol. 150, No. 4, pages 293–329.

DVDS

Russel, P. (2004). *The primacy of consciousness.* DVD: Amazon

INTERNET ARTICLES

https://www.academia.edu/35981689/The_Holoinformational_
Model_of_Consciousness_An_Extension_of_Pribrams_Monism
http://scecinfo.usc.edu/geowall/stereohow.html
https://www.ncbi.nlm.nih.gov/pubmed/22432419
https://www.frontiersin.org/articles/10.3389/fpsyg.2019.00210/full

ABOUT THE AUTHOR

I am based in Durban, South Africa and have an Honours degree in Philosophy and a Doctorate in Psychology from the University of South Africa. I am a long-standing member of the Rosicrucian Order, a brotherhood which is dedicated to spiritual and esoteric study and I have permission from the Grand Master to share certain information with you.

Insofar as my experience is concerned, I retired early and have since been a part-time lecturer in counselling skills, a part-time trauma counsellor and was a volunteer Lifeline crisis counsellor and trainer for more than thirty years. At present, I am an online tutor for Metavarsity in Cape Town as well as for psychology students at the University of South Africa.

I have written many books, e-books and articles on metaphysics as well as emotional, mental and spiritual wellness and spoken many times on radio stations and overseas podcasts. I presently give talks relating to my books to the public and interested groups.

I have placed several interesting articles on my website www.discoveringyourself.co.za

Contact me on Facebook https://www.facebook.com/Jimmy-Henderson-books-120112288020427/ or by email at jph@saol.com

TITLES BY THE AUTHOR

LET ME ALSO INVITE YOU TO HAVE A LOOK AT MY OTHER BOOKS AVAILABLE ONLINE:

In Search of the Oracle

Multi-Dimensional Thinking

Multi-Dimensional Perception

Effective Listening skills for Counsellors and Care Givers

How to Interpret your Dreams

Improving your Relationships

A Guide to Effective Parenting

Living on the Edge of Darkness

The power of Symbols, Ritual and Mystical gestures

A Comprehensive Guide to Crisis Counselling

Dealing with Trauma: An Introductory guide to sharpen your practical counselling skills.

www.ingramcontent.com/pod-product-compliance
Lightning Source LLC
LaVergne TN
LVHW051222080426
835513LV00016B/1368